'*Material Girl, Mystical World* make[s] accessible and cool, and reminds u[s] thrive we must learn to embrace our c[apacity] and spirituality, and engage with som[ething larger than] ourselves. With this book, Ruby Warrington is helping to redefine success for the 21st century.'

### Arianna Huffington

'I love Ruby's book! She writes about meditation in the context of spiritual activism in a way that makes it accessible and fun. The deeper message of *Material Girl, Mystical World* is one the world sorely needs in 2017 and beyond.'

### Bob Roth

#### CEO, David Lynch Foundation

'Ruby Warrington is the Malcolm Gladwell of the mystic scene! *Material Girl, Mystical World* is a bible for young women lusting after a deep and meaningful antidote to modern life, without disappearing from society.'

### Jasmine Hemsley

#### bestselling author and wellness expert

'I'm a massive fan of Ruby Warrington and her fabulous book *Material Girl, Mystical World*. It's a down to earth, current, relatable, and at times hilariously funny take on what it means to awaken in these times, also proving that you don't have to choose between the altar of Mother Mary or Chanel. Today you can actually worship at both.'

### Rebecca Campbell

#### bestselling author of *Light Is The New Black* and *Rise Sister Rise*

'I am a super fan of all Ruby does, and have been
a follower of *The Numinous* since day one. I loved reading
about her journey in *Material Girl, Mystical World*, which
both inspired me and made me laugh out loud!'

## Henry Holland

**fashion designer**


'For thousands of years, the "Spiritual Journey",
East or West, has been followed according to a rigid
tradition. But now that we're in the Aquarian Age – and
yes, it's for real – with its accompanying freedoms, each
student is responsible for mapping their own journey.
Consequently, Ruby's is unique to her. However, she details
its joys, agonies and miraculous moments with such
poignant detail that it will serve as both inspiration and
a guide for those who are eager to learn about spirituality
or, possibly, follow that path themselves.'

## Shelley von Strunckel

**astrologer and spiritual teacher**


'Ruby Warrington's intrepid exploration of the
mystical realm is sharp and refreshing. *Material Girl,
Mystical World* is a stylishly spiritual book for
people who are seeking more than just
the obvious explanations about life.'

## Ophira and Tali Edut

**The AstroTwins, astrologers for US *ELLE* magazine**

# MATERIAL GIRL, MYSTICAL WORLD

## The Now Age Guide for Chic Seekers and Modern Mystics

**RUBY WARRINGTON**

Thorsons

Thorsons
An imprint of HarperCollins*Publishers*
1 London Bridge Street
London SE1 9GF

www.harpercollins.co.uk

First published in the US by HarperElixir, an imprint of HarperCollins*Publisher*s
This UK edition published 2017

1 3 5 7 9 10 8 6 4 2

Text © Ruby Warrington 2017
Illustrations © Ina Stanimirova Tontcheva 2017

Ruby Warrington asserts the moral right to be identified as the author of this work

A catalogue record of this book is available from the British Library

ISBN 978-0-00-815117-1

Printed and bound in Great Britian by Clays Ltd, St Ives plc

MIX
Paper from
responsible sources
FSC™ C007454

FSC™ is a non-profi t international organisation established to promote the responsible management of the world's forests. Products carrying the FSC label are independently certified to assure consumers that they come from forests that are managed to meet the social, economic and ecological needs of present or future generations, and other controlled sources.

Find out more about HarperCollins and the environment at
www.harpercollins.co.uk/green

**For my Pisces**

# CONTENTS

# Part IV: Fashion & Beauty

# Part V: People & Parties

# COMING OUT OF THE SPIRITUAL CLOSET

*Brooklyn, NY. October 31, 2013.*

So what exactly do you wear to a séance? It's Halloween; my friend, the psychic Betsy LeFae, has invited me to a "Dinner with the Dead" at her apartment in Williamsburg, and I'm having a wardrobe crisis. On Facebook, my feed is filling up with people dressed as sexy nuns. But if Halloween fancy dress is about *laughing in the face of death,* I'll hopefully (gulp, *really?*) be spending my evening looking death in the face and asking who it thinks it is. Instead of a "meet the parents" outfit, I need a look to potentially meet and greet my dearly departed ancestors.

My instinct is to play it superwitchy and dress head to toe in black, even though I know it's considered more high vibe among spiritual circles to wear white. Apparently it raises your "auric radiance." In the end I settle on a long black Agnes B skirt I picked up at a consignment store in the East Village (just witchy enough), and I pair it with a sleeveless white silk blouse. A mouth of MAC's bright red Lady Danger lipstick completes the look. It's what I always wear when I want to feel properly pulled together. It's the same shade Alexa Chung wears (she told me when I interviewed her once), and I think it makes me look like a lady. A dangerously smart, sexy, and pulled-together lady.

In the street outside I can already hear the sounds of the impending zombie apocalypse as my fellow New Yorkers congregate outside the bars to smoke and flirt. Getting wasted and fornicating in the face of death is the other big theme of the evening, after all. Meanwhile, I think about all the spirits I won't be drinking but will instead be inviting to deliver their spine-tingling messages tonight, and I pick up the tray of tamari-roasted vegetables I'm taking as my dish for the potluck supper we'll be eating in silence after the séance. The idea is we'll be dining with any deceased ancestors who've decided to join us.

All of which, if I'm honest, has become a pretty standard Friday night for me.

Seriously, you should hear some of the conversations I have with my girlfriends these days. Women like Madeline, who used to work at *Nylon* magazine but left to go to psychic school in L.A. and is convinced she's a reincarnated mermaid. Raquel, a former fashion stylist who's devised a spiritual detox program to open your third eye and cleanse your chakras along with your colon. Or Marika, a financier turned modern shamanic practitioner who mainly wears Isabel Marant and introduced me to my spirit animal last summer.

And no, I didn't meet these women on some mind-bending plant medicine retreat in Peru. Although that's probably on their vacation wish list, along with swimming with dolphins, a trip to Burning Man, and a ten-day silent meditation Vipassana. Nor do my friends and I waft around in purple caftans (unless they're by Mara Hoffman), grow out our armpit hair, and imbibe only homegrown kombucha. Rather, the women I have been known to refer to as my *coven* are the hip, switched-on denizens of New York, L.A., and London, cities fast embracing the dawning of what I like to call the *Now Age*. As in New Age . . . but given a totally modern upgrade for NOW. And I connected with many of them after I launched my website, The Numinous, an online magazine where *Material Girl meets Mystical World*.

The by-way-of-intro e-mail often goes something like: "OMG at last. A platform that speaks to my twin passions—fashion *and* astrology!" And then we get into how a fascination with all things esoteric has opened up whole new worlds of inquiry about what it means to be thriving as a twenty-first-century woman.

Because from Ayurveda to the tarot and Tantric healing, on any given evening in Brooklyn, Venice Beach, Shoreditch, Sydney, or Berlin, Now Age curious seekers are flocking to workshops to waken our Divine Feminine, sitting in ceremony to welcome the New Moon, experimenting with shamanism, and getting seriously high on the vibes, man. The night I attended a pranayama breathwork session in a tepee in a park in Williamsburg last summer, I didn't come down for days.

Which sounds pretty woo-woo, I guess. But if embracing the New Age in the 1960s meant changing your name to Echo, rejecting your traditional upbringing, and running away to live on an ashram, in the *Now* Age, choosing to check out a more spiritual worldview is no longer seen as incompatible with an appreciation for fashion. If anything, the fact that we've evolved into such an exaggeratedly material, hypervisual, and device-dependent world has given these ancient *human technologies* a newfound allure. If social media, for example, has created what some people are calling a "disconnection epidemic," then esoteric practices like astrology and meditation become a (necessary) way to reconnect—sure, to each other, but not least to our*selves*.

And on the flip side, spending half our lives in the alternate reality we casually refer to as the Internet (I mean, let's take a step back for a minute; everything being "online" now, and existing somewhere in the Cloud, is actually seriously sci-fi) means we also get to investigate these Now Age practices from the comfort of our own living rooms. Not to mention the freedom it's given us to totally blur the lines when it comes to what a person who identifies as "spiritual" *should* look like. Um, have you checked out Miley Cyrus's IG feed lately? #GODDESS. The week I'm writing this, even Khloé Kardashian had penned an essay on her spiritual leanings for Lena Dunham's "Lenny" newsletter.

Enter mass meditations that devolve into networking events, spiritual speed-dating, and my friends and I discovering the joys of the "healing hang date." Also celebrities like Russell Brand (God bless that man) discovering yoga and going from Hollywood wannabe and recovering addict to total Now Age pinup. Oh, and his ex, Katy Perry, telling a reporter for *GQ* magazine, "I see everything through a spiritual lens. I believe in a lot of astrology. I believe in aliens. I look up into the stars and I imagine: How self-important are we to think that we are the only life-form?"

Well, I could *not* agree with you more, Katy, and astrology was my gateway drug into the Mystical World, too. I must have been about three years old when I discovered I'd been born in the Chinese year of the Dragon. Result! Most people got normal animals, like pigs or dogs, but lucky me had obviously been singled out for some pretty special cosmic treatment (not that astrology is for narcissists or anything. No, really, it isn't—as I'll explain in detail later on!).

Anyway, there followed a period of about six months where I'd scrunch my features into a "scary" dragon face and do this heavy breathing thing through my bared teeth, to show everybody how the mythical beast *lived in me*. And then my brother was born (year of the Sheep, yawn), and people stopped paying attention.

I also grew up knowing that my mum had my full astrology chart done by a family friend when I was born. I was an Aries, which meant I was "confident and extroverted, and sometimes quite bossy." Beyond the home environment I was definitely more on the shy side, though, and I was desperate to know what else the astrologer had said. But Mum was always frustratingly vague about it. "Ummm, you have a lot of planets in Cancer . . ." she'd murmur, balancing my baby brother on one hip while stirring a pot of buckwheat noodles.

If you haven't already guessed, she was kind of hippieish, and we ate mainly macrobiotic when I was a kid. I think mostly because John and Yoko did. The other families in the rural country village where I grew up were the same, a tight little clique of "alternatives" who embraced natural remedies, grew most of their own vegetables, and wore a lot of cheesecloth.

It wasn't until I started at the tiny village school that I realized there was anything *strange* about my mum taking my brother to see the fierce Dr. Singha, an Ayurvedic practitioner who cured his recurring ear infections by banning him from eating dairy, or us spending weekends at music festivals where I got pink henna streaks in my hair. But my flask of homemade adzuki bean stew felt decidedly *unsexy* next to my friends' pizza and fries at lunch, and even aged five I was acutely aware that my home-stitched smock dresses were no match for Claire Maplethorpe's shop-bought tutus. To my five-year-old eyes, not only did pizza and tutus look *waaaay* cool—it was also evident that without them in my world, I would always be on the outside looking in.

Up until that point I'd been completely satisfied with my social life too, which consisted mainly of hanging out with the fairies at the end of our garden, making mud pies, and tumbling down the rabbit holes in my imagination to explore magical, underground kingdoms. But now I wanted a Barbie. My fairies were mysterious and mischievous and very stylish in their own ephemeral way, but Barbie had long blond hair, an *extremely* covetable wardrobe, and a boyfriend called Ken, just like an actual princess. And I'd consumed enough fairy tales by this stage to know that princesses, even more so than little girls born in the year of the Dragon, got all the luck.

So what's this got to do with my adult interest in all things Now Age? Allow me to explain. If you think back, you'll remember there was a lot of talk about how 2012 was going to mean "The End of the World" as we knew it, due to it being the final year to be represented in the ancient Mayan calendar. And this was certainly the case for me. I want you to keep this deadline in mind as we fast-forward to a few months before D-day, when I was working as features editor at the UK's *Sunday Times Style* magazine.

I'd obviously decided at some point that the most direct route to getting my hands on a wardrobe like Barbie's and achieving as close to princess status as an outsider like me could really hope for was to pursue a career in fashion. I fell in love with magazines in my teens, which—by now the only "poor kid" (relatively speaking) in a progressive North London private school—found me grappling with the mother of all identity crises. And in shuffles a lineup of the usual teen rebellion suspects—early experimentation with drugs and alcohol, an eating disorder, and a six-year relationship with a much older, sexually domineering man (whom I'll be referring to as the Capricorn), who also managed to completely rob me of my sense of identity.

Magazines, and the glossily perfect world they represented to me, became an escape. And by the time I'd mustered the courage to leave the Capricorn and rebuild my life in the image of my own choosing, I became hellbent on pursuing a career as a fashion and lifestyle journalist. But after twelve years in the industry, I was dismayed to find that I was bored out of my mind.

Perhaps it was because landing a job on *Style* magazine pretty much represented the apex of my ambitions at the time. After all, a lot of the anger and frustration that lay in wait just beyond my tedium on the job was directed at *myself* for not being utterly satisfied with a position I'd worked so hard the past decade to achieve.

A lot of my friends were experiencing the sense of fulfillment I realized I was craving by having kids, but I'd decided long ago that I didn't want to be a mother (more, oh-so-much more, on this subject later). Whereas I had become increasingly aware that I was essentially trying to fill the creative *Source energy*, second-chakra-shaped void (the seat of our creative energy) that had appeared in my life with copious amounts of cocktails, designer clothes, and . . . cocaine. Yes, over the past decade I'd also morphed into the quintessential work-hard-play-hard party girl. In the beginning, it was a world that fueled my post-Capricorn desire to fill myself up with all the FUN I felt I'd been denied in my teens and early twenties—but lately, it felt less hedonistic, more like a way to numb my existential angst.

Sure, my "on paper" life was pretty fabulous—great job, great relationship (I'd since married the love of my life), great, generally heavily discounted, wardrobe. Loads of holidays, loads of freebies, and a home of my own on one of the most desirable streets in one of the most desirable parts of London. #Blessed. So why was it all tinged with the underlying sense of unease that something MAJOR was missing? Like, something fundamental to the purpose of me taking up space on the planet. Was writing about what T-shirt some celebrity was wearing or getting them to "open up" about the state of their relationship in an interview really all I had to contribute to the world?

I don't blame the drinking or the drugs, although they had become part of the problem. The morning after a binge, the anxiety and the despair, the anger and the frustration came on ten times worse. But essentially the nonstop party was just a way of distracting myself from the little voice that kept insisting, *It's not enough. It's NOT ENOUGH*. Because how dare I? This was what "having it all" looked like, wasn't it? How much more, exactly, did I want? No, the real problem was that as the months went by, and my anxiety reached a level that I actually sought professional help with a therapist, I continued to ignore the Voice. And well, 2012 was the year kismet decided to intervene.

I've since, thanks to my adventures in the Now Age, been able to understand exactly how dis(self)respectful it is to blatantly blow off the Voice (a.k.a. *your intuition, your soul, your higher Self, the Universe, um . . . God*), and I'm actually beginning to believe (more on this later too) that if each and every individual was in a position to truly honor this Voice, we might have the blueprint for world peace, right there.

Luckily for me, my soul wasn't going to give up that easily—instead, it led me back to astrology. Like: *Okay, why not learn astrology. Like properly, so you can read people's charts and stuff*, it said, while I was lying on Salinas beach in Ibiza, mojito in hand, pretty pissed off that I'd spent so much money on a new Missoni bikini that had begun to dissolve the first time I wore it in the sea. *You've always been into astrology, and it sounds like what you need is a passion project*. Because if my life was lacking anything, *it was passion*.

My childhood interest in astrology had bloomed over the years, and even my colleagues referred to me as Mystic Ruby, since I was the girl who always knew when Mercury was going retrograde (and all our writers were going to miss their deadlines and our photo shoots would fall through). Maybe our in-house astrologer, the eminent Shelley von Strunckel, would deign to teach me a thing or two?

Turns out she would, and soon I was being invited for dinners at her loft in Kings Cross where this grande dame of mystical glamour began filling my mind with stories of ancient spiritual folklore over bottles of biodynamic red wine. All the stuff that had been swirling in the background in my childhood, but which I'd locked away in a box marked "crazy, crunchy, and NOT VERY COOL"—along with the adzuki bean stew. Now Shelley was taking me back.

I was instantly in awe of her being so worldly and so well read—and not just in astrology but *all* things mystical! Shelley had traveled the world and experienced the magic of the Universe firsthand, and my heart thrilled at her vision. It was as if her stories were the missing link, as if she'd opened the door to a whole new world, which, conversely, I realized I'd been seeking all along—a Narnia she described as "the numinous."

"It means 'that which is unknown or unknowable,'" she explained . . . and I felt my soul swoon. Not even the hypnotic allure of a new pair of Miu Miu shoes could have inspired such tingles in me as the web of intrigue the word *numinous* wove in my mind. Having been raised atheist (I once had to walk out of a midnight mass in case I started yelling "cult!" at the top of my voice), it was kind of like getting the whole concept of, um, God, for the first time. (In fact, sometimes when people ask me what the word means, I have been known to reply: "basically 'awesome'—but in a biblical sense.")

Was this the moment I "woke up," as people in Now Age circles often refer to the day they finally decide to walk out on their corporate career and go train to be a yoga instructor in Bali? Well, in a similar vein, I basically decided there and then that beyond the study of astrology, my new side project was going to be investigating all things numinous for myself. And while we were at it . . . wasn't that a great name for a magazine?

Beyond the personal sense of "awakening" I was experiencing, this whole conversation was tugging hard on what had become my finely tuned journalistic sensibilities. I knew (also because the Voice told me) that in the face of such rapid/rabid technological evolution, I couldn't be the only one experiencing this deep sense of existential unease. From my fashion industry perspective, the whole esoteric shebang could use a bit of an *image upgrade* (all that patchouli and crushed purple velvet had been hanging around since the 1970s, after all)—but maybe *I* could have a go at that? The message that the "something more" we were all searching for was actually just sitting there, waiting to be dusted off and given a polish, was something I felt compelled to share. Before I knew it, I was envisioning a beautiful publication that would make it as cool to get to know your spirit animal as it was, say, to shop at Chanel. And lo, The Numinous was born!

Or conceived at least. There was no way in hell I was going to actually jack in my job on *Style* and start my own magazine instead (or more likely, due to my lack of funds or contacts with connection to funds, lowly blog). I was *waaay* too attached to the kudos and the baubles, despite the fact I was by now well aware that all the designer trinkets in the world were not going to make me happy. It's one thing to want to surround yourself with beautiful things (actually a very spiritual thing, since I've come to believe that "beauty" is simply the physical manifestation of "love"—a.k.a. *pure spirit consciousness*)—and quite another to, like, *literally* worship at the church of Chanel (as many a colleague had declared over the years).

It's actually been little surprise to me that a lot of the women in my Now Age coven describe themselves as "recovering fashion industry victims." Because isn't it also the definition of an addiction? When you keep reaching for the same magic potion (in my case yet more pairs of $350 shoes) expecting a different outcome—and ending up back at rock bottom?

I've also learned that as soon as you begin to pay actual attention to the Voice, however, and take even the most tentative steps in the direction it's urging you to go, the Universe will step in and take matters into its own hands. It's Law of Attraction 101. *As above so below . . .* thoughts becoming things. And it was only a few months later that my husband, from here on referred to as the Pisces, landed a job in New York—*starting January 2012*. Whether I'd go with him was a no-brainer, which meant it was time to leave the shiny baubles behind, woman-up, and step boldly into the Numiverse.

And here's the real kicker. Turns out when the Voice was whispering *It's not enough . . .* , it wasn't trying to tell me that I didn't *have* enough—enough stuff, enough success, even enough love. I clearly had buckets of all that; in fact, way more, on a global scale, than my fair share. The message the Voice was trying to hit me over the head with was that I wasn't living in alignment with my *truth*. Meaning I wasn't doing enough to work out all the crap—the karmic lessons, the conditioning, and the limiting beliefs—that was standing in the way of me experiencing a relationship with my most *authentic Self*. And, as such, a relationship with the Universal Source energy commonly referred to as "God."

I think I might have mentioned I was raised atheist, correct? And, well, as a result, the *G* word doesn't sit that comfortably with me (as you may have guessed). But if not having any religious beliefs drummed into me as a kid had never registered as a lack in my life, I have since come to see how the fathomless sense of emptiness I now found myself struggling with was essentially a lack of faith in the idea that all life on Earth is sustained and united by our connection to *the Divine*.

In the meantime, I'd been willfully plastering Band Aids over the other "wounds" I'd sustained over the course of my life. The superficial flesh wounds of being the weird kid in school and of my parents' divorce. And then the deeper lesions inflicted on my soul by my eating disorder, my relationship with the Capricorn, and my investing pretty much all my spiritual development and sense of self in glad rags and handbags.

But as I began to investigate all things numinous, it was as if every gong bath, every meditation, and every intuitive tarot session was clearing a path back to Source (my higher Self, the Universal one-ness . . . okay, *God*), and soon all the skeletons came screeching out of the closet, begging (in a kind of zombie apocalypse way at times) to be healed. Slaying them (*or, rather, putting them to rest, RIP*) has not always been pretty, but it has been consistently empowering, endlessly awe-inspiring, and often waaaay more fun than another Friday night *drinking my cares away* (because why would I want to wash *away* the things I *care* about?)—as we'll discover in the chapter on how, for me, *healing is the new nightlife.*

Another word on the concepts of "healing" and "wounds" here, too, since these are words you'll find me using a lot. Rather than be repelled by the idea that this suggests there's something "wrong" with you—how about leaning in to the concept that there's actually something very, VERY right with you, that needs "healing," meaning bringing into wholeness in order for you to be fully empowered.

As for the people you may encounter who prefer to dismiss all things numinous as "woo-woo" bullshit or a bunch of silly girls getting squeamish over their Ouija boards? (a), screw the patriarchal system that decided anything to do with divination and intuition has little bearing in the "real world." And (b), when not so long ago I was interviewed for British *Vogue* about the subject of astrology entering the mainstream, my response to a variation on the above objections went something along the lines of: "The world is divided into scientists and mystics—those who mainly ask 'how' and those who mainly ask 'why.' Left- and right-brain thinkers. I stand firmly in the latter camp (thanks in part to my Cancer Moon—lol), because, for me, without this kind of existential self-inquiry, life is meaningless."

Not that we don't need our fully-functioning right-brain faculties to navigate the daily task of being human, of course. But with no other word for "God" in my five-year-old lexicon, I can also see now that even as a child astrology spoke to a deeply *human* need in me—a need to know my place in the cosmos, in order to feel connected to my highest Self, to my fellow beings, and to the planet we happen to call "home."

Because you know, one of the best things about deciding to simply *embrace* the numinous, to marvel at the magic of the Universe, and then do the internal work it tends to ask of you, is that you get to align yourself with the beating pulse of our Mother Earth. And if there's anything we all know it's that we need to do everything in our power right NOW to foster a more harmonious coexistence with the natural world.

It also seems to me that it's only once we get truly happy in our *selves,* get *healed,* that we are in a position to stop with all the navel-gazing and reach out to help the people around us, too. As we all know, when the airplane is going down, it's essential to *put our own oxygen mask on first.*

So, before I send you on your own numinous journey, I ask you to consider this: if YOU are the greatest "numinous" there is, then accepting this mission could be the fastest route to unraveling *your* unique unknowables, tuning in to *your* own inner Voice, and excavating your happiest, truest, most empowered, and *empowering* self as a result. The sort of self who believes that maybe, just perhaps, you too have a unique and essential role to play in the future thriving of our species and our planet. Even if, for you, saving the world looks a little less Mother Teresa (since there can be only one of her) and a little more like simply being the best sister, daughter, lover, friend, and community activist you can be. BIG change has to happen one human at a time, after all.

I wrote this book to share the tools and ideologies, not to mention introduce the mystics and the teachers, I've found to be most inspiring in this not-so-humble pursuit, so you can use it as a road map of sorts. Some chapters have a more prescriptive, "how to" feel; others are more philosophical in tone. I encourage you to take copious notes, applying my experiences and observations to the transformations you're experiencing, or would like to experience, in your own life. Not to mention breaks between chapters to go out, have fun, and inspire others by walking the talk—for it is in the day-to-day, real-life experience of these practices that you'll make the greatest leaps on the path to a more high-vibe life.

Not that I claim to be any kind of a guru myself. Just a Material Girl in a Mystical World, who happens to think that if The Numinous was the new normal we might find ourselves inching a little closer to, you know, world peace.I

# PART I

# THE NEW AGE, BUT NOW

# 1.

# ASTROLOGY AS BASIC LIFE SKILL

One of the best things about being a journalist is the deeply random conversations I get to have with complete and utter strangers, many of whom also happen to be semifamous. Like the time I interviewed "plus size" supermodel (ridiculous, she's like a U.S. size four) Crystal Renn. It was supposed to be a basic Q&A for London's *Stylist* magazine, but the first thing Crystal wanted to know when we sat down were my Sun, Moon, and Rising signs. It turns out we were both astrology mad. *Soul sister!* I thought to myself, as the first thing *I* usually do when I get asked to interview someone is look up their chart.

Of all the wonders of the Internet, the fact that you can google most celebrities' birth details will never cease to be a constant source of entertainment for me. And by the way? For the student of astrology, this is also a great way to hone your skills. After all, once you've got their birth chart in your hands, the lives, loves, failures, and successes of the A-list are all out there just waiting to be analyzed.

For the uninitiated, your birth chart is essentially a map of the sky, showing the exact position of the planets on the wheel of the astrological zodiac at the moment you were born—that is, the moment your soul chose to incarnate this time around. Each placement of each planet is a window into a different aspect of a person's personality.

Back to Crystal, who loved astrology because as a model she found herself interacting with new people all day, every day. At every casting, every photo shoot, and every catwalk event, she would be faced with a whole new team—and what better way to break the ice, not to mention work out who the hell you are working with, than a little astrological inquiry? Knowing somebody's Sun sign (their intrinsic personality), Rising sign (how they come across), and Moon sign (deep-seated emotional needs and how they react to stuff) helped her find her place within the group, work out how to read different individuals, and, on a more advanced level, how best to communicate her own wants and needs. When the people in question (photographer, makeup artist, stylist) were responsible for how she was going to look in the resulting images, not to mention potentially recommend her for the next job, you can see how she'd found this to be a highly valuable life skill.

Sun Sign = Your Intrinsic Personality
Rising Sign = How You Come Across
Moon Sign = Emotional Needs and Responses

And in my book (this book, ha), it's not only supermodels who can benefit from getting a grip on the basics of astrology. Yes, it's fun to read a daily, weekly, or month-ahead horoscope for your own Sun sign, but it's when you learn some of the other key aspects of your chart and then apply this insight to your relationships with your Self and others that things get really interesting.

Astrology tends to get a bad rap from people who assume it's about trying to "predict" future events—and because it's based on something as seemingly random as the position of celestial bodies circling the Sun millions of light-years away. In answer to this, (a) I'd like to remind us all for a moment how profoundly our lives are affected by the seasons—not to mention the impact the daily weather forecast has on our mood. And if we can see the influence of the Moon in the ebb and flow of the tides, is it really such a stretch to believe that the other planets in our solar system might also affect life here on Earth? That the "cosmic weather" might also play some kind of role in our lives?

Meanwhile, (b) my take on astrology is that it's actually a complex *language of symbols* for describing the intricacies of human nature. After all, for anybody fluent in astro-speak, it's so much simpler to describe myself as having my "Sun in Aries" than go into a whole riff about how I can be self-interested, but at the same time am deeply loyal; or how I'm a born entrepreneur, prone to risk-taking, with a warrior soul that really, truly, underneath all the ego BS, wants to save the world.

For as far back as I can remember I have been fascinated with the way this mystical language just always seemed to make *sense*. That is, if I didn't spend too long trying to wrap my head around the concept that each individual life on Earth is shaped by the position of the planets at our time of birth. But for me, *how* astrology works isn't really the point (scientists versus mystics, remember?). I see it more as a tool for personal development, with which to interpret what, why, how, and when certain events, emotional states, and evolutionary processes are presenting in our lives. And all in the name of our evolution/karmic journey.

Yes, astrology can also seem like an extremely navel-gazing pastime. But I think the desire to know yourself and the world you move through better is essentially a drive to *be a better, more effective human being*. Not that it's there to be used as a scapegoat, either. Cultivating an awareness of the way certain astrological aspects *could* influence events is a very different beast to simply blaming all your shortcomings, your just-couldn't-really-be-assed-to-go-there fuckups, on the stars. This is where the concept of "free will" comes into play, the idea that while we are undoubtedly children of the cosmos and part of the Universal grand plan, we still get the deciding vote as to how our lives play out.

As my astrologer friends Tali and Ophira Edut, better known as the AstroTwins, put it, it helps to see your birth chart as kind of like your "factory settings." The cosmic blueprint you're working off in this lifetime.

How you then go about constructing your life depends on all sorts of external factors, including the people you meet, the opportunities you're presented with, and, ultimately, the decisions you make. But having that original blueprint on file to refer to is a great way to ensure that the foundations remain solid. As such, when you study the language of astrology as a tool for personal development, learning the basics of interpreting your own chart is a really great place to start. With this information at your fingertips, I guarantee you'll be granted a whole new perspective on your life, your relationships, and, yes, your karmic destiny.

It was the fabulous AstroTwins who lifted the lid on chart interpretation for me. Tali, who met and married her husband at Burning Man, studies shamanism in her spare time, and Ophira, whenever I visit her apartment in the East Village, has a pack of Angel cards out on the table. But they also write the horoscopes for *ELLE* and appear as regulars on *The Real Housewives*—in other words, they're a pair of Mystical Girls, making some seriously magical waves in the Material World.

*Numinati alert!* I thought when we first connected. (The "Numinati" being my affectionate term for my Numi coven.) And when I then discovered they were leading a Become Your Own Astrologer retreat in Tulum, Mexico, that summer, I knew I would move heaven and earth, not to mention all the freaking constellations in the zodiac, to be there.

This is where I first got a proper handle on basic birth chart interpretation, using what the Twins refer to as the "three-part puzzle" for examining each "aspect"—or planetary placement in non-astro-speak—in a chart. More on this to come. It was also where I got my first taste of comparing two people's charts (another of the Twins' pet subjects)—in the process uncovering some home truths about my chart in relationship to my mum's, for example, that have gone on to shape the way we understand and therefore communicate with each other, taking our mother-daughter connection to a whole other, more forgiving, level. Big stuff. And yet more fuel to my already burning astrological obsession.

## READING YOUR CHART

So first up, it's very important to understand that your Sun sign, which is the sign you read for when you check your daily horoscope, really only represents part of your nature, even though popular culture puts so much emphasis on it. But there are actually eleven planets at play in any one birth chart (including the Sun, Moon, and North Node, which aren't *technically* planets, but which astrologers treat as such), each of which has a bearing on said chart. As such, you also have a Venus sign, a Mercury sign, and so on.

And then there is your Rising sign, or Ascendant—the sign of the zodiac the Sun was rising in at the specific time of your birth—which also has a major role to play. Rising signs change every two hours, though, so it's only possible to calculate your Rising sign if you happen to know, to the nearest two hours, what time you chose to come into the world. But if you don't, never fear, it's by no means essential for calculating your chart.

Which, thanks to the aforementioned wonders of the Internet, you can do for free online. In fact, if you haven't already, go and do it now at www.astrostyle.com, the online home of the AstroTwins, where there's a link on the homepage for you to "Do your chart for free." If you don't know your specific time of birth, you can just enter 12 P.M. (this won't affect the other planetary aspects). It might also be a good idea to print it out, so you can take some notes.

Okay, got it? Good. And if you don't have access to a computer right now, here's what my chart looks like, to give you an idea:

| ☉ | Sun | ♄ | Saturn | ♈ | Aries | ♎ | Libra |
|---|-----|---|--------|---|-------|---|-------|
| ☽ | Moon | ♅ | Uranus | ♉ | Taurus | ♏ | Scorpio |
| ☿ | Mercury | ♆ | Neptune | ♊ | Gemini | ♐ | Sagittarius |
| ♀ | Venus | ♇ | Pluto | ♋ | Cancer | ♑ | Capricorn |
| ♂ | Mars | ☊ | N. Node | ♌ | Leo | ♒ | Aquarius |
| ♃ | Jupiter | ℞ | Retrograde | ♍ | Virgo | ♓ | Pisces |

Pretty technical looking, I know, and I'm not going to go into too much detail here. But there are four things to focus on for now.

First, see that circle in the middle? That's you. Or, if you're looking at my chart, that's me. Hi! Yes, pretty egotistical, since IRL, the planets actually revolve around the Sun. But in our birth chart, we get to sit center stage.

Now, look at the outer ring of the chart. This is the Zodiac Wheel, and as you can see it's divided into twelve sections, one for each SIGN of the zodiac, as denoted by the twelve different symbols or "glyphs" in the right-hand columns of the table opposite—which you may recognize from when you read your horoscope or see your Sun sign written about. My chart begins in Sagittarius on the left (or East) at "9 o'clock," where it says "A.C." (for Ascendant).

LEARNING NO. 1: The signs of the zodiac represent the different aspects of our personality, how we show up in the world and deal with situations.

Next up, you'll see that the middle ring is also divided into twelve sections. These are the different HOUSES of the chart, and they're numbered 1 to 12, beginning, again, at the nine o'clock position on the left. Each house is "ruled" by the sign it intersects—so my First house is ruled by Sagittarius, my Second house by Capricorn, my Third by Pisces (just), and so on. As such, each house will be colored by the personality of the sign it's ruled by.

LEARNING NO. 2: The houses represent the different areas of life that we operate in—love, work, home and family, and so on.

Finally, check out the symbols floating in the different houses. These represent the PLANETS, and the chart is essentially like a screengrab of their position in the solar system at the time of our birth.

LEARNING NO. 3: The planets represent our motivation in life, the things that drive us to act.

Basic chart interpretation lies in learning how these three elements interact with one another—planet, house, and sign—as they show up in different combinations in each and every individual birth chart. Here are a couple of examples to help explain what I mean.

As you can see in my chart, Mercury is in Aries in the Fourth house. Since Mercury is the planet of communication, and Aries is the sign of passion and all things new, it makes sense that I've always felt compelled to write about the next big trends! In my Fourth house of home and family conditioning, this could speak to the fact I feel most productive writing in my home environment (in fact in every magazine job I had, I did all my actual writing at home), as well as the fact that I was always encouraged to read as a kid.

On a deeper level, the Fourth house also rules women's issues, suggesting that my writing is destined to somehow impact the lives of women. Add my Moon (subconscious impulses and needs) being in Cancer (the sign ruling the feminine principle) in the deeply "mystical" Eighth house and, well, I bring you The Numinous. Um . . . confused yet?! As you are beginning to see, the "language" of astrology can get pretty complex, offering layers and layers of information to be interpreted. So, for now, let's get back to basics.

Before I move on to an overview of the different areas covered by each planet, house, and sign, a quick word about the Rising sign and house positions if you don't know your exact time of birth. Basically, it's impossible to get an accurate read on these without a time—but you will still know which sign each planet is in, plenty to work with as you begin to get to know your chart.

So once again, the rule to remember is:

---

## BASIC BIRTH CHART INTERPRETATION

Planet (motivation) + Sign (how you direct this) + House (the area of life where that motivation and effort will manifest).

As you'll begin to see once I get into the traits of each planet, sign, and house of the zodiac below, there's lots of crossover, all kinds of subtleties, and many, many different ways to interpret what the AstroTwins call this "three-part puzzle." And besides bucket-loads of experience, I believe the most skilled astrologers employ a degree of intuition, tapping into the *numinous* nature of this mystical science, when interpreting a chart.

As Julia and Derek Parker write in their brilliant *Parkers' Astrology* (a great beginner's book for anybody serious about the study of astrology): "The art of interpreting a chart is to look much more deeply—to consider the many different aspects shown by planets and signs and their inter-relationships, and weigh them so that one mitigates or strengthens the effect of another. You can, in this way, discover an in-depth portrait of yourself that is astonishing in its light and shade, its subtlety and persuasiveness."

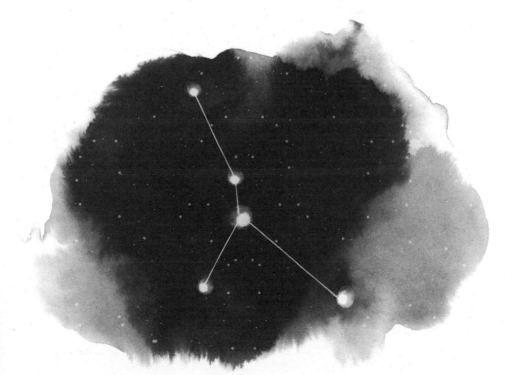

And, well, if that's the end goal, we all need to start somewhere—so here's a cheat sheet for you to refer to as you begin to look at your own chart:

## The Planets

☉ **THE SUN:** Self-awareness, personal power, life force, creativity, essence, self-expression, spirit, will, drive for personal significance

☾ **THE MOON:** Feelings, instincts, moods, response to things, gut reactions, emotional security, basic needs

☿ **MERCURY:** Communication, speech, thoughts, logic, analysis, ideas, intellect

♀ **VENUS:** Beauty, love, taste, harmony, aesthetics, attraction, charm, romance, sensuality, comfort

♂ **MARS:** Action, energy, desire, impulse, drive, strength, courage, anger, competition

♃ **JUPITER:** Enthusiasm, luck, fortune, optimism, positivity, generosity, benevolence, truth, outgoingness

♄ **SATURN:** Discipline, structure, wisdom, ambition, practicality, realism, responsibility, karma

♅ **URANUS:** Breakthrough, the unexpected, innovation, sudden change, insight, awakening, originality

♆ **NEPTUNE:** Imagination, ideals, sympathy, compassion, intuition, emotions, universal love, dreams, fantasy

♇ **PLUTO:** Fundamental transformation, change, death and rebirth, basic drive, regeneration, inheritance

☊ **NORTH NODE** (not an actual celestial body, but a point referring to the Moon's position in relation to the other planets at the time of your birth): Life purpose, destiny, personal growth, supportive people, potential

SOUTH NODE (this may not be shown on your chart but will always be in the opposite sign as the North Node): Old patterns, past-life experience, inherited traits, innate talents, cultural conditioning

## The Signs

Remember! Your chart will be influenced by ALL the signs to some degree—so no simply looking at your Sun sign and going: "Oh yeah, that's me." The traits of each sign show how you direct the energy of the planet it holds in your chart.

♈ ARIES: Self-starting, outgoing, active, forceful, entrepreneurial, self-confident, strong

♉ TAURUS: Stable, persistent, productive, deliberate, wealthy, practical, reliable

♊ GEMINI: Communicative, witty, adaptable, curious, many sided, variety seeking

♋ CANCER: Sensitive, feeling, receptive, nostalgic, security oriented, emotionally perceptive

♌ LEO: Expressive, self-aware, entertaining, playful, warm, childlike, creative, dramatic

♍ VIRGO: Analytical, logical, intelligent, detail oriented, sensible, methodical

♎ LIBRA: Balanced, just, tolerant, relationship oriented, sociable, cooperative, diplomatic

♏ SCORPIO: Intense, determined, thorough, energetic, secretive, passionate, forceful

♐ SAGITTARIUS: Enthusiastic, optimistic, jovial, friendly, generous, expansive, honest

♑ CAPRICORN: Organized, serious, practical, ambitious, hardworking, disciplined, realistic

♒ AQUARIUS: Friendly, intuitive, original, independent, unique, inventive, experimental

♓ PISCES: Imaginative, sentimental, sympathetic, compassionate, artistic, dreamy, escapist

## The Houses

FIRST HOUSE: Personality, physical body, self-image, personal self-expression

SECOND HOUSE: Finances, personal possessions, talents, earning ability, values

THIRD HOUSE: Communication, learning, information, discussions, siblings, transportation

FOURTH HOUSE: Home, family, the mother, nourishment, emotions, habits

FIFTH HOUSE: Creativity, love affairs, play, pleasure seeking, entertainment, art

SIXTH HOUSE: Daily work, health and wellness, diet, medical treatment, cleanliness

SEVENTH HOUSE: Relationships, partnerships, cooperation, social awareness, justice

EIGHTH HOUSE: Transformation, power, death and rebirth, sexuality, inheritance, taxes

NINTH HOUSE: Travel, philosophy, learning, aspirations, religion, spiritual teachers

TENTH HOUSE: Career, reputation, ambition, responsibilities and duties, the father, politics

ELEVENTH HOUSE: Friends, group activities, humanitarian interests, insights, rebellion

TWELFTH HOUSE: Healing, the subconscious, ideals, meditation, spiritual development

So once you've dug into your own chart . . . it's pretty much a given that you'll want to start looking at the charts of all the most important people in your life. Your family members, your lover, your boss. That irritating friend you can't help loving to death. There are specific ways to interpret how two charts interact with each other, but that gets kind of advanced to go into here. Suffice it to say that comparing the traits of, say, your Cancer Moon and your mother's Gemini Moon will begin to give you some insight into why, when it comes to certain basic needs, it can be difficult for the two of you to relate.

Yes, this is an example from my own life, and being able to "see" this in our charts was actually the first step on what has been an incredibly healing journey for my relationship with my mum. There'd never been a lack of *love* between us, but I was always frustrated by what felt like a fundamental inability to communicate on a soul level. I think one of the reasons I left home so young is because I spent a lot of time feeling guilty for not being the kind of daughter I thought she wanted: a.k.a. one who wanted to share every detail of my emotional life with her.

Following a checkered path juggling various jobs to try and make ends meet, she has actually found her calling as a psychotherapist (she studied the work of Carl Jung among others, the Swiss founder of analytical psychology who, by the way, was deeply invested in astrology as a tool for analysis). Makes sense, then, that her focus has always been on *airing your feelings* to heal—whereas I have always been deeply private about my emotional life, preferring to keep my feelings close to my chest until it feels safe to share. That's some not-so-friendly Gemini (her)/Cancer (me) Moon-sign friction right there.

You can add to this that her Gemini Moon is in her expressive Fifth house, while my Cancer Moon is in my secretive Eighth house! But guess what? Developing an awareness of this conflict through the lens of astrology has also helped me see the value in "her" way of doing things, and to therefore override my innate fear of sharing my emotions—a healing journey in itself.

And yes, considering all the different ways each aspect in a chart can be interpreted, an argument can be made that it's always possible to see what you want to. But I believe this is also the point: that you see (or choose to see) what you do in a chart *for a reason*. This is where the intuition part comes in. So long as you are fearless in following your gut to what *feels like* the truest reading for any particular aspect, no matter how inconvenient or ugly, you will be gifted with rough diamonds of self-awareness to polish and allow to inform your choices and actions going forward.

By using this technique to better understand my needs and my mum's, and the ways in which we move through the world as a result, our relationship has been transformed. For my part, developing the maturity to override my "crabby" Cancer Moon tendencies (Cancer is symbolized by a crab in its shell) and give her what she always needed from me—a real heart-to-heart—is what's been instrumental in moving our relationship on. Not overnight, not without us airing some difficult truths about our shared history, and not without buckets of tears. But we've gotten to a place where I know we both feel like mother and daughter in a way we were never able to before. It's this that's helped me evolve and open up about my feelings in other areas of my life too.

As the AstroTwins' Ophira puts it: "Astrology is a tool for radical forgiveness," and it's not like either my mum or I changed *who we are*. Rather, I've been able to see our differences from a whole more accepting perspective. She is she, I am me, these are our differing needs, *and that's okay*.

So if astrology in my book (this book) is for self-reflection, with a view to deeper self-knowledge, a few more words on what I do *not* believe it's for—and that's planning every move you make, every single second, of every single day.

You're no doubt aware of how some people act like the world must come to a standstill every time Mercury goes into retrograde (i.e., slows its path in the sky so it *looks like* it's moving backward). As the planet of communication, contracts, and technology, Mercury's roughly thrice-yearly retro phase is supposedly a time when things go haywire/backwards in these areas—and as you may well have experienced, this can definitely be the case!

But this is NOT a reason or an excuse to go hide under a rock until it resumes "forward" motion. Because guess what? *All* the planets are going retrograde and making all kinds of other "negative" aspects *all* the time, stirring trouble and rubbing one another the wrong way. If we put our lives on hold every time the cosmos was looking anything less than blue skies ahead, we'd never do anything. In fact, going back to my likening astrology to a kind of cosmic weather forecast, you don't cancel your plans because it looks like rain out—but you do pack an umbrella.

I also like the analogy used by Dr. Chee Ming Wong, an anesthetist I interviewed once who regularly cast his own astrological divinations: "If there's a bumpy road ahead, then it would be wise to slow down. Conversely, there will be moments that are potentially advantageous." According to wonderful Dr. Ming Wong (*scientifically trained Dr. Ming Wong*): "The scientific discipline is good at measuring observable phenomena. Yet, for all that remains a mystery, perhaps the way of the ancients, which includes astrology, provides a well-trodden pathway in exploring the science of the unknown."

Something to recite in the face of all those who will invariably treat you like a total Froot Loop for choosing to believe that the celestial bodies with which we share our place in space have any bearing on our earthly, human lives whatsoever. Along with this quote, a favorite of mine, from *Parkers' Astrology:* "The Universe is not only stranger than we think, but stranger than we *can* think." I rest my case, amen.

## 2.

# INTERPRETING THE TAROT THE NOW AGE WAY

This is an impression of me reading the tarot for myself: Shuffle the deck while tuning in to the energy of the situation I'm asking about. Shuffle the deck some more, and pick a card. Study the card briefly, and look up the meaning. If the message is positive, give myself a high five and go about my day with a spring in my step. If the message is negative, repeat above steps until I get a good one.

Thing is, more often than not the cards I pull in my admittedly amateur divinations suggest confusion, difficulties, and strife. They show misunderstandings up ahead or suggest that my own motives might be less than noble. None of which I really want to hear—and one of the reasons I've been slower to embrace the tarot when in search of insight, clarity, and self-knowledge.

In fact, when I first began to connect with the cards in any kind of meaningful way a few years back, I put them down again almost immediately. The Pisces had bought me the Rider Waite tarot a few Christmases ago, until recently the most famous and popular deck, and both the imagery on the cards and the descriptions of their meanings were often downright scary. Take the Devil card for example—which shows the classic "horned beast" punishing a naked couple bound by chains with a scepter of fire. I remember giving a "practice" reading to my niece after our holiday feast, and the look of abject terror on her eleven-year-old face after I pulled this card for her.

*Not for me,* I told myself, internally accusing the makers of the Rider Waite of scaremongering and manipulation. I would stick to astrology as my preferred method of cosmic weather forecasting, which felt so much more expansive and open to interpretation (i.e., easier to put a positive spin on things—after all, even a heavy Saturn transit is really about helping you build some rock-solid karmic muscle).

Plus, if truly understanding astrology is a lifelong study, akin to learning a whole new language, then the tarot appeared to be equally dense with meaning and tradition. I was well aware that perhaps my less than expert readings were the reason I wasn't able to glean anything but a face-value fear factor from the more "difficult" cards—but did I really have time to tackle a "minor" in tarot, when I'd already committed a large chunk of my study time to my "major," astrology?

Talk about lack mentality! What I've since discovered is that, in fact, astrology and tarot can be used to complement each other (more on this later), and that it's totally possible to dip a toe into the tarot here and there and still get plenty from it. I just had to ignore the impatient, perfectionist part of me (another trait of Sun and Mercury in competitive Aries, go figure) that was putting pressure on myself to learn the tarot overnight. Plus, I found I couldn't walk away from the cards that easily. If astrology had always been fascinating to me, the tarot held a similar allure. And, as I began to develop The Numinous, it also seemed to be gaining popularity in real time, with all sorts of beautiful new decks appearing on the scene.

To bring it back to basics for a minute, a tarot deck is composed of seventy-eight cards, divided into the Major and the Minor Arcana. The twenty-two cards of the Major Arcana incorporate "characters" such as the Devil and the Star, but also "concepts" like the Tower and the World. The fifty-six cards of the Minor Arcana are divided into four "suits"—Cups, Swords, Pentacles, and Wands—numbered Ace through King (a bit like a pack of regular playing cards). In a reading, the cards are shuffled and those selected by the person getting the reading, laid out in what's called a "spread." The positions in the spread usually relate to different elements of the inquiry—for example, the

# TAROT IS NOT FOR FORTUNE-TELLING BY LOUISE ANDROLIA

I believe we're most empowered and feeling our best when we're fully in our mind, body, and spirit. To get here, we need to be really clear about what our journey actually looks like. What is the ground we're walking on, and how connected do we feel to all the different elements of our self?

I use the tarot as a way to communicate with the most loving and truthful part of myself. When you turn a card over, if you see it as a reflection of your subconscious, then it can only be showing you something that, deep down, you already know. Using the tarot for myself, I often get a hit of, *Yes, I knew that*. And this in itself can be very comforting.

I see working with tarot as making a commitment to yourself. To paying attention to what's making you uncomfortable, to listening to your intuition, and exploring what's really happening in the present moment.

In this sense, the tarot is an incredible self-help tool—I don't like to use it for divination and fortune-telling. It doesn't serve anybody to be constantly trying to predict the future, since it leaves the present moment sort of flapping around, not knowing what to do with itself. Because also, the future is completely fluid and only NOW is real.

This means that the present moment is the only place we can act from, and our most empowered actions lie in our ability to take a risk and take a beautiful, brave step forward. The cards can show us what steps to take. This is often a humbling and heartbreaking process, because it often comes with a huge leap of faith and trust in our journey. Of surrender.

past, present, and potential future outcome of a situation (this is a classic three-card spread).

I've come to see that my misconceptions about tarot as a tool (an often scary one) for fortune-telling are shared by many. And based on the above depiction of a tarot "reading," it's easy to see why—for example, the Devil card appearing in the "future" position in a reading is enough to scare the bejesus out of anybody. Until, that is, you learn to interpret the tarot *the Now Age way*.

My dear friend Louise Androlia, an artist and mentor and one of the first people I shared my vision for The Numinous with, has been working with the tarot for almost twenty years, on both a personal and a professional level. And the first thing she will tell anybody is that, rather than a way to "predict" future events: "A reading is *a perfect reflection of your subconscious*." And as such, each and every card contains a valuable learning to help us navigate whatever stage we're at in our personal evolution. Yes, even the Death card—which corresponds with the energy of Scorpio, the sign embodying the cycle of death and *rebirth* (Lou's Sun sign, and one of her favorite cards). The Devil, meanwhile, points to addictive behavior patterns that may somehow be enslaving us—pointing, therefore, to an opportunity to recognize these and escape the "hell" of addictions.

Scary since: "Change and the unknown are two of the things humans are most afraid of, and as such learning how to change our habits is one of our most important lessons," Lou told me when I asked her more about it. "The Death card, meanwhile, is just a reminder that change is our natural state, since everything in nature goes through cycles of death and rebirth. There's something so comforting in that for me."

And so when Death shows up in a reading, it's not a sign you'd better watch your step since there's a body bag out there with your name on it. Rather, it can be read as an invitation to acknowledge where in your life an ending is occurring, to allow a *new* relationship/project/mind-set to come into being.

Lindsay Mack, another reader whose work I've come to know and love and who currently writes the monthly Tarotscopes on The

Numinous, reads this card as a death of the ego—what she describes as "the sacred fertilizer that's needed to help bring forth the new." See how this changes the energy around the card from scary to *exciting*?

And then there is the multitude of new decks blossoming like spring blooms all over my Instagram feed—what Lindsay describes as "evolved" decks: "meaning they're more feminine and holographic. A deck like the Rider Waite was created by men and based on Christian imagery. Motherpeace, the Medicine Woman Tarot, and the Starchild Tarot are great examples of more feminine and holistic decks." Lindsay even thinks the Wild Unknown deck, featuring the inviting yet mythical black-and-white artwork of Portland-based artist and yoga instructor Kim Krans, can be held solely responsible for what she sees as the tarot currently having a moment. "People are really drawn to Kim's style, which is so visually accessible and modern," she explained to me.

I also feel like tarot is gaining in popularity because it's kind of like *Google for your soul*. We have access to sooooo many answers in the Now Age, since regular ol' Google means we can get instant access to all the information that's ever been plugged into the Internet about every subject in the world, ever. But since very little of the information has been shared with our specific needs, questions, or journey in mind, things can very quickly become misleading—resulting in yet more confusion. The tarot, on the other hand, is a tool for tapping back into our own *inner knowing*.

Another deck I love is called the Thoth deck, named for the Egyptian god of writing, magic, and science and designed in the late 1930s by the famous occultist Aleister Crowley. And here's the thing: in the past, that reference would have just reinforced my fear of the tarot. "The Occult" sounds dark and scary, right? But the word *occult* actually just means "hidden." And what is the tarot if not a tool for excavating the hidden truths—*truths our higher Self wants us to become aware of*—of a given situation?

As for my personal practice? I'm still more inclined to celebrate and carry the message of the "positive" cards with me, but I'm learning

Tarot is a tool for tapping back into our own inner knowing.

not to shy away from the harsher-seeming messages too—just like my numinous journey overall is helping me accept and embrace every messy aspect of *being human*. So read on for twenty empowering Now Age lessons about the tarot that have helped me get to this place and incorporate the cards as a valuable component of my numinous toolkit.

## 1. The different kinds of cards—an overview.

If the Major Arcana are like the A-list players in a movie, playing the "parts," or higher forces, moving the action forward, then the Court Cards (King, Queen, Knight/Prince, and Page/Princess) of the Minor Arcana often represent our psychological state, as well as the actual people involved in a situation.

Meanwhile, the suits each correspond to an element and go something like this:

WANDS—Fire energy/passion/doing
SWORDS—Air energy/ideas/thinking
CUPS—Water energy/emotions/feeling
DISCS—Earth energy/work/making

As a rule, the Ace of each suit speaks to the energy of new beginnings, while the higher the number (2–10), the more extremely the element will be exerting itself in the reading.

This is a very rudimentary overview, and every reader I've met will agree you can do a whole two-hour class on the intricate meanings of just one card. But one step at a time. As Lou puts it, "Even just learning about the elements will give you an entire self-help practice."

## 2. It's all good.

The first thing to remember—as lovely Lindsay puts it—is that "nothing in life is happening *to* you, since everything is happening *for* you." For you to be empowered in your personal evolution, that is. This simple shift in perspective has been enough to reframe my relationship with the "scarier" aspects of the tarot. Plus it's kind of an amazing life lesson in general, so please keep this front of mind.

## 3. There's no such thing as a "bad" card.

When I first starting reading about the meaning of the different cards, I was shocked how many, like at least half, seemed to depict the shadow side of life: disappointments, frustrations, and unscrupulous individuals. But let's get really real—life *ain't* no bed of roses, and actually isn't the point of developing all this spiritual awareness to help us deal better with the inevitable thorns? In Lou's experience, the more "challenging" cards simply reflect the things showing up in our reality that we'd rather not deal with. Like the Five of Cups, for example—which speaks to feelings of sadness and loss. I love her message (spoken like a true Scorpio) that "part of our self-discovery is to look at our shadows and sit in our discomfort—as this is what deepens our levels of compassion towards ourselves and others."

## 4. Tarot is not a tool for prediction.

As I've explained, like a lot of people I came to the tarot with the idea that it is mainly used for "fortune-telling," and that this is where a lot of my initial fear came from. If my fate were somehow written irreversibly in the cards, what if I got a "bad" one? Rather, like with astrology, I've come to understand the tarot as a system of symbols that can be used to tap the Universal consciousness and access information from our highest Self. The cards and the messages imprinted on them are the "bridge" between our guides, God, the Universe, and so on, and our human understanding, and it is the reader's job (whether it's me or somebody else reading for me) to simply act as an interpreter for the information being delivered.

## 5. The tarot is YOU.

What a brilliant metaphor for helping to understand your deck! After all, you know better than anyone what a weirdo you are, right? Or rather, how many seemingly different weirdos you can embody in any given day, relationship, situation—veering from one emotion to the next, from crazy to rational thoughts and back, from lovable to needy and manipulative. (Please tell me this isn't just me.) Anyway, how about imagining each of the seventy-eight cards as a different facet of your/ our intricate human state? Like how the Fool is the naive part of us that will just say yes to anything and dive in with little regard for the consequences, or how the Two of Swords represents the way we can endlessly argue a point—with ourselves! According to Lou, "The more I look at the tarot, the more I understand myself, because I'm really just learning about the human psyche and our experience."

## 6. Pick a word, any word.

As you get to know your deck, Lindsay also suggests choosing one word that best represents the energy of each card for you. In the Thoth deck, the creators of the deck have gone ahead and done this for you—for example, the Six of Discs is also "Success" (representing material gain and power), while the Three of Swords is "Sorrow" (melancholy and unhappiness). You can also attribute actual characters to the court cards. When I asked another reader friend, the New Age Hipster, to write about the Queen cards for The Numinous, she attributed the Queen of Pentacles to Beyoncé, and the Queen of Cups to Bridget Jones. So you can see how choosing a character for each card can make it even easier to connect with its individual nature.

## 7. There's no right or wrong way to read the tarot.

Since the messages delivered by the tarot are all in the interpretation, it makes sense that each of us will see something different in the cards.

Beyond the basics—such as the different suits representing the different elements/areas of life—how we deliver and therefore interpret the information in a reading will depend entirely on our own life experience and unique worldview. In other words, what our higher Self chooses to show us *is* the message.

## 8. Because the tarot is also a mirror.

While the best readers I know wouldn't necessarily call themselves "psychic," they are gifted intuitives—since being tapped in to your inner Voice / higher Self is a prerequisite for delivering an authentic reading (see above). In this sense, the tarot, and the reader delivering the information, can also be understood as a mirror—reflecting *out* what's going on with*in* the person getting the reading. Lou sees the role of the reader as an interpreter, as well as a teacher. As she puts it, "The cards are showing you something you already know, but perhaps aren't aware of because of all your anxieties layered on top. A reading is really an opportunity for my client to be reminded to look at their life through their own loving lens, which they may have forgotten is always available to them. In a session I also encourage them to be part of the reading. I am not there to 'tell' them things. The days of disempowered fortune-telling are well and truly over, and it's time to trust the power we have within."

## 9. The tarot is an invitation to evolve.

In Buddhist philosophy, the only constant is change—as illustrated beautifully by the cards of the Major Arcana. The Majors are said to represent the different stages in the evolution of consciousness, from the Fool depicting birth/inception (of, say, an idea, project, person, or relationship) to the World signifying completion, fulfillment, mastery— or even enlightenment. This process shows up throughout different spiritual traditions and is also sometimes called "the hero's journey." Meanwhile, the Minors depict the cycles of said evolution. Seen this way, the message in *every* card, Major or Minor, carries an invitation to step into and participate with the evolutionary process of being human. Not all of which was ever going to be easy, rewarding, or pretty.

## 10. We still get to choose.

Because of free will, the tarot is still only an *invitation* to evolve. In the same way astrology can be viewed as a sort of cosmic road map, with plenty of opportunity for self-directed detours, whether we choose to follow the guidance offered by the tarot is entirely up to us. Pull the Fool when you're wondering if you should quit your job and start your own business, and the Universal energies are suggesting that the time is right to *just go for it*. But you totally get to keep your cubicle if for whatever reason you still don't feel ready. A.k.a. free will!

## 11. Pick a pretty deck.

Along with the Wild Unknown by Kim Krans, three of my favorite decks are the Starchild Tarot by Danielle Noel, the Serpentfire deck by Devany Wolfe, and the Invisible Light Tarot by Brandy Eve Allen. Visually enchanting (to me at least), they are also infused with a sexy, upbeat energy I find attractive, inspiring, and compelling. The imagery of the Rider Waite deck never really resonated with me, and it's no surprise really. It was designed in 1910, and although it must have seemed modern then, dumbing down the even heavier religious overtones of previous decks, times and attitudes have certainly a-changed. But again, each to their own. Lou loves the Rider Waite, finding infinite meaning in the artwork. Which leads me to . . .

## 12. Let your deck choose you.

Lindsay says decks are like the wands in *Harry Potter*—they choose who they want to work with. The Thoth deck found me through PR guru and *America's Next Top Model* judge Kelly Cutrone, who I persuaded to give me a reading while on a press trip in Denver. In a past life (not literally—it was back in the 1990s), Kelly worked as a professional tarot reader on Venice Beach. To this day, she ONLY reads with the Thoth, telling me how the illustrations actually shape-shift in front of her eyes to deliver specific pieces of information.

Lou says the same thing about her favorite deck, the Cosmic Tarot: "The archetypes—the people cards—actually come to life for me. The faces morph into the faces of people I've known. Sometimes they even appear to turn their heads to look at me." Cosmic indeed! And most readers will say that once you truly connect with a deck, it will in some way "come alive" in your hands.

The Starchild Tarot has actually become my go-to—first because I find the artwork to be truly enchanting, and second because every single card I pull, for myself and others, offers an immediate and (what feels like) true answer to the situation in hand. In other words, it *just speaks my language.*

### 13. Begin with a one-card pull.

Perhaps the simplest way to get familiar with the energies and symbolism of the seventy-eight different cards is to commit to a daily one-card pull. As in, ask a question, pull a card, and interpret the message. (And then don't get *too* attached to it, continuing to exercise your free will!). What I have found completely fascinating about this practice are the patterns that emerge: like pulling the same card for myself day after day, but in relation to seemingly different situations. It's also totally cool to pull a second, or even a third card if you're not getting what feels like a clear message right away. But be aware that each card you pull will have informed the final reading. Generally speaking, a card's meaning is strengthened when you pull another card of the same suit. Meanwhile, cards of an opposite nature are weakened: Swords are opposed to Discs; Wands oppose Cups. Likewise, Swords are friendly to Cups and Wands; Wands like Swords and Discs.

## 14. How you ask is everything.

As Lindsay Mack puts it: "As a human I like to think I'm pretty awesome, but I always ask for guidance from a higher power when I do a reading." And duh—since we're looking to access the *Divine intelligence* within us, why would you not dial up your guides and ask the Universe to please pay attention as you pose your question? These are busy entities, after all, and so asking nicely for them to be present for you is just kind of polite. You can keep this process simple or get as ritualistic as you like, using whatever language feels right for you. But to cut to the chase, Lindsay also suggests asking for information containing "the Truth with a capital T."

## 15. No question is too small.

Don't feel like every card you pull for yourself has to be about a major life transition or hard-core relationship inquiry. Since you're reading this book, I'd hazard a guess that you're pretty invested in your personal development, and so it's likely you're the kind of person who feels compelled to dig beneath the surface. But while you're practicing, a few days playing in the shallow end of the pool will help build your confidence for the deeper dives. Plus tap you into one very important (for me anyway) truth about the tarot—it can be a lot of fun!

Lou is always talking about how ridiculous it is to be human sometimes, and actually when you take a step back and check out the kind of stuff we get our knickers in a twist about, it is often kind of absurd/hilarious (with hindsight at least). Sure, your higher Self is primed with all the information you need to navigate the sharper bends in your path, but she/he/they also want you to enjoy the journey. So what if all you really need to know today is what shoes to wear to a party? She/he/*the tarot* can help with these kinds of questions too.

## 16. But be expansive with it.

Instead of asking, "Kale salad or vegan sushi rolls?" (which limits you to just two options), try an open-ended question. "How will the kale salad make me feel?" opens up the playing field, inviting a more expansive worldview. Like, a Whole Foods salad bar of options. Being expansive in how you ask will lead to more questions, and therefore more cards, so also know when to stop. It's one thing to inquire, and another to use the tarot as a tool for endless procrastination. As with the Whole Foods salad bar, know when you've had/asked enough.

## 17. Now design your own spread.

While the one-card pull is a great place to start, it can also get kind of limiting, and once things start to get a little bit more advanced, the reading becomes about how the cards interact with each other. There are many books detailing the different kinds of "spreads" (where multiple cards are placed in different positions to inform different parts of the reading), from a three-card "past, present, future" reading, to the classic "Celtic cross" (which also takes in "self," "others," "hopes and fears," etc.).

But I love what Lou suggested to me recently, namely that "you get better insight when you're really specific with a spread, designing positions and questions that really go in deep." For example, this could look like a three-card spread with cards that ask: "Is this a great time to expand our family?" "What would I need to prepare me for motherhood?" "What kind of mother would I be?" No prizes for guessing what was on my mind when we had that particular chat.

## 18. The astro-tarot connection.

When I tried learning Spanish, whenever I couldn't remember a word my brain would automatically sub in the French (which I had studied in high school)—and I find it similarly difficult to separate my understanding of astrology and the tarot. Luckily, there are all kinds of crossovers! Officially, each of the major arcane *is* linked to an astrological sign—as outlined in Rachel Pollack's book *Tarot Wisdom,* widely recognized as something of a tarot bible. As mentioned, Death, representing transformation, is ruled by Scorpio. The Fool, the first card in the deck, is pure Aries: naively headstrong, and also the first sign of the zodiac. And then there's how the different suits represent the four elements, which in turn are embodied by the twelve signs of the zodiac. And then there is the way the cycles in the tarot (numbers 1–7, 8–14, and 15–21 representing different evolutionary phases in the Major Arcana, for example) could be said to mirror the waxing and waning phases of the Moon.

## 19. Numerology is also at play . . .

. . . as are different religious symbols, figures from ancient Greek, Roman, and pagan mythology, the teachings of the Kabalistic Tree of Life, et cetera. In fact, the tradition of tarot is INCREDIBLY rich with history and infused with layers of meaning and symbolism. Way too complex to go into here, which leads me to . . .

## 20. If you're serious about the tarot, then study it.

Buy a few books, or even take a proper class. As with learning any new language, there's really no substitute for discussing each card in depth, in a group setting, for delving into the many possible meanings and getting these teachings to stick. I've heard Lou describe the tarot as "an infinite well of knowledge" and "like having a therapist with you always." As I called it in the intro, the tarot is kind of "Google for the soul"—and what a brilliant investment in your emotional well-being to be able to add this ancient system to your spiritual toolkit.

# MATERIAL GIRL, MYSTICAL WORLD TAROT SPREAD BY LINDSAY MACK

The perfect layout to create a balance between both worlds and divine what's going on above and below.

CARD 1: The matter at hand

CARD 2: What's swirling beneath the surface?

CARD 3: What am I moving on from?

CARD 4: What is ready to manifest in its place?

CARD 5: What is the deepest medicine and wisdom available to me at this moment?

CARD 6: Outcome

# 3.

# "YOU KNOW YOU'RE PSYCHIC IF YOU HAVE A BODY"

When I first met Betsy LeFae, I knew she was my kind of medium. And if she's taught me anything, it's that first impressions, gut feelings and hunches—about a person, or a job, or a potentially soul-destroying relationship for that matter—are *really* worth going with. Even if going with them means walking away from a killer "on paper" opportunity, pissing a bunch of people off, or making yourself look like a total idiot.

Betsy and I were introduced by my friend Jules, a downtown New York jewelry designer who makes pieces for Rihanna and Beyoncé and who has a healthy appreciation for the mystical herself. (She's the kind of girl who goes to Iceland on vacation and winds up naked in a sweat lodge.) Anyhow, Jules had hired Betsy to do palm readings at the launch of a new collection, and when I told Jules all about my plans for The Numinous, she insisted we had to meet.

I'd had limited success with psychics in the past, having mainly been exposed to them as a journalist at product launches (like Jules's event, I guess), where you get a ten-minute reading after some publicist has plied you with wine and your brain's all soggy anyway. When I went for a proper session with the psychic all the fashion people in London go to, her "predictions" were so ridiculous ("a former airline pilot named Pete will have the key to your new apartment . . .") it felt like I'd been punked.

My one good experience was with a woman called Katie Winterbourne, when I was about twenty-five and having a hard time trusting my decision-making processes. It actually felt more like a therapy session. She used a tarot deck to divine the root of the issues I'd been facing, and I just remember crying buckets and walking out feeling like I had all the answers I'd been looking for. What she'd essentially done, and what I've come to realize is the job of any psychic worth their crystal ball, is tap me into my *own* intuition.

Which brings me back to my first meeting with Betsy, who had invited me for an almond chai latte at a café near her apartment in East Williamsburg. We'd been chatting about ways she could contribute to The Numinous, and so far the cute-as-a-button, tattooed woman in front of me was about as far removed from the clichéd image of a psychic as you can get. There was no bejeweled turban, and no "mysterious" glint in her eye. She'd also been telling me about the time she read for Andrew W.K. and channeled the spirit of Steve Jobs for Vice TV. If my mission with The Numinous was to create a mainstream conversation about the Now Age, she was *beyond* perfect. Thank you, Universe. And Jules.

Betsy had also been hosting something called the Weekly Williamsburg Spirit Séance at her home for the past two years. Every Thursday, Betsy and her boyfriend, Bryan (they met on Okaycupid.com and bonded right away over spirituality, sacred geometry, and music for plants, of course), had invited eleven total strangers, along with their deceased ancestors, into their space. And all for a $10 donation. *Are you insane?!* was my first reaction. Since we'd just met, I didn't say this out loud. But seriously, there were some bona fide weirdos out there and this was New York freaking City (a.k.a. weirdo central).

The image that immediately flashed in my mind's eye when Betsy told me about her séances was of a group of, I dunno, voodoo-wielding screwballs?, descending weekly on her one-bedroom walk-up—an example of the prejudice I believe so many people have about all things Now Age. And having embraced this mystical path myself, and crossed over to the "other side," I've also found myself on the receiving end. I can see it in people's eyes sometimes when I explain what I do ("oh you're one of *those*") and hear it in an editor's tone of voice when he or she politely declines a story on, say, high-vibrational furniture made with crystals, designed to shift negative energy. On these occasions, I consciously choose to *not* try to "convert" the naysayers. If the New Age was about rebelling against the status quo, the Now Age way is simply to lead by the example of your fabulously mystical life.

But back to the notion of hosting a weekly séance in your home, wasn't it a little, um, dangerous? We've all seen *The Exorcist,* right? There's some gnarly energy out there in the spirit world, so surely you need to proceed with extreme caution. I soon learned, however, that Betsy was on a mission to set the record straight. She saw it as her unique contribution to the world to show each and every one of us that *we were all psychic too,* and that working with our *own* intuitive voice—as Katie Winterbourne helped me to do—was the first step to leading an ultimately fulfilling life. Rather than the portal to a scary-Mary supernatural experience we often associate with the word, the weekly "séance" was her way of reaching the masses with her message.

When she asked if I'd like to come along the following week, it was obviously an invitation I couldn't refuse (and little did I know I'd even get invited back for the "experts only" Halloween séance I wrote about in the introduction). My Numinous research was still in its infancy at this stage, and here was Betsy presenting me with an opportunity to go behind the "veil," the illusion of separation that detaches us from the "subtle realms" where pure spirit energy connects, and is accessible to, us all. This was exactly what Shelley von Strunckel was talking about, the place where even Miu Miu shoes paled into tacky, man-made insignificance in the face of true numinosity. And my gut was already telling me that Betsy would be a loving, conscientious, and informative guide. Gulp. It was a yes from me.

*  *  *

Cut to two weeks later and I've rounded up Simon (the Pisces) for moral support and a photographer to capture exactly how cute and nonpsychic-y Betsy is. I might have sounded all gung ho just then, but secretly I'm shitting myself—part of me, the Material Girl part who still has one Miu Miu–clad foot very much in the "real" world, is still convinced I'm about to find myself being confronted by the spirit of some long-forgotten, malignant ancestor in the company of a bunch of complete and utter freaks. But soon I and my crew (the other freaks are yet to show) are all sitting on Betsy and Bryan's big blue sofa while they prep the space. The scent of burning sage, used in shamanic traditions to cleanse negative energy, is heavy in the air as Bryan uses a fan made of macaw feathers to waft smoke from a lit bunch of the herb into every corner of the room.

As if she's reading my mind (funny that!), Betsy explains how this is a vital part of the process. "We want to make sure that only positive spirits of pure love are invited into the circle tonight," she says, and although Bryan is obviously a total expert with the wafting, I can't say this helps me feel any more at ease. An altar in the center of the room is also laid with crystals, and the blinds are drawn on the lingering heat of the midsummer's evening. It's 90 degrees outside, but that isn't the only reason my palms, my pits, and the creases behind my knees are pooling with sweat.

Soon, the rest of the guests are piling into the apartment. Who turn out not to be weirdos at all, but a bunch of completely normal-looking hipster kids—most of whom seem as nervous as me. There are sheepish grins all around, and questions hang unspoken in the air. If I really am psychic, my guess is that most of them are also thinking something along the lines of: *OMFG, WTF have I got myself into?* I take a few deep breaths and remind myself that Betsy does this every week, and there have been no reports of a boom in exorcisms in East Williamsburg to date.

Apart from one woman who's been before, it's everybody's first séance, and once we're all seated, Betsy starts by explaining what to expect. The idea is she'll open the circle with a prayer to protect us all with white light, call in our ancestors, state our positive intentions, and give gratitude, before leading a guided meditation to tune us all in to the Voice of our intuition / higher Self. Then, she'll go around the room and deliver a minireading for each of us. "And I invite you to share any messages you're getting for people in the circle too," she says. Huh?

"I like to say that you know you're psychic if you have a body. So . . . does everyone here have a body?" She grins. We look at one another. We nod. We do. "Spirit is actually giving you messages all day every day, and the way you receive them is through your body. So you might see an image, or hear a voice or another kind of sound. Maybe you smell burning when there's nothing on fire—that could be a message from the other side. *Your* job is to interpret what it means," she explains.

In psychic circles, these different ways of receiving information are known as the "clairs" (think "clear")—and there's one for each of the six senses. You've probably heard of somebody being "clairvoyant," which means they get clear "visual" messages (as in the French verb *voir,* meaning "to see"). Meanwhile, a "clairaudient" will clearly hear things, and a "claircognizant" will simply "know." Most people, Betsy explains, will be stronger in one or two of the clairs.

When an "impression" (image, smell, sound, taste, sensation, simple knowing) comes through, she goes on, it's actually just a *symbol* for the real message. The trick is to then attach a feeling to that symbol based on what it means to you and your personal life experience. So, say I'm

---

## THE SIX PSYCHIC SENSES

Clairvoyance: The ability to see psychic visions

Clairaudience: The ability to hear psychic messages

Clairgustance: The ability to taste psychic impressions

Clairalience: The ability to smell psychic impressions

Clairsentience: The ability to feel psychic sensations

Claircognizance: The ability to simply *know*

reading for somebody (or looking for a sign for myself) and out of nowhere I get Beyoncé's "Crazy in Love" playing on a loop in my head. Well, that song came out the year I got married and I really *was* crazy in love, with my Pisces, with my first magazine job, and with my life. The feeling in that song for me is one of celebration—so the message is that whatever we're talking about in the reading is something to be celebrated, or to make a commitment to. Perhaps, to get more specific, there even *is* a marriage proposal in the pipeline!

Are you following in the back? The way Betsy's explaining all this is making total sense to me, but the hard part, she's saying now, is then trusting your interpretation enough to actually share it.

"Nobody wants to look stupid, but the only way you'll know if you're right is by getting a confirmation from the person. So"—she looks around the circle—"I invite you again to share."

But first, the guided meditation part, in which Betsy talks us through a group visualization to clear and protect our energy, as well as call in our spirit guides, angels, and the ascended masters.

Then, a bit like a game of psychic spin the bottle, Betsy allows "spirit" to dictate the order she delivers people's readings—and the whole time I'm scanning my body for any out-of-context impressions that might actually be a message from somebody's dearly departed grandma. By now I'm so psyched I might actually be psychic that I'm actively willing spirit to use me as its channel. And then it comes.

Betsy is speaking to the woman directly across from me when my mind's eye fills with the color purple. And a very specific purple too: the deep magenta used to advertise a brand of cigarettes called Silk Cut, back around the time I thought it would be cool to start smoking in the early 1990s. I immediately go to the feeling, which is one of creeping unease, bordering on disgust (how I generally feel about smoking now). A lull in Betsy's reading means it's time to speak up: "Um . . . I'm getting . . . I wonder if . . . are you trying to give up smoking?" Epic fail; the woman shakes her head. But I get encouraging looks from Betsy and my fellow "students," and we continue.

Finally, Betsy turns to face me. She smiles.

"When I look at you, Ruby, I see flowers turning to fireworks . . ." And I swear on my mother's life that as she utters the word *fireworks,* the whole apartment begins to boom with the sound of a firework display starting up just outside the window over the East River. Even Betsy looks totally shocked and we're all obviously freaking out, but in a "holy shit this is awesome" way. The firework noises continue throughout my whole reading, interrupting Betsy over and over with their whiz, pop, bangs, and at one point she pauses to tell me: "That's all you, you know."

The message she delivers is that something in my life is beginning to "bloom" and "take off." Which of course I relate to the fact that, having been *thinking* about creating The Numinous for some time now, here I am actually walking the talk and researching a story for my brand-new website. "Whatever it is will be a huge success, bigger than you can imagine right now."

By the end of the evening, I've got that elated feeling that always comes after facing something you're afraid is going to (a) challenge all the belief systems you've carefully put in place to keep you safe in the world or, worse, (b) make you look like a total idiot. If we're all made of chemicals that reward us with good feelings when we do things that are good for us and our fellow humans (sex, helping people, not drinking a bottle of wine every night), then following our curiosity (*another example of our intuition at work*) despite being afraid has got to be one of them, right?

And as I'm bouncing around feeling all excited about The Fireworks, the girl I got the Silk Cut purple impression for sidles over to me. "You know, I didn't want to say this in front of the whole group, but this week I decided to stop smoking weed," she tells me. Wowzer. So my message was kind of spot-on.

## SYNCHRONICITY IS ALSO YOUR PSYCHIC VOICE

It was Carl Jung who first did any in-depth study into "meaningful coincidences" such as The Fireworks, which he termed "synchronicity." Jung—also an advocate of astrology as a study of what he saw as the "archetypes" of our "collective unconscious"—was a proponent of the idea that, rather than a series of random events, each and every human life is actually the expression of a *deeper cosmic order*. He and Wolfgang Pauli, the Swiss-American pioneer of quantum physics, called this the *Unus Mundus,* from the Latin for "one world"—describing an underlying unified reality, from which everything emerges and to which everything returns (Source, the Universe, oneness consciousness . . . God, etc.)

Jung also believed that synchronicity, glimpses of this cosmic order in action, shifted a person's egocentric conscious thinking ("we are all in this alone") to that of a greater wholeness ("everything is connected")—granting temporary access to the "absolute knowledge" that resides within us all. A.k.a. your intuition or "psychic" inner Voice!

Louise Androlia, a gifted intuitive herself, is also deeply invested in shifting the perception of "psychic" phenomena away from being a tool for "predicting" future events, and rather something that we all have access to, all the time, to be used for the highest good of both our human selves and of the collective. "The sixth sense is for us all," she once told me. "In fact, we're all very tuned in as kids. Having had an imaginary friend or pet as a child is a classic example of somebody just being very energetically sensitive. I think whether this carries on into adulthood depends on the rate we forget." Or that it's conditioned out of us by a society that decides it's "weird."

Remember what I said about tarot being like "Google for the soul"? It reminds me of a conversation I had with Brooklyn-based intuitive Lisa Rosman, who told me: "It's our natural birthright to be able to tune in on deep levels to each other as well as what yogis call the 'divine intelligence' of the Universe. But the less we have to communicate on that level, the less we do." Lisa went on to describe how she believes our reliance on modern devices—from computers to clocks—is partly to blame. "Rather than merely using cell phones or the Internet as shortcuts, we've been using them as a substitute to true communion with ourselves and each other. And yet in our dreams and disorders our deeper wisdom is still, always, clamoring to be heard." Not to mention in the serendipitous synchronicities we kind of *just know* are there to tell us something, but which often get brushed off as "just coincidence."

## HOW TO LISTEN TO YOUR INTUITION

And so, since that night at Betsy's, I've been actively practicing tuning in to my intuitive Voice, a.k.a *going with my gut*. After all, Jung's theory suggests that this is actually how to live *the life that has been cosmically designed for us*. I also love what astrologer and modern mystic Gahl Sasson said about this when I attended his Become Your Own Psychic workshop, how "you only know it works when you *don't* go with your gut and everything goes wrong." Because how many times have you found yourself trying to wriggle out of a predicament you know in your *heart of hearts* (yes, your gut) could have been prevented if you'd been brave enough to go against all logic (peer pressure, expectation, EGO) and just trust your instincts instead?

One huge telltale sign that you're about to go against your own intuition / the cosmic order is when you have to keep asking other people if they think it's a good idea or not. An example from my life is when I recently walked away from what seemed like a really prestigious and potentially quite lucrative opportunity. It had taken a good two months to negotiate the terms, during which time I had laid the whole deal out in front of everybody and anybody who came into my path. I told them I wanted their "advice," when actually I think my inner Voice was trying to find somebody, *anybody* to back up its pleading argument *against* me taking the job. *Your freedom is way more important to you than a regular salary! And besides, you've got your soul project to fulfill!!!* it kept insisting. But my ego would always drown it out with stuff like: *But this will look awesome on your résumé, and not having a regular salary is REALLY SCARY.*

After months of anguish, not to mention boring everyone to tears with my massive first-world problem, I used one of Betsy's techniques to really feel into my decision. She calls it *Stop, Drop, and Roll,* and it goes something like this:

## STOP, DROP, AND ROLL:
## HOW TO LISTEN TO YOUR INTUITION

- Take one of the two (or more) scenarios you find yourself faced with, and use your *imagination* (yet another word for intuition, since where else do your "imaginings" come from?) to play out the scenario from start to finish in your mind. Go into as much detail as possible, seeing the colors, hearing the sounds, and mentally interacting with the other people involved.

- Then, when you have a really clear picture of the outcome in your mind's eye, STOP the movie, DROP into your gut, and take note of how it feels. Write this down if needed.

- Now repeat for the other scenario(s). Whichever makes you feel the most content, confident, and excited—the one that feels like *home*—is the one to go with, regardless of which looks better on paper. That's the "just ROLL with it" part.

Of course, it can be hard to distinguish between some gut feelings, like, say, fear (usually of the unknown, and as such no reason not to go for it) and anxiety (usually about a less-than-ideal future outcome your spirit senses is potentially up ahead, suggesting probably not such a wise move). One breed of butterflies in the gut can look a lot like another after all, especially if you've been drinking a lot of coffee or you're really hungover, 'cos there's a whole other species of stomach-dwelling creepy-crawlies right there. In his workshop, Gahl suggested another fun exercise to help distinguish the difference (see box opposite).

To simplify things even further for you, having done my own extensive work in the (unified) field, the best analogy I can come up with is this: the "right" decision always feels to me like the *truth*. Which suggests that every time you go *against* what your intuition is telling you . . . it could also be said you're living a lie.

## INTUITION VERSUS FEAR:
## HOW TO TELL THE DIFFERENCE

> "How do you know if it's your gut or your fear telling you to act? The sensations can be similar so train your body to tell the difference."
>
> —GAHL SASSON

- Download some music you know you will really hate. For some people this might be gabber house; for others, anything by Justin Bieber.

- Force yourself to listen to it, loud.

- Take note: Where do you feel the sensation of disgust in your body? What does it feel like?

- Repeat with a piece of music you really love.

- Take note: Where do you feel the sensation of pleasure and happiness in your body? What does it feel like?

- Remember the difference between your physical experiences of *aversion* and *attraction*. This is your body's way of communicating what you need to know.

(N.B. This experiment can also be conducted using food.)

## FEEL THE FEAR . . . AND PRACTICE BEING PSYCHIC ANYWAY

As Betsy hinted at during the séance, it can take years of practice (or rather unconditioning) to really begin to trust your intuition—not least because many of us have learned to be "afraid" of delving into our psychic or intuitive abilities, "mainly because we're afraid to look inside ourselves," she says. But also because "we're all afraid of dark places. And are there darker forces in the spirit world? Absolutely. But you'll only attract them to you if you're fearful of them. I always think about Cesar Millan, the dog whisperer, and how he can transform a dog's energy with his energy, which is always calm and assertive. It's about a shift in thinking toward 'I have the power.' Which, in the spirit world, we always do."

As with developing any "muscle," she continues, "the practice of feeling into the meanings of symbols (psychic impressions) isn't easy, but it gets easier with time and repetition." When she decided to develop her gift, she took classes at the Spiritualist Church of NYC and has even developed her own six-week course to help others do the same—but there are some simple ways we can all begin to dial up our inner Voice in our everyday lives.

First, to bring it back to astrology, Gahl Sasson suggests looking at the area of your birth chart ruled by Pisces—the sign that rules our connection to Carl Jung's "collective unconscious." In fact, "wherever Pisces shows up in your chart is where you will benefit most in life from what your intuition is telling you" (in my chart, Pisces rules my Third house of ideas and communication, for example). Meanwhile, "any activity that gets you closer to your inner Pisces is a good way to get your intuition flowing—so go for a swim, take a salt bath, take a yoga class, or read some poetry." Yep, I've had many a flash of insight doing laps in the pool!

Another way to begin to recognize the psychic "hits" we're getting all the time is to keep an intuition diary to make a note of symbols, noises, and smells that light a psychic spark in you, so you can track the daily musings of your higher Self. Same goes for taking note of the "messages" in your dreams, since Jung (not to mention his colleague Sigmund Freud) was also a staunch believer that our nighttime visions (also ruled by Pisces) are direct communications with our unconscious, Universal Voice.

The tarot, as discussed, is another way to spark this kind of internal "conversation" with your higher Self—while Gahl also suggests opening a book at random, selecting one sentence from the page, and using this passage to work with your intuition (what he describes as "the 'tuition' that comes from with 'in' us").

And whatever ways you discover to get more intimately connected to this Voice—for anybody invested in living the full TRUTH of their divinely ordained purpose in this life, it is my humble suggestion that you take whatever opportunities you can to get tuned in.

## HOW PSYCHIC ARE YOU?

Louise Androlia shares four ways your soul may already be speaking to you.

- Scent memories. Have you ever suddenly had the scent of, for example, your grandmother's perfume waft into a space? This is a way of connecting to people who have passed.

- Knowing that someone is about to call before they do. This is you being tuned in to the energy of friends and family, so you have simply picked up their intention.

- Picking up a mood or feeling from a person or a space. This is an example again of being tuned in to a person's energy, which is all psychic ability is. When you feel sad because your friend is, that's a perfect example of "tapping in."

- Songs. Often when you get a song in your head from nowhere, making a point of listening to the lyrics often gives you a useful message that you can use.

# 4.

# DO YOUR DHARMA, FIX YOUR KARMA

Public speaking is most definitely not my jam, and here's why. No matter what kind of group I'm speaking to, the moment I vocalize anything that feels remotely meaningful to me (which is most of what I think about and want to speak about, so), my voice cracks, my face collapses, and I begin to cry.

And when I say "meaningful," I'm not necessarily talking about baring my soul or revealing my most personal inner truths—this could be anything from reading a killer quote out loud to mentioning a particularly potent astrological aspect and the way I feel it is impacting our lives. To be honest, I think it's one of the reasons I became a writer for a living: I'm just so much more comfortable expressing myself in the written, as opposed to the spoken, word.

So you can imagine my relief when my first real public speaking gig, for the spirituality "un-conference" Higher Selfie, was scheduled to take place over Skype. When the day came, this meant delivering my talk into my laptop, with the Skype camera directed at nothing but a blank white wall on the other end. It was more like talking to myself than a room of 250 expectant faces. But as it turned out, it didn't make any difference with the crying.

I still had to choke back sobs as I made my most heartfelt points, which cemented my theory that it wasn't necessarily nerves that got me so worked up. More likely it was all the heavy-hitting planets (the Sun, Moon, Saturn, Mercury, and Mars) in the watery, emotional Fourth and Eighth houses in my astrological chart. Meaning, I just can't help really *feeling* stuff. Plus the fact that my Third house, the area of my chart governing communication, is ruled by Pisces—the biggest emo of them all! (I threw in this last part for you to practice your astro skills by the way. You're welcome.) But you know what? The crowd loved it, and I got dozens of messages afterward from people thanking me for being so "real."

The talk itself was on "doing your dharma," a spiritual concept that links our destiny, or life purpose, to an act of service. The topic was actually given to me by the organizers of the event, since they apparently felt that The Numinous was an example of me doing *my dharma*. And the concept *had* been a bit of a theme that year. The first article I published on the site in January, setting the tone for the new year, had been a piece on dharma by a yoga instructor named Naomi Constantino. In her piece, she included this quote from Yogi Bhajan, founder of the Kundalini yoga practice: "You have made very deep promises between your Soul and your Self. Now is the time to carve your place into the memory of this planet earth and serve this promise. May your journey complete its way to your destiny. And may you understand the preciousness of your own life."

This *did* speak to how I felt about The Numinous. What had begun as an idea for a fun side project, something to bridge the fulfillment gap I was experiencing in my journalism career, had become so much more. It had taken on a life of its own and had become something—as being asked to speak at an event like Higher Selfie had helped make me aware—that was also having a positive impact on the lives of others.

Cue major waterworks when I read this quote out during my talk . . . and OMG, it's even happening now while I'm writing about it! (But then the moon IS in Pisces today, go figure.) And the fact that this idea

"You have made very
deep promises between
your Soul and your
Self. Now is the time
to carve your place
into the memory of
this planet earth and
serve this promise.
May your journey
complete its way to
your destiny. And may
you understand the
preciousness of your
own life."

—YOGI BHAJAN

moves me so very deeply—the idea that living your destiny is a way of realizing the "preciousness" or value *to society* of your own life—suggests to me that it gets close to answering the Big Question: the question of why we're all even here anyway, on both a personal and a human level.

## SO WHAT IS "DHARMA" ANYWAY?

I first heard the word *dharma* when I read about the Dharma Punx in *i-D* magazine, while I was researching feature ideas for *Style*. Based out of L.A., Noah Levine and Josh Korda were a pair of tattooed former punk rockers, preaching meditation and other teachings from Buddhist philosophy as an aid to addiction recovery. This was way before my numinous awakening, but still I was deeply intrigued (since my spirit *intuition* evidently recognized a pair of absolute soul brothers).

But not having heard of dharma before, I simply added it to the list of mystical-sounding words that lived in the file in my brain marked "to be investigated one day" (along with words like *Shakti* and *mandala*). Since dharma rhymed with "karma," maybe it was something to do with . . . destiny?

It wasn't until Naomi wrote her piece for The Numinous that I gave the concept much more thought. But reading her take on it, I realized that "doing your dharma" is about answering your *soul's calling*—and even better, it encapsulates the idea that in doing so, your work will automatically be contributing to the greater good.

The Dharma Punx named themselves as a way to honor the Buddhist tradition of delivering a "dharma talk," a sort of sermon on the teachings of Buddhism, and a way of sharing the positive impact the teachings have had on you. And having gotten sober using meditation and by following the Buddhist philosophy that separating from attachment to material things is a way to quell addictive cravings, Noah and Josh were doing their dharma by helping others to do the same.

The concept of dharma appears with varying subtleties in meaning throughout different strands of Eastern religion. For Sikhs, the word *dharma* means the "path of righteousness." The Hindus see it as the "right way of living" leading to Universal harmony. In Buddhism, meanwhile, it gets stripped right back, with *dharma* simply describing a sense of "cosmic law and order"—my favorite definition, not least since it was becoming increasingly clear that all the numinous practices I found so compelling were actually in service of bringing each individual human soul back into alignment with this cosmic code.

Take astrology, for example. If, as the AstroTwins put it, your birth chart is like a "blueprint" for your soul journey, then learning about the strengths, weaknesses, and challenges of your chart and really making your life choices in accordance with this information (i.e., *living as your absolute authentic self*) will naturally lead you to do the work you were born for. And by the law of dharma, this work will also, in some way, be of help, or service, to others.

The same theory can be applied to working with the tarot, to developing your own intuitive powers, or to healing your emotional and energetic wounds, since all these practices are designed to help clear the conditioning and the fear that's keeping you stuck in a life of your parents', your ego's, or society's choosing—as opposed to following the path of your Universal calling—with the conviction that comes from developing a clear and open channel to your highest Self.

## DISCOVERING YOUR DHARMA

So chances are you might be sitting there contemplating your life and thinking, *Oh, man, I am so not doing MY dharma . . .*, a realization that often begs the question, *Because how am I even supposed to know what it is?*

This is where I invite you to travel back in time, back to when you were, say, five to seven years old. What were you happiest doing? And please don't say, "Watching Disney movies on TV." This is likely an example of the first way your soul found to soothe itself (adult versions of this include shopping, cocktails, and dating apps) when you got told off or put down for practicing what you *really* came here to do.

Let's say this was . . . playing dress-up. Or making mud pies. Going back to the Psychic Betsy method of communicating with your higher

Self, close your eyes and picture your five-year-old self engaged in whatever your favorite activity is. Now take it one step further, and *feel into* what it is you love so much about it. What emotional need does the activity fulfill? What aspect of it fascinates you? If your thing was playing dress-up, was it the look and feel of the clothes themselves you loved, or the way you got to experiment with playing different roles? Or telling different stories? And now play it forward. How is your *innate attraction* to beautiful clothes, or characters, or storytelling being met by the life and career choices you've made as an adult?

When I think back, I remember being a really shy child, and happiest with my nose in a book. But my mum, on the other hand, says she used to call me "Radio Ruby," since from the day I learned to string a sentence together, I would deliver a rolling commentary on the contents of my head. I reckon she actually found this pretty annoying (fair enough, I would too!). I also remember her admonishing me for "telling tales" on my brother when he'd done something naughty (i.e., practicing my reporting skills).

Anyhow, as a result, I was encouraged to flex my fledgling researcher/reporter muscle through reading and writing instead, rather than driving my mum batty and tattling on my brother. Naturally, since it was my (soul's) favorite thing to do, English became my best subject in school. And years later, having decided that I wanted a career in fashion (I did also love playing dress-up), when I went to study styling at the London College of Fashion, it was actually the journalism component of my course—a component I wasn't even aware of when I signed up—that came *most naturally* to me.

And then one thing led to another, and well, here we are. My point being that when it comes to your dharma, your soul has a way of getting things back on track when life (your parents, your ego, society) knocks you off your path. IF, that is, you're doing what it takes to recognize and heed the voice of your highest Self and are actually prepared to follow the signs being waved in your face.

What do those signs look like? They're mainly the positive feelings that tell you, *Yes, keep doing more of this!,* and the negative ones that are screaming, *Quit this job/activity/relationship now; it's killing you!!!* I repeat: your job is not supposed to make you feel this way. If it does, THIS IS YOUR HIGHER SELF ADVISING YOU TO QUIT AND DO SOMETHING DIFFERENT. Seems pretty obvious, right? But it's amazing how we're conditioned to look away from our personal truths when following through might mean a period of uncertainty and discomfort, looking stupid or pissing some people off.

On a lighter note, there are the little coincidences and serendipities of life, which we can't help get all excited about since we know deep down this is the Universe illuminating the way.

As for more specific insights about the actual next right steps to take in fulfilling your dharma? Some of my friends (quite a few actually) report having heard actual voices in their heads delivering specific

---

## HELLO, HIGHEST SELF

Connect to the Voice using any one, or a combo, of the following:

A regular meditation practice. Here's another of my favorite quotes from Yogi Bhajan: "Prayer is when you talk to God; meditation is when God (a.k.a. your highest Self) talks to you." (More, much more, in the chapter on meditation.)

Investigating your soul blueprint by getting to know your astrology chart and applying this to your career and other life choices.

Using divination tools such as the tarot to help you tap into your intuition—and then following through with the actions that *feel* right (that feel like home and/or the "truth").

Seeking to heal any emotional wounds that are keeping you stuck in learned behaviors, versus fearlessly walking the path that's right for *you*.

Choosing to surround yourself with people who *ask,* as opposed to *try and tell you,* what's best for you.

"downloads," such as: *Create THIS online course; Move HERE in the fall and start teaching yoga.* Less cosmically inclined folk might simply term these "ideas," which doesn't make them any less special. My advice, if you have an idea about what it is you're maybe just supposed to be doing with your life, then you owe it to your (higher) self to at the very least investigate what it would take to make it happen.

Ignoring the feelings, the signs, and the flashes of inspiration about how to get back into the path of your dharma will likely result in you remaining in a similar cycle of anxiety and numbing I found myself in at *Style* magazine. In which instance, it's highly likely that God/Goddess, the Universe, and so on may serve you up what is commonly referred to in recovery circles as a "rock bottom" experience. Closely followed by the classic breakdown / breakthrough / *spiritual awakening*.

## WHAT MAKES YOU COME ALIVE?

When it comes to discovering your dharma, here is another one of my favorite quotes on the subject, from civil rights leader Howard Thurman: "Do not ask yourself what the world needs. Ask yourself what makes you come alive and then go do that. Because what the world needs is people who have come alive."

I love this quote because it encapsulates the idea that "what makes you come alive"—that thing you stay awake thinking about at night (in a good way), that gives you tingles, and that you could bore people to tears talking about at parties—could be literally *any*thing. This is an important point to remember, since it's also way too easy to confuse the idea of dharma as being tied to some kind of creative "gift."

*That's easy for you to say—you're a writer, and* that's *a creative gift!* I hear you cry. Well, here's how I actually see it. I am an observer, a reporter, and a storyteller. This is my dharma. I got good at writing through *practice,* since I needed a way to tell my stories—and as I have explained, vocalizing stories out loud doesn't exactly come naturally. And yes, perhaps this is because my mum preferred studious, bookish Ruby to having to listen to "Radio Ruby" all day when I was a kid!

"Do not ask yourself
what the world needs.
Ask yourself what
makes you come alive
and then go do that.
Because what the world
needs is people who
have come alive."

—HOWARD THURMAN

(See how easy it could have been for you to be knocked off the path of your dharma, too?) And if it's true that writing, through practice, has become what you might call a "talent" of mine (something I got good at), consider that I've also tried writing fiction and failed miserably. I could never make my characters "come alive"—since writing that way is not an expression of my dharma.

When it comes to creativity, simply how we use our *life force energy,* this isn't confined to "inventing" things anyway. In *Big Magic,* her brilliant book on the subject, Elizabeth Gilbert writes: "When I refer to 'creative living' . . . I am talking about living a life that's driven more strongly by curiosity than by fear." *Curiosity* being another word I use for *intuition,* remember?

Other people with a similar dharma to me might have gone into PR, or qualitative research, or wound up making documentaries. And if doing this with their days lights up every cell of their being and makes them feel their most alive, then there is no doubt in my mind that they are also playing their part in bringing about the perfect cosmic alignment of all humanity. As I said, I think I got partway to fulfilling my dharma with my magazine career, particularly after I landed the job at *Style* and finally got to write about more stuff I was really interested in (it wasn't all reporting on celebrities' outfits). But still only half the stories I got to tell made me *come alive*—and my soul (higher Self, the Universe, law of cosmic order, etc.) knew this wasn't good enough.

First, this manifested in feelings of acute boredom, which morphed into a period of major anxiety, sleepless nights (in a bad way), and numbing out with shopping, drugs, and alcohol. In other words, the mini breakdown / breakthrough / spiritual awakening that led to me seeking "a fun side project" to bridge the dharma gap.

Which is also where the F-word comes into play, since following the truest expression of your dharma will also feel like FUN (hence why *boredom* could be one of the first signs your coordinates are off). Also why my next question to the Universe went something along the lines of: *Well, what's the one thing I could never get bored of researching, thinking, and talking about*—ever? And the answer came almost instantaneously:

*ASTROLOGY.* A.k.a. my gateway drug to an altogether more cosmic worldview and a giant, Vegas-style neon signpost from my intuition, lighting my way to the *Numiverse.*

## DISCOVER YOUR "ORIGINAL MEDICINE"

Cherie Healey, a life coach I did some work with while writing this book, has another way to describe dharma. "In Native American tradition, they say each soul is born with its own 'original medicine,' something unique to them that is their healing gift to the world," she told me. Going on to explain how it will be *a loss to humanity* if this "medicine" is never fully expressed.

This suggests that the fact that we all have different interests, talents, and, yes, creative gifts (not to mention personalities and birth charts!) is no accident—that humanity was designed this way, since we all have an individual role to play in maintaining the "cosmic law and order." The same way every cell of every living organism has *its* own role to play in keeping said organism alive. I love visualizing humanity this way, like a giant people patchwork, with each and every one of us a vital stitch helping keep it all together.

The problem is, not all dharmas, or medicines, are created equal in the eyes of our parents, our ego, or society, and so we often end up following whichever path is considered most profitable (society) or most glamorous (ego) or will result in us experiencing the greatest material stability (parents). It can seem that we've become so fearful of never having enough (money, recognition, security) that we've forgotten the Universe has been *designed* to support us when it comes to fulfilling our dharma. Because this is what makes the *Universe* come alive.

I once interviewed the jewelry designer Satya Scainetti, whose career is a brilliant example of this principle in action. Growing up in a family of talented "creatives," she always felt left out, since as far as she could tell her gift was "making people happy." This led to a career in social work, which she found ultimately unfulfilling, because the reams of red tape meant she never felt like she was really helping anybody.

Burned out (breakdown / breakthrough / spiritual awakening), she took a sabbatical to do something *just for fun:* a yoga teacher training. And it was on the last night of the training, having been gifted her "spiritual name"—Satya, meaning "all truth"—that evening, that she had a vivid dream. "In the dream, I launched a line of spiritual jewelry called 'Satya,' of which I donated a percentage of the profits to charity," she told me.

The next day she called a friend to share her vision, and despite having no previous experience in jewelry design, the pair of them began work on the collection the minute she returned to NYC. By the time I met Satya, twelve years later, she'd donated over $1 million to children's charities all over the world—and made *thousands* of people happier as a result.

This isn't to suggest that your unique medicine has to psychically heal the world, have a spiritual angle, or "give back" quite so literally as Satya's, either. Just as it's not everybody's dharma to create inspiring pieces of art, or make music that gets the whole crowd at the Coachella main stage singing along, not everybody is here to be the next Mother Teresa. Gandhi had his unique medicine, and Lady Gaga has hers—both have "helped" millions of people in their own way.

The week of my talk on dharma, an astrologer I follow named Rob Brezsny wrote a horoscope for Aries (my Sun sign) which encouraged his readers to take on the idea behind the motto of Benedictine monks – *Laborare est Orane*, which means 'to work is to pray'.

Which makes me think about what "angel whisperer" and author Kyle Gray says about "*undercover light workers*." He makes the point that if your dharma, like Satya's, is to make people happy, then even working as a receptionist in a doctor's practice, bringing happiness to each and every person who walks through that door with your sunny attitude, will *at the very least* help contribute to them having a better day.

Which is also when you pass the baton and allow the Universe to step in. Because, who knows, the knock-on effect of this added spring in their step could be them feeling good enough about themselves to finally trust the inner Voice advising them to do more of what makes

Gandhi had his
unique medicine, and
Lady Gaga has hers.

them feel that way. Which means, ultimately, you will have been instrumental in them discovering *their* dharma too.

## BEWARE THE S-WORD

Not just because I'm an Aries who likes to get my own way, but *should* is one of my least favorite words—and it's become something of a red flag for me. Whenever I find myself using the S-word, I know I'm about to embark on something that can't be for my highest good. This is since doing something because you "should" pretty much always implies that you're doing it for somebody else's benefit—and that part of you, rather than being thrilled to help, to follow along, or to fulfill a loving duty, is begrudging and resentful of the fact. And in my book (this book), resentment is one of the most toxic, soul-corroding emotions to be carrying around with you.

And so, in matters of dharma, any time you find yourself using the word *should* (I should *take the job I feel less passionate about because it pays so much better; I should postpone my round-the-world life research trip until my mom's health improves*), try replacing it with the word *must* and see how it impacts your priorities. Personally, I find it virtually impossible to use the word *must* unless I really mean it—and so, for me, a *should* becoming a *must* instantly creates the perspective I need to feel empowered about making the "right" decision. In the case of the above, I wouldn't take the job and I would stick around for my mum. And despite how uncomfortable it makes me, public speaking, in connection to The Numinous, is also a definite "must" for me.

I also believe that people pleasing—wanting to be a good girl and appear "nice," so we'll be loved and accepted—can be one of the biggest stumbling blocks to women in particular when it comes to fulfilling our dharma. In fact, I think men experience almost the opposite—even if it actually stems from the same place, a place of "put up or shut up." For some dudes, wanting to appear invincible can mean it almost becomes a badge of honor to override feelings of fear, anxiety, or being overwhelmed—when actually this is another example of their higher Self despairing: this is SO NOT YOUR FREAKING DHARMA, MAN!

In my experience, defying our people-pleasing tendencies is about cultivating what I like to think of as a kind of "healthy (higher) self-ishness," which brings us right on back to all the practices I believe engender true (higher) self-respect. As in, the highest levels of respect for and trust in the ultimate Universal wisdom of your most authentic Self (your soul).

For me, this again means being actively engaged in a conversation with this part of my being: using tools like astrology, the tarot, and my intuition to decipher the symbolic messages being beamed from my higher Self (God/Goddess, the Universal oneness, etc.) into my everyday consciousness.

And on a more practical level, it's been about making the necessary lifestyle changes to keep the cosmic airwaves free of static. Not to mention the fact that doing your dharma might just take you *waaaay* out of your comfort zone (like me with the public speaking), and you'll want to be feeling your most gladiator fit when that happens.

For me, these changes have included but have not been limited to cleaning up my diet to heal my digestion (how else am I meant to feel my gut reactions?); steering clear of mood-altering substances (since "moods" are messages in themselves); meditating regularly (like Skype time with Source energy); and engaging in daily physical movement (to shift stuck energy that's clogging up the channel).

In fact, if we are advised to "dress for the job you want"—I say take it one step further. How about you eat, drink, think, and *live your life* for the job you want? Or rather, for the dharma you were born to do?

# #SHITNUMINOUSGIRLSSAY

"I feel like this is the year I'm gonna start using a moon cup."

"I got offered this white powder and she kept saying: 'It's all natural, it's from the earth.' I was, like, 'So is peyote.'"

"Sorry, can you repeat that? I totally just lost track of what dimension I was in."

"How do I explain the rose quartz in my bra to my Tinder date?"

"I am SO done with this planet. I cannot reincarnate here again."

"I was thinking Wednesday too. Why do we even text when we can just psychic schedule?!"

"I think a lot of the time I'm hungry, I'm just craving energetic nourishment."

"Yeah, I know Erica; she used to be my smudge priestess."

"Ruby, you just became friends with 11 other people, you have 11 music likes, and 1,111 friends on Facebook #angelmessages #nbd."

"I'm at the stage where I'm even saging before sex."

"I had a gulp of cannabis almond milk before I read your e-mail, so I hope all this makes sense."

"Sometimes without that masculine energy it just becomes this Goddess soup, y'know?"

"It could be more of an Amma style altar if you think sex temple is too much."

"I'm so bummed I wasn't Cleopatra in my past-life regression."

"My Kundalini teacher told me my bangs are obscuring my third eye."

"Of course she's fine to drive; all she's had is some cacao!"

"I find it SO hard to be productive during the waning Moon phase."

# PART II

# HEALTH & WELL-BEING

# 5

# CONFESSIONS OF A RELUCTANT YOGI

So, okay, first a confession: yoga does not come naturally to me. You know those people who claim to experience straight-up ecstasy when they so much as step onto their mat? The ones who say they've never felt more whole, who can only find true peace, or who have experienced miraculous healing of mind, body, and spirit, as a result of their practice? They're everywhere, and I am endlessly inspired by them. But I am most definitely not one of them.

Rarely does yoga feel like a balm for my soul, or a way to transcend my Material Girl concerns. At best, it feels like I'm getting a good stretch; at worst (and more often than not), I spend the duration of the class in varying degrees of physical discomfort with one eye on the clock. For the most part, I find yoga to be tedious and frustrating, an endeavor resulting in a serious effort/reward deficit. Also majorly intimidating, since surely you have to be an actual acrobat to achieve certain postures. And yet still I maintain a regular practice.

To the point, in fact, that just recently I had something of a yogic breakthrough—or what master yogi Baron Baptiste might describe as "a break *with* to break *through*." This speaks to the most ancient yogic philosophy, described in the *Yoga Sutra* (the original text on the practice) thus: "Yogas chitta vritti nirodhah"—which translates as "Yoga is the removal of the fluctuations of the mind." Said "fluctuations" are all the mental patterns, the conditioning, and the limiting beliefs we bring onto the mat. Such as: *This hurts, I'm bored, I am* never *gonna be able to do this right so what's the freaking point?* (um, all of which can also be applied to *life in general.* Read them again).

And well, my *break* with these has looked something like reframing the discomfort and the frustration as simply signifiers that I have a body and that I am *alive.* The break *through* has been embracing the difficulties of the practice as a precious opportunity to expand my conscious understanding of how I—my highest "I"—inhabit my body, and, as such, my physical interaction with the cosmos. So y'know, pretty major! And not something I ever expected would result from my sketchy history on the mat.

Because truthfully, I was always in it for the same reasons I presumed everybody else was—for the lean, toned limbs, the cute outfits, with maybe a few moments of "inner peace" (whatever that meant) on the side.

It's a little over fifteen years since I attended my first Hatha yoga class, in a neon-lit rec room at a public swimming pool in Brixton, London. Then I joined a fancy gym and there was a strenuous Ashtanga phase (if it worked for Madonna . . . ), followed by a pretty serious commitment to the sweat-fest known as Bikram, where classes are performed in rooms heated up to 104 degrees Fahrenheit, to aid flexibility and encourage detoxification.

With Bikram, I could finally relate to the yoga zealots. I was a convert! But mainly because the copious sweating meant it felt like a "proper" workout, while the heat made me bendy enough to ace poses I could never do in a regular studio. I would leave class high as a kite, with a clear head and a courageous heart, ready to take on the world. But according to the high-and-mighty yoga community at large, Bikram is not the real thing AT ALL and should not even be going around calling itself "yoga" in the first place. Besides the multiple sexual harassment cases against the founder, Bikram Choudhury, real yoga is all about the *pranayama,* they say, the breath, which it's impossible to control properly in the heated room. The heat is also the "cheater's" way of advancing fast through difficult postures (dang), not to mention a serious drain on the *jing* ("life force" in Eastern medicine).

And so the fact that I only came close to experiencing yogic bliss in the hot room was obviously only further evidence that I just didn't "get it." And considering the ubiquity of yoga among the Now Age spiritual

## YOGA IN THE USA

What's the right style of yoga for you? Here's a quick overview of the systems that are popular in the USA today:

HATHA YOGA. Refers to all styles of yoga, but where the emphasis is placed on aligning mind, body, and spirit. Best for: preparing the body to sit in meditation.

ASHTANGA YOGA. A dynamic set sequence of poses incorporating arm balances, headstands, and multiple vinyasas (see below). Best for: if you want Madonna arms.

VINYASA YOGA. Describes any class where a "vinyasa" sequence—Chaturanga to Upward-Facing Dog to Downward-Facing Dog—is used to transition from one pose to the next. Best for: getting creative with your flow.

HOT YOGA. Any style of yoga practiced in an intentionally heated studio (from 85 to 105 degrees Fahrenheit). Best for: sweating out toxins while you stretch.

KUNDALINI YOGA. Blends physical practice with active breathing techniques, chanting, and meditation. Best for: expanding consciousness and transcending the ego mind.

RESTORATIVE YOGA. Incorporates just a few poses, held for five minutes or more, where the body is supported by props such as blocks and blankets. Best for: total relaxation.

set, perhaps, a voice whispered deep inside, this meant there was something majorly wrong with *me*. A missing link in my mind-body-spirit connection that no amount of carefully monitored *pranayama,* practiced at the correct room temperature, would ever heal.

Which is right about the time I attended my first Kundalini yoga class and had my mind, along with all my preconceptions about yoga, blown. Talk about a break with conditioning—there weren't even any "postures" as such, just a series of seemingly random repetitive movements and breathing exercises. Then there was the chanting ("oh man," went my terribly reserved and thoroughly British ego), and the dancing (ditto).

Yet the aftereffects were undeniable—I felt "awake" in a way I can only describe as "double espresso with a Prozac chaser." I've since had some truly mind-bending experiences with Kundalini yoga too, like deep, *deep* psychic stuff (the time I had a full-on vision of exactly what I needed to heal in my relationship with my dad, and how to do it). But still it's not my go-to. I find it too intense, and too much in the head.

So it's safe to say that over the years I've tried it all. And the practice that finally "worked" for me? It's the yoga I've found myself doing at home—no dogma, no adjustments, no mirrors. The yoga I practice with the help of an online library of classes, called YogaGlo.com (YouTube would work just as well), that is essentially something to make me stand up (or lie down, depending on my energy levels) and take a break from my Mac. Yoga that's a way to "break with" whatever task I've been stuck in for however many hours, and "break through" to the next part of my day.

Which sounds so prosaic, doesn't it? And so *not* the door beyond which nirvana lies. However, as Einstein himself once noted: "Things should be as simple as possible, but not simpler." And it's been stripping it back to the basics—just me, my mat, the postures, the breath—that's finally allowed me to transcend the hype and discover yogic bliss. Here's how I think it happened.

## NO EGOS ALLOWED

So one of the major "break withs" of my home practice has been the removal of any expectation about it looking a certain way. After all, the downside to my lack of dedication to one style of yoga over another is that I never progressed very fast (except when I cheated in Bikram, obv). Like I still can't do a Crow pose (a nifty little arm balance where your shins rest on your upper arms, feet lifting off the floor), and I've pretty much given up on headstands and handstands altogether. Actually, that's not true. One day I plan to take a dedicated "inversions" workshop and nail those babies—mainly for my *ego's* sake.

Because the way I see it, that's what the fancier poses are often about. Sure, inversions are also said to improve circulation and calm the nervous system—but it's the same part of me that writes things on my to-do list after I've done them *just so I can cross them off* (anybody?) that decided yoga had better be about acing the perfect standing split. That part of myself also known as my ego / inner critic / perfectionist—and essentially the part of myself that yoga is about learning to transcend (a.k.a. STFU). Also a part of us *all* that tends to get a lot of airtime versus the more loving, forgiving, and accepting voice of our higher self. And I can see now that one of the biggest gifts of yoga is the way it forces us to confront the ego head-on (*"a break with to break through . . ."*).

Confronting the ego is pretty much the core teaching of Kundalini yoga. In fact, I often think founder Yogi Bhajan designed the practice to be as uncomfortable as possible (meaning as weird, as painful, as frustrating, and as silly) with the sole aim of getting into a stand-off with the voice that says: *No WAY, this is too weird/painful/frustrating/silly* (yep, the ego). Hell, one of the most popular Kundalini "meditations" is even called the Ego Eradicator!

I also think this is why self-help author Gabrielle Bernstein, a certified Kundalini teacher, describes it as "a way to get my body involved in my spiritual practice." Because at the core of Gabby's message is the teaching that the way to connect to our higher self (spirit, Source energy, the Universal oneness . . . what she names simply *love*) is to separate from the ego, the fearful part of us that gives voice to all judgment, all comparison, all *hate*.

And so these days I like to remind myself that it's okay if I can't do a lot of the poses (while also questioning the ego's assertion that this is because I'm simply too weak of mind and body). Why let the fact that I'll probably never be able to transition to Chaturanga via handstand (just google it) put a stop to me even stepping onto a yoga mat? It's why a lot of teachers like to remind us (often in the midst of transitioning to Chaturanga via handstand): "It's called yoga practice, not yoga perfect!" To simplify, as Baron Baptiste might put it, "Don't worry about doing it right, because you're not."

## A BREAK WITH THE MAINSTREAM

I had the honor of practicing with Baron, a true yoga preacher (more on them later) whose parents opened the first ever American yoga studio in San Francisco in the 1960s, on a retreat called The Immersion. Hosted by Lululemon, it was a weekend-long . . . immersion . . . into what, as a brand, they see themselves promoting as the core teaching of yoga: that what goes down on the mat is actually just "practice" for becoming our best (perhaps even highest) Self.

Ironic, since Lululemon is also one of the brands at the forefront of bringing yoga to the mainstream—and, as such, often accused of making it *all about* how the practice looks (since the company is in the business of selling expensive clothing to do yoga in). Elsewhere, the commercialization of yoga has seen the rise of celebrity teachers selling expensive courses and retreats, blingy studios with expensive memberships, Instagram yogis with "perfect" bodies doing pretzel poses, and even yoga asana championships. In other words, all the stuff the ego eats for breakfast.

Because what the ego wants is to compare and compete, since what the ego fears is that (without the $100 yoga pants and the perfect Scorpio pose) I am *not enough*.

There's a fine line for me between feeling inspired by the super-bendy yogis I follow on social media and being intimidated out of practicing altogether (again, my OWN ego in full effect). But on the other hand, becoming aware of this and separating from the need to "fit in" with the mainstream yoga community has kind of been a yogic practice in itself!

After all, as Eddie Stern, another wonderful yoga teacher and philosopher (and the man responsible for *those* infamous Madonna arms) reminded me: "When you just observe those (beliefs) without getting attached to or distracted by them is when yoga is happening. When you dwell in your own true nature, as the observer and not the participant." Even better; "We then get to choose (the beliefs) which are supportive of something like liberation, or knowing who we truly are, whatever that might be."

Now *that's* a philosophy I can buy/bend into (and which doesn't cost a thing). Thing is, selling the masses on yoga as exercise—something you need all kinds of kit for, and that will make you look good and feel, like, so blissed out, man—was always going to be an easier win than inviting people to take up a practice that's designed to make you confront the conditioning and the limiting beliefs that are stunting your personal evolution. Because that stuff can get downright messy. After all, any kind of growth—physical, mental, emotional, spiritual—is usually preceded by the discomfort of *out*growing what came before. No pain no gain, correct?

This is actually the revelation I got in my classes with Baron at Lululemon's Immersion: ironically, that yoga is absolutely not about your outfit. That, in essence, it is a way for us humans to experience the very nature of evolution, or *creation* itself. A.k.a. HUGE.

Which can, of course, also be applied to working toward the more difficult poses. As Eddie puts it: "You *could* want to put your leg behind your head because you want to explore the boundaries of what your body is supposed to do. And that could make you look at the world in a whole different way."

## MY BODY IS A TEMPLE

"The body is the temple of the soul." Is there a bigger New Age cliché? And, well, I'm sorry, but I actually kind of love this one, and I'm going to reclaim it for the Now Age, too—not least because in finding my yogic bliss, I can finally *relate*.

Because I've mentioned my body image issues, right? Basically six years grappling with an eating disorder I barely felt was worth acknowledging once I "grew out of it," since so many women I knew had a conflicted relationship with food on some level. Plus, by the time I hit my middle twenties I'd found my groove with eating "healthy," and in doing so healed myself. Or had I?

The truth is, overexercising had always been the evil twin to my anorexia. And even after my years obsessing over every calorie consumed and then burned off were a distant memory, my workouts were generally fueled by the same thing: keeping my body looking a certain way. Yes, the way most women's bodies are portrayed in the mainstream yoga industry—thin, toned, and with a gravity-defying butt.

I remember being inspired to pick up my lapsed practice (*again*) after I met a photographer who specialized in nudes, who told me: "The best bodies are always the yoga bodies." And I've already mentioned how I fell for Bikram, since the sweat and the way the heat made my heart race were enough to convince me I was getting a "proper" workout (i.e., one that would torch calories and get me ripped). How ironic, then, that it was in the "hot room" that the actual practice of yoga began to slowly chip away at a lifetime's conditioning about what a "perfect body" looked like.

Operating somewhat outside the mainstream, Bikram yoga actually attracts a pretty diverse crowd. As in, less wealthy, white, juice-detoxing yummy-mummies, more bodies of all shapes, sizes, races, and genders. Ditto Kundalini, actually, which is less intimidating to the less-than-bendy masses since the majority of *kriyas* (a series of postures) are practiced with the eyes closed and can also be performed wearing long flowing robes if you're feeling less than confident about showing off your non-gravity-defying butt. One reason founder Yogi Bhajan dubbed it the "householders'" practice.

But back to Bikram, where I was given an opportunity to study all different kinds of close-to-naked yoga bodies, all performing incredible feats of strength, focus, and flexibility, in real time (as opposed to in air-brushed advertising images, or artfully posed and filtered Instagram posts). The message was beautiful and Einstein simple: it's not about how a body looks, but what a body can do, and how a body can feel. Talk about a balm for the temple of the soul.

Which ALSO brings me to the #fatyoga movement—the in-your-face hashtag that's gained momentum on social media as a statement against the lack of body diversity in the mainstream marketing of yoga. If the unattainable pretzel poses aren't enough to convince you "yoga isn't for me," then the fact that all the yogis we see in magazines and advertising images are yet more "skinny white women" isn't exactly going to encourage a person of color, or a fat person, or a man, or a senior citizen for that matter to check out their local studio.

And trust me, the #fatyoga community won't be offended by my use of the F-word—since, as the frankly awesome yogi and self-declared "fat femme" Jessamyn Stanley once reminded me: "If (the word *fat*) makes you uncomfortable, it's because you're projecting self-hate onto a word that's essentially just an adjective." That kind of beautifully nonreactive observation is also the result of a regular practice!

If yoga was designed to nurture the well-being and enlightenment of *every* body, then believing that a yoga body has to look a certain way is also not a good situation for *any* body—since, speaking as a "skinny white woman" myself, the images of this yogic "ideal" also feed the kind of perfectionism that had long-fueled my own body image issues. A lose-lose scenario all around.

Which brings me back to my home practice—where, crucially, there are *no mirrors*. Where yoga has become *all about* what my body can do, today; how my body feels, today. And what the yoga looks like is irrelevant.

What Does My Body Want?

So since my psychic awakening with Betsy, I've also gotten really into and very well practiced at listening to the physical sensations in my body/soul temple that cue me in to the voice of my intuition. This applies to everything from "Should I take this job?" to "What should I have for dinner?" and is equally applicable to physical exercise, which I've been working toward making a *nonnegotiable* in my daily life. As in, something I do every damn day.

And no longer in a fearful "gotta earn that gluten-free paleo brownie" or a type A "gotta get my SoulCycle on" kind of way, but because of the stats that tell us the average office worker in America is seated for ten hours a day—and that being sedentary is linked to significantly higher risk of pretty much every major disease going. The Mayo Clinic has even coined the term "sitting disease"—ick! And considering I write for a living, meaning my desk time likely clocks in at the top of the scale, my "daily movement" mandate begins to sound like simple common sense.

As for listening to my body, this is my first port of call when it comes to what kind of workout to do today, since it's my body that's going to be working out! And wouldn't you know, despite the discomfort and the frustration, at least half the time what my body wants is YOGA. But then it's a question of, *What kind of yoga* do you want today, body? As I touched on in the intro, there are many, many, many schools of yoga, and I still prefer to worship at the broad church—mainly because what my body wants and needs can vary wildly from day to day.

And so the inquiry often goes something like:

- How long have we got?

- Where are my energy levels at?

- Where is there tightness (*physically, mentally, emotionally, spiritually*)?

And also not to mention:

- If this was going to burn zero calories, *then* what would I choose?

Sometimes it's all about some fast, flowy vinyasa, to shake things up and help me break a sweat. And some days, the anxious days, I need the opposite: long, deep holds to ground my energy, get me back into my body, and help me get cozy with my discomfort (the physical a mirror for the mental, emotional, and spiritual). And sometimes, my body takes me off on a brisk walk across Williamsburg Bridge, the sun on my face and my favorite SoundCloud mix on my headphones. And since it's often on *these* "movement breaks" that I feel most connected to my breath, most in tune with the jing pumping through my limbs, and get the most sparklingly specific downloads from my higher Self (yes, "ideas"), I've decided to call this "yoga" too.

After all, when somebody at The Immersion asked Baron Baptiste what his daily practice looked like, he replied that it was less about the asanas themselves, and more about the "substance"—what he was getting out of it. Ideally, a "break with to break through"—through to the essential yet ever-evolving you, that is.

## HAIL TO THE YOGA PREACHERS

So my final beef with the way yoga has been packaged for the mainstream is that the spiritual nature of the practice often gets stripped right back in the name of keeping things PC. Yoga is NOT a religion, got it?! But the lack of emphasis on the ultimate goal of yoga being *union with the supreme being* (the literal translation of "yoga" being "union") also comes back to my point about it being easier to sell it to the masses as exercise that makes you look good (along with all the cute yoga pants you'll need to do it) than a spiritual exercise that requires any kind of introspection (often kinda messy).

But at its core this *is* a spiritual practice—which, beyond the doctrines of organized religion, can simply be anything Louise Androlia defines as "a practice that connects you to your spirit." Or what I might define as *life force*. After all, the last of the "eight limbs" of yoga as described in the *Yoga Sutra* (only one of which is the physical asanas) is *samadhi*—a state of transcendent ecstasy, when the individual (highest) Self merges with the Universal oneness. And on the rare occasions I do get myself to an actual yoga class, my favorite yoga teachers are what I call the yoga *preachers*—the ones who say screw the PC committee, we are *going* there.

Teachers like Baron Baptiste, who describes yoga in his latest book, *Perfectly Imperfect,* as "the ultimate excavation tool for the soul." Or like Elena Brower, who speaks of the body/soul temple with such reverence that her vocal cues to breathe into its different rooms and corridors are like an invitation to prayer. Also like my favorite Bikram teachers, who use the empty moments between giving practical instruction to remind us that the faith, focus, and determination we develop in the hot room (and therefore within ourselves) are in the service of strengthening our sense of self/spirit out in the world.

## HOW YOGA IS YOUR LIFE?

The eight "limbs" of yoga actually describe a mind-body-spirit system for living a life of meaning and purpose—with each designed as the foundation for the next step toward enlightenment. So, how yoga is your life?

**1.** YAMA: Integrity. First up, are you a (wo)man of your word? Giving good yama demands that we do unto others as we would have them do unto us. Even when it's elbows at dawn at the rag & bone sample sale.

**2.** NIYAMA: Spiritual self-discipline. Yes, this is where to get real about your "lapsed" meditation practice. The good news? Getting regular with *any* kind of ritual that connects you to your higher Self totally counts as doing your niyama.

**3.** ASANA: Physical practice. The "yoga" part of yoga, since the postures—or asanas—of any yoga class are actually designed to help cultivate the discipline and concentration necessary for meditation. Yes, your body *is* the temple of your soul.

**4.** PRANAYAMA: Breath. Or, rather, the ability to recognize the connection between the breath, the mind, and the emotions—and learning to master this life force energy. In other words: breathe before you speak.

Like all the most charismatic gurus, a true yoga preacher has a way of reading the room and then delivering precisely the right words, at precisely the right point in the proceedings, to guide you down the numinous pathways of your being and unlock memories, emotions, and insights that it turns out have been begging to be released. Cue the kind of psychic visions and realizations that can leave you weeping on your mat.

My all-time favorite? New Jersey–born Seane Corn, cofounder of the charitable organization Off the Mat, Into the World, who weaves her vigorous Vinyasa flow classes with wisdom like this (from an interview in the 2012 documentary *Yoga Is*):

---

**5.** PRATYAHARA: Sensory transcendence. Learning to take a step back and observe the physical body, as a way of separating from earthly desires—particularly if they're distracting from your spiritual growth. Like, is it really *you* (a.k.a. your highest Self) reaching for that third glass of pinot?

**6.** DHARANA: Concentration. Potentially the most difficult of the limbs to practice in our fragmented modern lives; when was the last time you maintained sustained, single-minded focus on a single object, sound, or . . . social media feed, even?

**7.** DHYANA. Meditation. The natural result of extended periods of dharana, in yoga, meditation is described as the uninterrupted flow of concentration. The distinction between the two? A truly meditative state means being aware *without* focus—a.k.a. attaining the famously elusive empty mind. Struggling? The thing to keep in mind (or not—ha) is that it's all about the process . . .

**8.** SAMADHI: Ecstasy. A.k.a. enlightenment. To achieve samadhi, the meditator transcends the body to realize a total connection with the Divine (spirit, the Universe, oneness energy, etc.). We're talking the realms of the saints! But maybe even you, lowly soul, have experienced this ecstasy in your human life. Another word for samadhi could be simply *peace*.

People are awakening at this time in our culture to the power of the grace that exists in our hearts, which a lot of the time we shut down. When we shut down, we can't feel, and when we can't feel, we can't surrender—and the way to God is through surrender. Through the yoga practice, you open, you begin to expand, and you begin to feel. Feelings lead to vulnerability, vulnerability leads to surrender, and there you go, you open up to God.

Yep . . . more #waterworks every time I read this. And sure, she uses the G-word. But God, the Universe, Source, oneness energy . . . call it what you will, personally I like to be reminded that yoga *is* a way to connect to the part of this energy that resides in my physical being, or else it is just exercise. And if we're simply talking strength and balance and flexibility, my body still prefers other ways to work on that.

Earlier in this chapter, I described yoga as "a workout for my soul"—and the big reveal for me has been how, actually, my whole perfectly imperfect journey on the mat has been exactly that. That all the years I struggled to find a practice that worked for me were actually part of the process, part of the practice itself.

# 6.

# HIGHLY MEDITATED

A little while back I tried to book Andy Puddicombe, creator of the crazy popular Headspace meditation app, for a brand job I was consulting on. After initial interest, we were told he was just too busy after all—with a book to finish, and a new baby to bond with. The last thing he'd said yes to, I was told, was a conference hosted on Necker Island, where Richard Branson had brought together the most important minds outside of politics to brainstorm future solutions for the problems being faced by the human race. Not only was Andy in high demand, he had evidently perfected the art of prioritizing and had exceedingly sturdy boundaries in place to boot.

It seemed a far cry from the first time I met Andy, in a nondescript business suite in a gray building on the outskirts of London's financial district back in 2010. Headspace had launched a few months earlier, as an events company dedicated to bringing meditation to the masses. Andy, who had graduated from university with a degree in circus arts, had only recently returned from studying Buddhist meditation and living as a monk in the Himalayas. But his fledgling brand was already beginning to create a buzz, and with the *Sunday Times* about to go online for the first time, I'd approached Andy about creating some guided meditations for the website.

# WHAT IS MEDITATION?

The word *meditate* means "to think," and so anything that makes you consciously aware of your thoughts could be termed "meditation"—since the word literally speaks to the act of monitoring the thoughts in your head. In spiritual circles, the act of meditation is generally used as a way to distinguish between these thoughts— often referred to as the output of the "ego" or "monkey mind"—and a higher level of conscious awareness, a.k.a. our higher Self, the Universe, God/Goddess, et cetera.

Was meditation going to be the next big thing? It felt like it could go that way, and so when he invited my colleague and me to come in for a session after I'd pitched him my idea, of course we went along. Cut to me—back straight as a ruler, feet planted on the floor, hands resting lightly in my lap—sitting in a chair in his office, following Andy's soothing instructions to count my breath in, and out, while gently observing any thoughts that came along "as if you're sitting in a deck chair under a tree, and the thoughts are just traffic driving past."

The stillness in the room felt crystalline, Andy's lovely, friendly voice sounding farther and farther away. "Now you can stop counting your breath, and just let your thoughts go wherever they like," he instructed. And as I did, I felt a surge of energy pulse through my body, as my heart did a double backflip. My breath began to come so hard and fast I was overwhelmed with a sense of vertigo, and I had to flutter my eyelids open to make sure I wasn't keeling over in my chair. I was experiencing what I can only describe as a mini panic attack.

The feeling subsided after a few more seconds, leaving me cold and clammy and nauseated, but I was too embarrassed to tell Andy what had happened. He was so nice, and it was meditation for goodness' sake! It was supposed to be deeply relaxing—what the hell was wrong with me? But then I HAD been extra stressed out lately; maybe I was just exhausted. Or perhaps it was the triple-shot cappuccino I'd had before our meeting.

Needless to say, when my astrologer friend Shelley von Strunckel invited me to try meditation again six months or so later, I was fairly apprehensive. But Shelley was the person I'd asked to guide me on my mystical studies—she was the mentor helping me germinate The Numinous—and I trusted her. She had made it clear to me that, along with a daily yoga practice, regular meditation was absolutely key to "tapping in" to the numinous realms. How could I say no? She was also hosting the invite-only meditation lessons at her luxurious loft apartment, which I had been visiting regularly of late, so the setting itself also felt safe. And well, things went pretty differently—in fact, I can actually pinpoint this evening as the first time I officially "met" my higher Self.

A group of around five of Shelley's fabulous friends had gathered (she's one of those women who collects interesting characters), and we each found a spot on one of her plush velvet sofas, with cushions to help us sit upright. Her instructions were very simple: to close our eyes and concentrate on the sensation of our breath moving through our body. "Every time a thought comes, simply observe it and go back to your breath," she went on.

I closed my eyes with some trepidation, half expecting a repeat of my experience with Andy. But we meditated in silence like this for I don't know how long (I think Shelley told us afterward it had been about three minutes), and when I opened my eyes, I actually felt . . . deliciously stoned. It had been years since I'd smoked a joint, and I'd stopped because it only really ever made me paranoid. But the physical sensation I was experiencing now was one thing I *did* like about weed—a tingling sense of bliss, of absolute ease, and of expansiveness. Like I'd just woken up from a deep, unbroken sleep. And after just three minutes? I couldn't stop smiling.

But then came the best bit. "Did you notice the thoughts come and go?" asked Shelley. We all nodded. "I'll ask you again, and this time consider *who,* or what, exactly was noticing those thoughts," she said, smiling like the Cheshire cat. The point she was making was that our awareness was entirely separate from the thoughts in our head. Which must mean that what I called "I" was not necessarily *all there was to "me"* at all—and, even better, that the rest of "me" evidently hung out somewhere in the void of absolute tranquillity it had felt so *good* to drop into.

Back then, this was nothing short of revolutionary for me—opening a portal to my understanding of my *self* beyond my physical body and my ego mind. *As spirit.* What was this intangible part of "me" made of? What was *its* perspective on life? And how could I connect with *this* self more often?

## WHY IS IT SO HARD TO SIT?

The above revelation that my whole self stretched way beyond my physical body and ego mind is the reason many believe a regular meditation practice is the absolute entry-level requirement to living a more spiritual life, an existence that's aligned with the needs of your highest Self. Or, in layperson's terms, a more peaceful, less stressful, and generally happier and more fulfilling experience of being human. All the great teachers—from Deepak to the Dalai Lama—will tell you the same thing, and the good news is that evidence suggests the world is slowly waking up to (or perhaps remembering) this truth. But this doesn't make it any easier to actually get on that cushion and meditate.

Did I begin meditating every day after my experience at Shelley's? I did not. Numinous contributor Ellie Burrows, who runs the MNDFL meditation studio in lower Manhattan, likens meditation to going to the gym: "I would spend fifteen minutes deciding whether to meditate in the first place, just like sometimes the hardest part of working out is getting into your workout clothes," she told me, joking that she built a whole meditation studio to "seduce" herself into a regular practice.

And I know I'm not alone when I say I can totally relate. Over the years, I've tried meditating with Andy's Headspace app, I've attended Zen Buddhist meditation classes at various centers in NYC, I've found guided meditations on YouTube, and I've signed up for Deepak and Oprah's 21-Day Meditation Challenge, all in the name of trying to find a practice that would stick. Having met my higher Self and experienced that intoxicating sense of calm when I meditated with Shelley, I knew this had to be good for me, on every level (physical, mental, emotional, and spiritual). So the fact that when it came time to actually close my eyes to go "within" I would find literally anything to distract me (clean the bathroom, send just . . . one . . . more . . . e-mail) made me worry that my soul was seriously unevolved. Plus, I rarely came even close to achieving that same state of deep relaxation as when I meditated with Shelley. Maybe I just wasn't ready.

I took some solace when I interviewed Elizabeth Gilbert—perhaps, with *Eat, Pray, Love,* one of the first mainstream voices to really discuss the benefits of meditation—and she told me that even her practice was currently "lapsed." After all, in *Eat, Pray, Love,* she writes at length about the *boredom* and *discomfort* she experiences meditating, as well as the *discipline* it takes. Not exactly words to entice anybody to sit.

Because the thing is, our minds don't *want* to meditate. Our minds want to think. As Ellie reminds us: "The mind thinks involuntarily, like the heart beats, and the lungs breathe. Heart and lungs stop, you're dead. Mind stops, you're in a coma or brain dead." So it makes sense that evolution has made it pretty darned difficult to switch the mind off!

Of course, as most meditation teachers like to remind us: *this isn't about turning the mind off.* It's about simply learning to *observe and detach* from our thoughts. But then how come in the same breath, the same teachers will also often explain how the *goal* of meditation is a "quiet" or even an "empty" mind? Which sounds quite like a mind that's been put on stand-by mode to me.

## THE RIGHT WAY TO MEDITATE?

You might have also heard the saying, *There's no right way to meditate.* Which essentially speaks to the fact that, as with yoga, different styles or approaches to meditation work for different people. But Ellie thinks the reason so many of us have a problem maintaining a regular practice is that too many of us are trying to meditate like Buddhist monks—who spend years meditating for hours every day with the ultimate aim of achieving *nirvana,* a.k.a. transcendence from the human experience of suffering. It is in this state of *integration with pure spirit,* say the monks, that we're able to full-on communicate with God (the Universe, Source, oneness consciousness, etc.). And that the way to get there is by removing all earthly thoughts from our heads—or at least detaching from them so thoroughly we no longer notice they're there.

There's a name for this approach: Focused Attention, which involves actively monitoring every single thought that pops into your head and kindly (these are Buddhists, after all) asking it to retreat. Or else simply disregarding it by remaining focused on the breath. Anybody who's tried this will know that it is extremely difficult. Not least because the mind (well, my mind at least), tends to go: *Aha, a thought! Ignore it and go back to the breath . . . Oh . . . wait . . . now I'm thinking about ignoring that thought . . .* And so on. Which very quickly (for me) becomes the definition of frustration, and most definitely not something I'm likely to make time for every day.

Focused Attention is a technique I tried at the Zen Buddhist center in Manhattan, and it is the kind of meditation that Liz Gilbert writes about in *Eat, Pray, Love.* It's also the kind of meditation Andy Puddicombe would have learned in Tibet. Which comes back to Ellie's observation. While emptying the mind of all thoughts with the view to creating a clear channel to God is a very noble pursuit, it's not actually what little old me, a Material Girl still going about my daily business in the Material World, is really in this for. Yes, I want to feel connected to my higher Self, but mainly so I can make better choices and have a better time here in the earthly dimensions.

Enter Mindfulness meditation, or Open Monitoring Thinking. This approach is slightly less intense, since the aim is to simply become aware of and observe the thoughts as they come and go, without actively trying to make them go away. Because this is far easier than maintaining full-on Focused Attention, Mindfulness meditation has become way popular—for example, it's the approach behind Andy's Headspace app, which has had two million downloads (and counting). But still, the degree of effort involved in mindfully monitoring my thoughts is still enough of a deterrent to doing it daily. It's also not exactly fun—kind of like being monitor in a kids' playground in charge of keeping a lid on the action. Which brings me to . . .

## FINDING MY ZEN WITH TM

So for about five years or so I dipped in and out of the above techniques, all the while telling myself this was enough, actually. The same people who insist "there's no right way to meditate" will also tell you that just a couple of minutes a day (or week, even) is better than nothing. After all, the people with the most dedicated practice—teachers like my friend Gabby Bernstein, or my shaman Marika (who you'll meet in the next chapter)—were also the most committed (in kind of a monklike way) to their spiritual path, having embraced teaching and healing with spirituality as part of their dharma.

Plus the fact that even what I *was* doing seemed to be having an effect. After experiencing life (a.k.a. my thoughts) from the perspective of my higher Self firsthand, I naturally found myself stepping back to observe the contents of my head *all the time*—particularly in stressful situations. Instead of getting carried away on a fast train to anxietyville, the internal conversation would go: *Oh look, anxiety. Who invited you?* I was less reactive and undoubtedly more connected to my sense of self. Overall, I felt I could give myself a pat on the back for embracing meditation at all.

This part of the book was essentially going to confirm that, yes, ANY meditation, even the "moving meditation" of yoga, IS better than no meditation, especially as you begin to carry the teachings of mindfulness, equanimity, and (higher) self-awareness into your daily life. Which I still believe to be absolutely the case, and which is still essentially what I want you to take away from this chapter.

But then I discovered Transcendental Meditation, or TM, and everything fell into place.

TM is a five-thousand-year-old mantra-based meditation technique—meaning that rather than trying to make your mind go sit obediently in a corner while "you" (your higher Self) have a grown-up conversation with the Universal oneness, you give it something—a mantra—to distract it. As if the ego mind is kind of like a restless five-year-old, and doing TM is like playing it a Disney movie—giving me a few minutes' blissful respite from its constant demands for attention.

Forty minutes per day, to be precise—split into twenty-minute sessions, morning and afternoon, as recommended by the school of TM. Considering that finding even five minutes to sit had always seemed daunting, the time requirement alone had been enough to put me off, as well as being the reason I'd always considered TM to be the big kahuna—the real deal—a style of meditation for absolute pros only. But turns out it's the opposite. If concentration and mindfulness techniques were made for monks, then mantra-based meditation (also called *Vedic meditation*) was designed for us "householders." Just like Yogi Bhajan's Kundalini yoga.

I decided to learn so I would have all bases covered before writing about meditation here—and what d'you know, it's the practice that's stuck. And not least because *it feels so freaking good!* That tingling sensation of relaxation and ease I got meditating with Shelley? I experience it every single time I practice TM—ample incentive alone to set my alarm twenty minutes earlier in the morning or stop whatever I'm doing to fit in my afternoon session. A couple of weeks in, I described this feeling to my teacher, Bob Roth, as "like sinking into your sofa at the end of a hectic day." The whole body and mind relax, transported on a cloud of comfort. I have also been known to describe it as "like a massage for the mind."

Bob is the director of the David Lynch Foundation, which he set up with the *Twin Peaks* director (a TM practitioner since the 1970s) to teach TM in prisons, schools, and homeless shelters, and the word he always uses to describe the technique itself is *effortless*—versus the *intense effort* of trying to empty or control a mind that has no intention whatsoever of shutting off or shutting up. Rather, TM is about accessing a part of the mind that is quiet, calm, and relaxed *by its very nature,* in every human, always, no matter what's going on "up on the surface." Which is why Bob claims he can teach anybody this technique—regardless of demographic or spiritual beliefs. "You don't need to believe anything for this to work, like you don't have to 'believe' in gravity. It's just a law of nature," he is fond of saying.

He also uses the analogy of an ocean to describe the mind: "There will always be waves, or thoughts, on the surface. Sometimes these will be huge, and overwhelming. But deep down at the bottom of the ocean, the water is always still." Um, if I were my higher Self, I know where I'd be hanging out. The *mantra*—the word literally translates as "mind vehicle"—is the submarine we use to go visit. It's a trip our minds want and are designed to take, and used to embark on of their own accord, says Bob. Before every waking minute of each and every day got infiltrated with enticing pieces of information for our synapses to pick up and color with curiosity, anxiety, possibility, and desire. A.k.a. e-mails, tweets, YouTube clips, and social media "likes."

They used to call it "daydreaming"—letting the mind wander when there was no new information to process—and I have vivid memories of dropping into this state as a kid. When lying in the garden, or on my bed, I'd allow myself to become *entranced* by the way the light moved through the leaves on a tree, or so absorbed by a new word I'd learned that I'd repeat until it became an abstract sound. Likely not the case for so many "kids these days."

Another reason TM felt less accessible (despite being by far the easiest technique) is that it's taught one-on-one by a certified meditation teacher. This can be expensive (even if, in the case of the David Lynch Foundation, fees also cover free tuition for hundreds of thousands of people in at-risk communities). But there are several reasons for the need for individual attention.

For one, being given your mantra verbally, and in private, helps it to remain an abstract sound. Essential if it's to remain an effective "mind vehicle" to distract the monkey mind (versus a word it can attach meaning, and therefore yet more thoughts, to). Second, the technique is so deceptively simple it's easy to think you're doing it wrong. Learning over a series of sessions gives your teacher ample times to address all the questions you may have about this. And finally, it's just really beautiful to know that your teacher will be there to support you in your practice for life. All that alone time with the contents of your head can get a little solitary, after all.

## MEDITATION IS THE NEW EXERCISE

So Bob, who's been practicing TM for almost fifty years and teaching the technique since 1972, could not be a better advertisement for the practice. An exceedingly kind, calm, and attentive individual, he told me he became a TM teacher because he's "an activist kind of guy" with a desire to "ease the suffering of others." Which brings us back again to Yogi Bhajan, and a very Now Age ailment he termed "computer sickness."

It's pretty much common knowledge that our increasing reliance on and integration with technology hasn't exactly resulted in us thriving as *happy, healthy human beings,* so check out this very truncated list of the scientifically proven benefits of (all kinds of) meditation:

Less stress

More focus

Less anxiety and impulsivity

Enhanced self-esteem and self-acceptance

Increased memory retention and recall

Better decision making

Helps manage ADHD

Reduces blood pressure

Um, which essentially makes meditation sound more and more like an actual magic pill for managing the adverse side effects of living in the digital age. As I said, I can physically feel the relaxing effects of TM, and in terms of meditation's benefits, the theory goes something like: quiet or detach from the ego mind; save a BUNCH of energy; redirect this energy toward the project and/or physical healing at hand. For example, Ellie Burrows credits her Vedic meditation practice with how quickly she healed from a recent whiplash incident, which astonished her chiropractor. "It's like the body is relaxed enough to do its thing," she explained.

As Bob also told me: "I think human beings *must have quiet* to survive. And we have to go inside ourselves to find peace now, because the always-on nature of modern life means there is no more quiet on the outside." Enter, *computer sickness*. For which there is also a more scientific-sounding name: adrenal fatigue. A particularly twenty-first-century malaise, adrenal fatigue results from chronic overstimulation of the adrenal glands—which secrete the "fight or flight" hormone cortisol as a stress response.

I was diagnosed with adrenal fatigue during my darkest days working at *Style* magazine. I was exhausted but wired, often stressed out to

---

## ADRENAL FATIGUE: A LIFE CYCLE

The body experiences stress (emotional, mental, or physical) → the adrenal glands secrete cortisol, designed to give us extra energy to combat the stress → the cortisol itself causes a stress response in the body → the adrenal glands secrete more cortisol → cortisol supplies, and energy, run low → we reach for coffee, sugar, alcohol, etc., to compensate → these substances cause a stress response in the body → the adrenals secrete more cortisol.

The problem is that modern life exposes us to way more daily "stressors" than the adrenals are designed to deal with, including, but by no means limited to, deadlines, nasty e-mails, "push notifications," traffic jams, air travel, FOMO, no Wi-Fi, processed food, light pollution . . . You get the idea.

the point of tears, and I couldn't sleep through the night (all the classic symptoms). I was advised by a nutritionist to cut out coffee and sugar as a first response to manage the situation, which actually worked like a miracle (since *any* overstimulation of the nervous system—from caffeine, sugar, and other drugs, for example, to *too much screen time*—can trigger the adrenals).

Which brings me back to my first experience of meditating with Andy Puddicombe. I was operating at probably my *most* adrenally fatigued at that point—and self-medicating through the tiredness and the anxiety in all the wrong ways: coffee, alcohol, sometimes cocaine. I mean, yikes! But also totally par for the course for my profession. And then along comes Andy, with his slow, controlled breathing, and his soothing instructions to detach from the incessant chatter in my mind—my cortisol levels drop instantly . . . and my body *freaks the F out*. Not to mention my higher Self gets WAY overexcited that I might finally be ready to tune in, after months of trying to get my attention by . . . making me feel anxious and overwhelmed by life (please refer back to the chapter on dharma, and the messages to change up our current situation that our higher Self sends our way as *feelings*).

I actually think about that incident now as an example of just how powerful meditation can be. Whereas, speaking of magic pills and their side effects, modern medicine has failed miserably when it comes to addressing many of the issues mentioned above. For example, prescription drug abuse now kills more people than car accidents in the United States, while deaths by overdose of prescription painkillers have quadrupled since 1999 (about 50 Americans *every day*). Which is another reason I say TF for TM. If the message is becoming more and more clear: *meditate before you medicate,* then hallelujah for a style of meditation that makes it easier for everybody to get on board.

We've all gotten the memo by now that we need to move more, right? (Remember "sitting disease"?) And if hitting the gym may not feel like fun at first, we do it anyway because we know it's good for us (and then, surprise, it often becomes fun too). Sadly, since there's so much money in modern pharmaceuticals, governments are unlikely to get behind meditation in the same way. But who needs government guidelines when your *higher Self* knows it to be true: do meditation anyway, because it's good for you.

## THE BIG PICTURE (AND THE BIG FISH)

Even better, meditation is also good for *us,* as in the human race, and the planet we inhabit. When I asked Bob what he thought the world would look like if everybody meditated, he told me: "If even one percent of the population learned to meditate, as well as less stress and disease, there would be less divisiveness, and less violence. There would be more consensus and willingness to work together and be collaborative."

Which is a whole lot BIGGER than the answer I was expecting, and one that speaks to the role of meditation in the global shift in consciousness that's the hallmark of Now Age thinking. On a more microlevel, here's how Bob has seen this at work when people begin to meditate in families and other community settings: "When a family meditates, everybody becomes more accepting of differences, and so everybody gets along. When I'm feeling good and confident about myself, it doesn't matter if somebody likes a different style of music or has a different opinion to me." Meditation facilitates this because, as David Lynch writes in *Catching the Big Fish,* his book about TM: "The thing with meditation is: You become more and more you." More connected to your higher Self, that is.

Lynch also writes about TM being a way to access the ocean of pure consciousness known as the *unified field*—a mystical concept the ancient Vedic scholars of India spoke of as the origin of all living things, including thoughts and ideas. Lynch's "big fish" are the ideas you have to dive deepest into the unified field to catch. Time for another great Einstein quote: "I think 99 times and find nothing. I stop thinking, swim in silence, and the truth comes to me."

And there's more insight into this cosmic element of *being human* in my favorite TED talk ever, by Jill Bolte Taylor, a brain scientist who suffered a devastating stroke and was able to use the experience to gain living, breathing insight into how the brain actually works. Since the stroke occurred in the left side of her brain, the side that rules logical thinking, she proceeded to observe as all left-brain functions (anything relating to the ability to process information) shut down one by one, leaving her to experience life from an entirely right-brain perspective. Or, it could be said, from deep within the unified field.

Her most profound insight? "I am an energy being connected to the energy all around me through the consciousness of the right hemisphere (of my brain). *We* are energy beings connected to one another through the consciousness of our right hemispheres as one human family. . . . We ARE the life force power of the Universe."

The implication of *millions* of people getting on board with this idea—that we are, in essence, all connected by this *universal Self*? In terms of the impact this could have on the world stage ("less divisiveness, less violence . . . more consensus and willingness to work together and be collaborative"), why else would Richard Branson have invited Andy Puddicombe to his supermind summit on Necker Island (and what I wouldn't give to know what was discussed!)?

And so, in conclusion on this subject, however you make a regular meditation practice work for you, MAKE IT WORK FOR YOU. For yes, I too have come to see how it is the entry-level requirement for reestablishing your connection to the universal, unified Self of all humanity (spirit, God, the oneness, etc.), as you take your seat in an evolution of consciousness that is already beginning to reshape our world.

## 7.

# YOU, THE SHAMAN

Undoubtedly one of my most profound and moving numinous experiences to date was the first time I met my spirit animal—over Skype. I was living in a high-rise apartment in the East Village in NYC at the time, and the encounter took place on a gray spring day at about 4 P.M. in the afternoon. One minute I was sitting on my sofa, being led into a deeply relaxing guided meditation . . . and the next thing I knew, I was standing in a clearing in the forest of my subconscious, my arms around the neck of a beautiful black stallion, with goose bumps all over my body and tears of love and gratitude streaming down my face.

I'd also met a hedgehog, a kaleidoscope of butterflies (the official term!), and even a unicorn along the way—"the way" being a vivid psychic trip, down into the core of the earth and out into a lush natural landscape representing my inner Universe. But it was the goose bumps and the tears, which had sprung from nowhere, that told me this horse was my *power* animal.

And the message he had for me in that moment was one of absolute, unwavering inner strength. Coming across him, standing proud and quiet in the deeper, more shadowy reaches of my psyche, I knew without question that all the courage, resilience, and loving support I would ever need in this life were *within me*.

My guide into the spirit animal kingdom was Marika Messager, a modern shamanic practitioner based in London (hence the Skype situation) who had used hypnosis to take me there—her preferred technique for "journeying," or accessing what she called a "shamanic trance." The journey into the subconscious, numinous realms to seek "answers" to Material World problems forms the foundation of the shamanic healing tradition. And it was in this altered state of consciousness, Marika explained, that her clients were able to connect to their animal guides—totems that symbolize the different aspects of human psychology (a little like the different human archetypes represented by the signs of the zodiac).

## YOUR SPIRIT ANIMAL AND YOU: WHAT DO THE TOTEMS MEAN?

When our spirit animals show up, they're said to be a symbolic representation of different aspects of the human psyche and/or the soul journey. As well as in a guided meditation, you can also tune in to your highest Self at any time and ask to meet an animal guide—and then be on the lookout for the first "animal" that appears to you. While this may be an actual creature, it may also appear as an image on a billboard or in a magazine, or perhaps just as a strong psychic impression. Your animal could be anything, but here are some popular animals and their meanings:

BUTTERFLY: transformation, lightness of being, and transcendence from earthly concerns

DEER: sensitivity, innocence, and a connection to the inner child

HORSE: personal drive, passion, and a desire for freedom

OWL: intuition, wisdom, and a harbinger of transition or change

SPIDER: creativity, particularly writing, patience, and the darker side of feminine energy

The idea was to then research that animal, its habits and physical traits, as a reminder of the innate qualities we have access to in times of need. For example, the stallion is known for its rock-solid strength and unflagging will. It also represents freedom—since wild stallions are notoriously difficult to tame. Meanwhile, the butterflies I had seen represented transformation; the little hedgehog, the spiky armor we often wear to mask our more vulnerable emotions. And as for the unicorn? I think my mind's eye might have conjured that one for fun. Although having looked it up since, the unicorn is said to represent faith—so maybe she appeared simply as an invitation for me to *believe*.

Generally, when I've experienced something as genuinely and undeniably magical as my journey with the spirit animals, I immediately want all my friends to do it, too (my researcher/reporter dharma in action). So fast-forward to two months later, and The Numinous is hosting a group spirit animal meditation at Celestine Eleven, a high-fashion boutique meets metaphysical bookstore and natural apothecary in East London. The response has been outstanding, and over twenty curious seekers, including a handful of my old magazine contacts (many of whom I haven't seen since crossing the numinous divide) have gathered at the space. Meanwhile I am waiting nervously for Marika, who I've asked to facilitate the event, to arrive.

Nervously, because beyond the smiling face on Skype, I honestly have no idea what to expect. All I know about this woman is that she's French, she used to work in finance, and now she hooks people up with their spirit guides for a living. What does a "modern shamanic practitioner" *wear* anyway? I'm imagining flowing robes, perhaps some kind of headdress, and a lot of burning sage. Considering the people in the circle tonight, this event could be enough to convince the whole of London I have officially gone completely woo-woo.

And then in saunters Marika, dressed in leather pants, a fur gilet, and a pair of kick-ass Isabel Marant boots, with strands of diamond-laced mala beads around her neck. *Marika, I love you,* I think silently to myself. And of course she dresses this way. Marika's clients are lawyers, bankers, and CEOs—not the kinds of people who are going to swallow anything as downright mystical as spirit animals without a spoonful of first-world glamour to help the medicine go down.

In fact, since my encounter with Marika I've worked with several Western "modern shamans" (as Marika calls herself, to distinguish her practice from traditional shamanism)—a former Sony exec and a couple of ex-Ibiza party girls among them—to the point where my initial preconceptions about this ancient Earth magic, and the people who practice it, have been completely shattered. And based on my experiences and subsequent research in the field, I've also come to believe that the medicine of the shamanic traditions is perhaps the ultimate balm for our Now Age ills. "Medicine" we actually *all* have at our fingertips.

As for the group spirit animal meditation? It went down a storm, and everybody left with that spooked-in-a-good-way look you get when you've encountered actual freaking magic in action—a.k.a. a shift in perception that defies all reason and logic, and which opens a portal to another belief system or way of being. For Marika and her fellow shamanic practitioners, the kind of revelations that are all in a day's work.

## SO WHAT EXACTLY IS A SHAMAN?

When I asked Marika to explain her practice to me, she laid it out like this: "A shaman is basically somebody who is able to get (themselves or their client) into another state of consciousness. This is called a 'shamanic trance,' and in this state you are opening the door to another reality. You go here to get some insight, some healing energy, and some wisdom about the current situation you or your client is facing."

This "trance," she went on to explain, can be accessed many ways— through dancing, chanting, drumming, and, at the more extreme end of the spectrum, the use of hallucinogenic medicinal plants (a *whole* other Now Age trip in itself, which gets a full chapter of its own later on). Marika, however, having come to shamanism herself following years of psychotherapy, prefers to use hypnosis. "In Native American culture, for example (where shamanism is still a dominant force), there is no doubt that there are *many* realities, and that the reality we live in is equally as valid as the dream reality, the trance reality," she explains. "But I was, like, 'I need to understand how the subconscious mind actually functions.'"

Because let's face it, beyond the analyst's couch, modern society—let alone modern medicine—doesn't exactly give much credence to what goes on in the further reaches of our psyche. The author and philosopher Graham Hancock talks about this in his "censored" TED talk, *The War on Consciousness* (which TED staff explained they had relegated to an obscure discussion forum following "due diligence" of scientific research): the fact that Western civilization only values the "awake and productive" state of consciousness that enables us to build empires and win wars (what you could call "survival consciousness"), which in turn is fueled by our sanctioned consciousness-altering substances like sugar and caffeine.

The shamans meanwhile are ALL ABOUT the other, more nebulous (or *numinous*) states of human consciousness, since this is where we gain access to intuitive wisdom channeled directly from the Universe, God, the spirit world, and so on. Jill Boyle Taylor's right-brain states. And when it comes to healing, this philosophy encapsulates the belief that all the tools, the "medicine," we need to cure *ourselves* are also available to us within these subtle realms, versus available in pill form, as concocted in a lab and prescribed by your MD.

Which is not to say that shamans don't have their own potions, tricks, and tinctures up their sleeves. Flower essences and oils, crystals, sound tuning forks, hands-on healing, Human Design, and the tarot have all featured in various "shamanic" healing sessions I've experienced. This is because, as Marika puts it, "shamanism is very holistic. It's working on your mental body, your emotional body, your physical body, and your spiritual body." The idea is that perfect "health" is the result of all four bodies being in alignment.

As a result, it's said shamanism can be used to "heal" mental and emotional problems, such as addictions, anxiety, and depression, as well as physical conditions like sleep disorders and chronic pain. Traditionally, Marika tells me, it was the role of the shamans to maintain "the ecological, the spiritual, and the social balance of their community." In which case, I'm also interested to know what qualifies somebody—her, for example—for the job?

At this stage, it's important to emphasize again that Marika uses the term "modern shamanic practitioner" to describe herself, as opposed to straight-up "shaman," since in some South American tribal cultures, for example, you must be born into the correct lineage and be trained in the shamanic traditions from childhood to earn the title. "It's serious stuff," she says. But she also believes that the future of shamanism is for the tradition to blossom in a different, more accessible way in Western culture, since "it's really up to us now if we want to do our work and connect with ourselves." In essence, this means that: *I think there is a shaman in each and every one of us.*

Marika's own study of shamanism stemmed from a deeper than average interest in and understanding of human psychology, and a commitment to walking the path of what she calls "the wounded healer" (i.e., using her experience of healing her own life to help others' lives heal). But other than this: "I have no special powers." Rather: "I think the best way to describe myself is I have learned to find my own way through the dark, so I can guide you."

## SHAMANISM IN PRACTICE

So how do you choose a shaman to work with? Well, The Numinous is always a good port of call for information on trusted practitioners of all healing modalities. Once you have some names, I suggest engaging with an intuitive three-step process based on Betsy LeFae's Stop, Drop, and Roll technique (see box opposite).

Marika has some further advice too, which is to look at how this person is living *their* life. Which essentially means: Are they walking the talk? In her case: "I always try to keep my four bodies completely clear, clean, and aligned. On a physical level, this means I don't drink, smoke, or take drugs, and I am vegan like 80 percent of the time. Mentally, I am mindful of my thoughts, and I have a therapist and coach to supervise me in this. Emotionally, when I experience an emotion, I stay with it,

ASK YOURSELF:

Is this person's work in support of my highest good? ("Stop")

Do I get a sense of absolute trust when I engage with this person? ("Drop")

And then *listen* to what your body has to say on the subject. ("Roll with it")

and I learn from it. There is no numbing, no denying. And in a spiritual sense, I do everything to live my life with integrity, with transparency, with kindness, and with courage."

Which is actually a pretty good summary of my personal Now Age lifestyle #goals.

And then, of course, there is personal recommendation. The most extensive shamanic work I've done has been with Manex Ibar (also French, and the dude who used to work for Sony). Manex was recommended to me by two separate sources, one of whom—a fashion writer at *Harper's*—had recently been on something called a "vision quest" with him. An ancient shamanic rite of passage, the object of a vision quest (which can include four days out in the wilderness, alone, with no food and no shelter) is to retreat from society to allow the subconscious (or spirit Self) to rise fully to the surface, but also to rekindle a sense of trust that nature can and will provide.

The general consensus from the two intelligent, impressive women who suggested him was basically: "Manex is the best." A vision quest felt a little extreme for me (although my *Harper's* friend reckons it's the one experience in her life that's truly and fully connected her to her personal power source), so I decided to try his signature shamanic "prescription" instead.

This would take place over three sessions, scheduled roughly three months apart (since Manex travels between New York, London, Paris, and L.A. seeing clients), and meeting him for the first time was a bit like being on a date with Indiana Jones. As in, all six feet, four inches of him turned up at my apartment wearing a leather trilby with a feather tucked into the bow, and carrying a small canvas briefcase containing his tuning forks, his notebooks, and his essential oils. And a "date" because Manex is one of those guys who sounds like he's flirting with you no matter what he's talking about (or maybe it's just the accent).

The sessions themselves incorporated an overall reading of my energetics, chakras, and ancestral wounds, a dive into my psychology by way of the tarot, and a shamanic journey to meet my spirit guides. There was also "homework" involving flower essences and essential oils, and some meditation practices. But since I didn't go to Manex with a specific problem (it was less "let's fix this," more "so what can you do for me?"), it's hard for me to say if the sessions actually "worked."

Looking back, it's undeniable that things have shifted in a big way since our work together—there's more abundance in my life, and my relationship with my family feels loving, open, and stress-free. But as anybody who reads The Numinous (or even this book thus far) will suspect, I experiment with all sorts of healing modalities, often on a weekly basis, making it hard for me to pinpoint one particular practice that's gotten me to this point in my journey toward feeling more whole. My view on this? Each and every piece of my numinous puzzle has been an essential part of the process—including my sessions with Manex, in which he also delivered some incredible insights about my life and my journey.

Plus, we had some in-depth conversations about the nature of shamanism and its place in Western society, and he agrees with Marika on one very important point about modern versus traditional shamanic practice. "(Traditionally) a lot of shamans do the journeying part themselves, on behalf of the client, and then deliver the messages they receive to them," he told me, whereas both he and Marika think it's important for the individual to walk this path for themselves. "Otherwise I am demanding that you take me as your authority, which creates a massive dependency," he explained.

And it's true. Had *Marika* met my stallion in a trance and simply informed me that he was there for me, I'm pretty sure there would not have been any goose bumps and I would not be able to summon his presence myself so readily in times of need (which I totally do all the time!). In her observation: "Now more and more shamans are guiding people to enter the trance state themselves, so that they find their *own* answers. It's very empowering to have this experience yourself."

## ROOT CHAKRA PROBLEMS: SHAMANISM FOR THE NOW AGE

Listening back to the tapes of my first session with Manex (I record most readings and healing sessions to help join the dots further down the line), his immediate diagnosis had been that two of my chakras were closed: my heart chakra and my root chakra. Um, come to think of it, the two chakras directly related to the areas of my life that have shown the most improvement over the past two years: abundance, support, and feelings of open, authentic, and loving connection to others.

This was also a common diagnosis among his city-dwelling clients, he said, and one that manifests in all the classic modern malaises: depression (most prevalent in Paris); anxiety / never enough time (NYC); emotional frigidity (London); and trust issues (L.A.). And the common thread running through all this? A profound sense of disconnection, from ourselves and from each other.

According to Brené Brown, a shame and vulnerability researcher and author of the brilliant (seriously, if you haven't already, then please read) *Daring Greatly,* "Connection is why we're here. We are hardwired to connect with others; it's what gives purpose and meaning to our lives, and without it there is suffering." And if they say it's impossible to love others until you learn to love yourself, I think it's also impossible to connect fully with other people until you have forged a true and authentic connection to your (higher) Self.

Which is essentially the basis of shamanism—and why I believe this ancient *Earth medicine* is gaining so much traction in the Now Age.

As Marika puts it: "Shamanism is the work of connecting to your own truth, of understanding and releasing all the patterns and inherited conditions that are blocking you from realizing your true and full self." Meanwhile, on a deeper level: "Connecting with yourself and finding that everything is within, we are reminded that there is a part of Source, of God, or whatever, in each and every one of us. And that therefore, we are *all connected*."

This also describes the role of the shamans, with their animal totems, plant medicines, and reverence for the elements, as a reminder of our innate and divine connection to Mother Earth herself—our disregard of this being an issue some, including the shamans themselves, would say is at the *root* of the disconnection epidemic in modern society. Which brings me back to Manex and his root chakra problems—which he says he sees in 90 percent of his clients (with the other "lower body" chakras—sacral, solar plexus, and heart—following close behind).

You'll find a chart explaining the full chakra system on page 118, but the root chakra represents safety, home, and material security. In our day-to-day lives, this translates as family or tribe, shelter, and finance—and when this chakra is closed, there's a sense of panic that there will *never be enough* of the above. Brené Brown sees this in her work; that is, how "everything from safety and love to money and resources feels restricted and lacking. We spend inordinate amounts of time calculating how much we have, want, and don't have, and how much everyone else has, needs, and wants." A.k.a. your classic comparison trap—the "me versus them" culture this creates being yet another example of our disconnection epidemic (i.e., *heart chakra problems*).

According to Manex, "This means we put so much pressure on (the pursuit of the above), we forget to *trust life*." Because, from a shamanic perspective, our root chakra problems are a symptom of our disconnection from nature, from the earth, and the planet that literally supports *all life*.

It seems to me this has created something of a vicious circle. We seek to address the "lack gap" by earning more money, so we can buy more stuff. The capitalist system both resulting from and fueling this wreaks devastation on the natural world (through the burning of fossil fuels, as one example). We become yet more fearful that there are not enough *natural resources* to support us. Our root chakra problems are further exacerbated.

Graham Hancock talks about this in his TED talk, too—how when he asked the shamans he has worked with about the "sickness of the West," they replied: "It's quite simple. You guys have severed your connection with spirit." Meaning the all-loving, all-knowing life force (God, the Universe, our higher Self / consciousness, etc.) that manifests in and as the forces of nature that sustain life on this planet as we know it.

So how do the shamans propose we go about forging what they see as a vital *re*connection to Source? One way is to literally commune with nature. "Shamanism is, like, 'go and spend two hours with water.' It sounds really boring, but when you do it, it's amazing," says Manex. "The river begins singing to you, and bringing you all these messages. And you start to realize that what is spoken about in ancient myths wasn't about imagination, or hallucination. It's actually like 'wow, they *were* talking to the elements.'"

## YOU, THE SHAMAN

So now I want you to meet Tamara, a twentysomething former hair-dresser from Essex in the United Kingdom who discovered shamanism as a way of managing the chronic anxiety that was manifesting in her life as panic attacks, insomnia, and an eating disorder. (Um, sounds familiar.) She told me that after she began practicing meditation, "I would experience these animal visions, that unbeknownst to me at the time were actually my spirit guides." Exploring further, she said she was guided "by some very loud Universal signposts" to travel to Bali to apprentice with a shaman there and immerse herself in the practice more deeply (a journey you can read in her account on The Numinous).

On a personal level, Tamara says discovering shamanism means: "I no longer suffer from anxiety, my eating disorder feels like a distant memory, and my sleep is restful." She also describes how the practice of shamanism has taught her not to be fearful of the world. "Life is in constant flux, so I still have occasional moments where I feel overwhelmed," she went on, when I asked about this. "But thanks to (shamanism), I have the tools to ground myself, which makes life feel easier and lighter than ever before."

# THE CHAKRA SYSTEM: AN OVERVIEW

*Chakra* literally translates as "wheel" in Sanskrit and is the word used to describe the seven "spinning" energy centers in the body. Beginning at the tailbone and continuing to the top of the head, each chakra is represented by a color (reflecting the spectrum of colors in a rainbow) and is said to be the power source for the energy required for different organs to function—which in turn "power up" different elements of our life.

Optimum health requires all the chakras to be open, allowing for our energy to flow freely to where it is needed—and as such, just one chakra being "closed" or blocked can throw the whole system off, leading to physical, mental, emotional, and spiritual dis-ease. As well as in shamanism, all yoga and meditation practices seek to bring the chakra system into balance, and developing awareness around how we cultivate and expend our own energy can help us balance these life force centers within ourselves.

### Root Chakra

*Color:* Red
*Location:* Base of the spine

Powers our survival instinct and regulates the systems that keep the physical body alive.

### Sacral Chakra

*Color:* Orange
*Location:* Just below the navel

Powers our creativity and sexuality and governs how we feel about ourselves and others.

Tamara has even gone on to follow the path of the wounded healer herself and make shamanism her work as well as her personal practice. She goes by the name Wolf Sister, after *her* power animal, and told me how, for her, "shamanism encompasses my love of Earth magic, wild

---

Solar Plexus Chakra
*Color:* Yellow
*Location:* Just above the navel
Powers our willpower and self-esteem and rules our overall sense of satisfaction with life.

Heart Chakra
*Color:* Green
*Location:* Center of the chest
Powers our capacity for compassion, devotion, and unconditional love. The Heart Chakra is also the "bridge" that connects the lower (physical) and upper (spiritual) energies in the body.

Throat Chakra
*Color:* Blue
*Location:* Center of the throat
Powers communication and self-expression and holds the desire to speak and hear the truth.

Third Eye Chakra
*Color:* Indigo
*Location:* Middle of the forehead
Powers the imagination, knowledge, and intuition and is the gateway to spiritual awakening.

Crown Chakra
*Color:* Violet (sometimes white)
*Location:* Top of the head
Powers the higher Self and our connection to spirit. The Crown Chakra integrates the energy of all the lower chakras, allowing us to experience human life from a spiritual perspective.

nature, crystals, ritual and ceremony, divination, and intuitive practice." Which essentially reads like a shopping list of many of *my* favorite tools for self-discovery and healing too—the same tools I see being embraced by Now Age seekers everywhere.

Which makes me think about what Marika said about there being a shaman *in every one of us.* Also, how the way she lives her life—using her diet, thoughts, and daily practices to keep her four bodies in alignment—mirrors the way so many of us are making lifestyle changes that are as much about nurturing a sense of wholeness, and a connection back to our authentic Self, as they are about getting the kind of body we want, or rocking the latest Reformation dress.

Consider what my research has led me to identify as the keystones of the shamanic tradition:

*Reestablishing a connection to the authentic self*

*The use of tools such as divination, crystals, meditation, ritual and ceremony*

*Living with, and with respect for, the forces of nature*

*Believing that there is more than one reality or way of seeing the world*

*Trusting and acting on messages from spirit, God, the Universal oneness, etc.*

These are themes and practices that come up again and again as I witness people switch on to a Now Age, or numinous, way of thinking and being in the world. Which, more often than not, looks like taking responsibility for fully feeling, healing, and therefore dealing with whatever is keeping us from stepping with conviction onto the path of our highest human potential—as individuals, and as part of our global community.

The way I see it, in the Now Age *we are all our own shamans-in-training.* And when it is difficult to find our own way through the dark, I believe it is part of our journey to seek counsel and guidance from the mystics and the wounded healers who walk among us.

# PART III

# LOVE, SEX & RELATIONSHIPS

# 8

# CALLING IN NUMBER ONE (ON SELF-LOVE)

When it comes to love and relationships, I feel like I'm both the most and the least qualified person to talk on the topic. On the one hand, I've spent the past seventeen years in a blissful relationship with the man, the Pisces, who is undoubtedly the love of my life. And on the other, I haven't been on a date since 1999 (yes, waaaay before there were apps for that). But then "dating" (based on my own limited experience, plus years spent observing my friends go at it) isn't necessarily how you meet a partner anyway. Both times I've met the person I've wound up sharing my life with—once with somebody who literally made me feel like a ghost in my own body, and once in a way that has allowed me to express my true Self in ways I never could have imagined—I wasn't actively looking for a relationship. Rather, it's like we were magnetized to each other by an irresistible cosmic force.

Which, whoa there, is already getting way ahead of myself, since this chapter is supposed to be about *self*-love, right? About the relationship we all know is the most important one of all—your relationship with number one. After all, as Guru Meher Khalsa writes in his brilliant book on emotional healing, *Senses of the Soul:* "You live with yourself 24/7 for your entire life, so it's time to work things out in that relationship." And in no way do I want to imply that the *goal* of getting to a place of deep appreciation for your own sweet soul is snagging somebody who's then going to somehow "complete" you.

I have actually never felt more "complete" than during the brief six-month period of singledom that came between mustering the courage to show the Capricorn the door (or rather walk swiftly out the door, slam it behind me, and never once look back), and falling down a velvet-lined rabbit hole of bliss into the arms of the Pisces. Complete, because it was a window in time when I got to be 100 percent, unapologetically, ME. Because all relationships, good and bad, require a compromise, a concession of the needs of the *self,* to accommodate the needs of an *other*.

Which is where the self-love piece comes in—which I have come to believe is about truly acknowledging *what it is you need.* Since in identifying your deepest desires at soul level (like, beyond your material desires for Celine shoes, or a partner who brings you breakfast in bed), and then seeking for them to be fulfilled, is another example, like doing your dharma, of you playing your unique role in weaving the fabric of the Universal oneness. Which, in turn, is how we experience a *Universal* kind of love and connectedness.

The cosmic magnet effect I mentioned? They also call it the law of attraction—and we all know by now that *like attracts like,* right? In which case it makes sense that when I was going around bursting with pride, absolutely *in love with myself,* for finally leaving the Capricorn, I magnetized in a person who expressed the same sense of unconditional appreciation for me. And who continues, to this day, to be my biggest cheerleader. Also, somebody whose steadfast energy and no-BS attitude has provided the anchor my headstrong yet vulnerable Aries-Sun-Cancer-Moon combo *needs* to feel safe to go out there and do my dharma.

Which again, I apologize, may suggest that attracting a partner is perhaps the end goal when it comes to cultivating self-love—which is not what I meant at all. Rather, I use my own situation to illustrate how attracting anything we truly desire, anything that answers our *fundamental needs,* requires us to (a) acknowledge what it is we truly want; (b) be brave enough to go for it; and (c) value ourselves enough to trust that our needs will be met. That *we're worth it.*

After all, the Universe knows how precious you are—which reminds me of an amazing quote I heard recently: "Your birthday is the day the Universe decided it could not go on without you."

And so there follows an exploration of some practices and principles I believe will help you to believe this about your SELF. To learn to recognize and prioritize your unique and lovable *needs.* Practices and principles I invite you to embrace regardless of your relationship status (or even your desired relationship status)—since my own journey also illustrates how NO relationship is infinitely preferable to a relationship founded on anything less than the highest levels of respect and utmost admiration for number one.

## Self-Love Is . . . Way More Than Bubble Baths and Buying Yourself Flowers

Beginning a conversation about self-love, it's easy to go straight to all the external stuff. Like, how would my ideal lover treat me? He or she would tell me I'm beautiful, cook me delicious meals, buy me gifts, and rub my feet at the end of a stressful day. So I want you to take all this and assume it as a given. Like, *of course* you're going to pamper yourself and treat yourself nice. The thing is, unless you look at what's going on on the inside, at how you can learn to love yourself on an emotional and spiritual level, it's all just empty gestures—more Hallmark than heartfelt. The journey to true self-love is not necessarily this fragrant or this pretty; in fact, it can get downright messy.

## Self-Love Is . . . Self-Awareness, Self-Acceptance, and Self-Forgiveness

This is because to truly love yourself, you must first seek to forge a loving relationship with every part of yourself. Waaaay harder than it

Self-love is about
acknowledging what
it is you need—and
seeking for this to be
fulfilled at soul level.

sounds, as this inevitably requires shining a light on all the dark or ugly impulses, thoughts, feelings—a.k.a. signifiers from your higher Self that needs are going unmet—we're generally taught to shove away under the carpet (since we're taught to believe these unattractive, perhaps "too demanding" parts of our Self will ultimately make us unlovable—the irony!). Which brings me back to . . . astrology.

When the AstroTwins describe birth chart interpretation as a tool for "radical forgiveness," this is because identifying the more difficult aspects of your chart can be one way to cultivate awareness as to where your gremlins might be hiding out. Because chances are you've gotten pretty good at pretending they don't exist (by drowning them in a half bottle of wine every night, say). You can also do this in psychotherapy, through journaling, or even getting really deep and dirty with your tarot practice.

The work, then, is learning to acknowledge your jealous streak, or your anger issues, or your competitive impulses—with a view to welcoming these traits as part of your makeup, and ultimately forgiving yourself for, you know, *being human*. Which, by the way, is not the same as issuing yourself a get-out-of-jail-free card and continuing to engage in any associated low-vibe/mean behavior. This is about acceptance and forgiveness with a view to *transmuting* low to high vibes.

## Self-Love Is . . . the Self as Love

My friend Jennifer Kass, a life coach who teaches self-love as the basis for personal development in every area of life, takes this one step further. On the very deepest, most spiritually advanced level, she says that to know and love oneself is to foster a connection to our inner or higher Self as a pure expression of the Divine (spirit, God, the Universal oneness, etc.).

She actually uses the words *God* and *love* interchangeably (also describing herself as the kind of person who, before her breakdown / breakthrough / spiritual awakening five years ago, "would not be your friend" if you told her you believed in God) and says the trick to truly experiencing and therefore knowing this cosmic force as the most elemental part of your Self, the bedrock of your being, is to completely transcend the ego mind, a.k.a. the plant where all the ugly stuff I mentioned above is produced. "And then BOOM, you're there. Because beyond the ego, the higher Self IS love," she says.

## Self-Love Is . . . a Daily Practice

And how do we do this? "Simple. Through meditation and our daily spiritual practice," says Jennifer. Which we all know can be easier said than done—but when it comes to truly knowing your Self and your unique needs, deep *self-listening* is key. As I explained in the chapter on meditation, when I first experienced the practice, I was genuinely astounded to discover that I could actually *hear myself think,* followed by the attendant realization that this meant "I" must somehow be a separate entity from my thoughts. And this "I" is the Self we're angling to embark on a mad passionate love affair with. The Self that Jennifer encourages us to recognize as the expression of *love itself.* Why a daily practice? Because this "I" can be a whimsical beast—and so what I need can change dramatically depending on what kind of shit went down in I's day!

## Self-Love . . . Takes Time

Conventional wisdom is that it takes twenty-one days to form a new habit, although a 2010 study by University College London showed that it took anywhere from 18 to 254 days for lifestyle changes such as going for a daily run to feel automatic. And since what we're talking about here can mean making a fundamental change to the coding of our operating system (learning that our needs not only count, but are of *paramount importance,* for example), depending on your levels of commitment I'd go right ahead and triple that.

Because you can set all the intentions and recite all the positive affirmations you like, but you still better be prepared for life—mainly in the form of self-sabotage, media messages, interactions with other people, and generally living in a human suit—to stall your self-love progress. Sure, you could make like Elizabeth Gilbert and disappear on your very own *Eat, Pray, (Self)-Love* pilgrimage, and get back in touch with your fundamental needs that way. But this option simply isn't available (or even appropriate) for everyone, and chances are you'll be feeling your way there, one step at a time, while navigating the life and the lessons you've been given (or rather, your soul chose for you). And for every two steps back? *Self-awareness, self-acceptance, self-forgiveness.*

### Self-Love . . . Can Be Measured in the Quality of Your Relationships

Going back to the giant cosmic magnet theory of like attracts like, "One of the biggest aspects of my awakening was watching my relationships transform as I transformed, and watching my relationships heal as I healed," Jennifer told me. So if you're actively staking out your self-love pilgrimage but are having a hard time working out how far you've come, then take a look around you at the people in your life.

And not just the people you're romantically involved with. Which friends and new acquaintances are you gravitating toward, and whom do you naturally find yourself having less time for? The higher your self-love vibe, the higher-vibe people you'll attract—people who in turn make you feel better about and therefore more inclined to feel lovingly toward your Self. (N.B. And please not one crumb of guilt about cutting the haters off completely.)

But also, and very importantly, how are things improving in your existing relationships? Like the one with, say, your mom (not the easiest for a LOT of women I know)? As discussed, I used to find it extremely annoying that my mum always wanted to know how I was feeling, and to tell me how she was feeling. Couldn't she just leave me *alone*? And why did she have to be so *needy*? These days, I consider myself extremely fortunate to have a mum who wants to talk about what's *really going on*—not to mention one who has learned to make *her* needs top priority, and ask for them to be met.

This is because since beginning to work on my *self-knowledge, self-acceptance, and self-forgiveness,* I'm no longer so afraid of revealing my demons (unattractive needs), which in turn means I no longer feel so "exposed" by (and defensive about) her probing. What I used to experience as criticism on her part ("you're emotionally repressed, you don't care about me") I now see as loving concern and a desire for connection. Exactly mirroring the shift in my relationship with my Self.

## Self-Love Is . . . Dating with Integrity

Elyssa Jakim is a healer and intuitive whose work is focused on sexual healing, and she arrived at her self-love journey thus: "Dating in a way that was not in integrity with my (spiritual) Self ultimately shone a light on what needed to be healed in me, which was my sense of self-worth, and self-love."

Having moved to NYC to be an actress, she'd wound up having a LOT of Tinder sex to make up for being a late developer and not having dated much in high school. And not that there's anything wrong with sex for sex's sake—in fact, if that's what you want and need, then dating with integrity for you could simply mean "acknowledging, accepting, and forgiving" your inner slut (let's also reclaim that shameful little word while we're at it), and being up front with your casual hookups that that's essentially what your encounters are.

But in her case, Elyssa realized the resulting lack of intimacy and respect was essentially reflecting a lack of intimacy and respect in her relationship with her *Self,* which is when she decided to make a declaration to the Universe.

"Any time a guy wanted just sex, I would tell him: 'I'm actually looking for a relationship now, and I can't have sex without that.' It became like a spiritual practice," she told me. "In declaring this, I was both setting an intention and reminding myself I was worthy of the kind of relationship I truly desired." Not to mention making herself way more attractive, according to the law of attraction that *like attracts like,* to the kind of love she wanted to experience with a partner.

## Self-Love Is . . . Self-Pleasure

Okay, this is a big one as it gets a bit sciencey, and is kinda juicy, so let's hang out here for a while.

When one friend was embarking on her self-love journey, she lamented: "But it's probably going to mean no sex life for at least six months." And this feels like a missing piece in the puzzle to me. Like OF COURSE waiting for the kind of sex that's going to fill you up as opposed to make you feel like a used condom is a way of cultivating self-love . . . but you want to get off while you wait, right?

Damn right. Chinese medicine specialist Sandra Lanshin believes that women's bodies are designed to receive and feel pleasure, including sexual pleasure. As in, it's essential to our well-being. The hormone oxytocin (a.k.a. the "LOVE" hormone or cuddle drug), released in women during orgasm, reduces stress, lessens the chance of obesity and psychotic behavior, improves cognitive function, and decreases breast cancer risk. (And p.s. it's released *any* time the uterus contracts—like when you give birth and even when you have your period.)

The best part? In most women, clitoral orgasms—meaning orgasms resulting from clitoral stimulation alone, which have no role whatsoever in the reproductive process, and which you are perfectly equipped to administer yourself—are the strongest. And the stronger the orgasm, the more oxy is released. Yay!

But, MAN, is there some stigma around women and masturbation. It's not "ladylike"; it's shameful; it's self-indulgent. My theories about this are way too complex to really get into here, but think about the way women are taught to feel about sensual pleasure in general. How from food to physical exercise, denial and discipline are good—and without pain there can be no gain. Or how indulging in things we want is a "guilty pleasure." I love the fact that Sandra often prescribes her clients "a thirty-day self-pleasure diet"—an orgasm a day, for thirty days—as a way of getting women to address this taboo. (Yes, you might want to try it!)

Now consider this. The ancient Taoists referred to self-pleasuring as one of the nine tenets of "self-cultivation"—"sexual sagehood" lining up alongside surrender, harmony, simplicity, grounding, integrity, transformation, immortality, and spontaneity. I found this beautiful description referring to "solo meditative sexual alchemy" online: "(using) our tangible sexual essence to *capture and crystallize the invisible essence of our spirit.*"

For me, this idea speaks to the fact that our sexual energy resides in the second, or sacral, chakra, along with our creative energy. And so getting in touch (literally) with ourself as a sexual being is also a way of stimulating our creative self—or powers of manifestation. This theory is the basis of a practice called Sex Magic, or what sex educator Annie Sprinkle calls "medibation": the act of self-pleasuring while holding the image of something you want to call in, or create, in your mind.

Consider this quote from Chakrubs founder Vanessa Cuccia, whose company produces beautiful crystal dildos (for real!): "When we're truly rooted in our pleasure, comfortable and excited, our minds go into a state of meditation [N.B. So much easier without a partner's pleasure / our "performance" to worry about]. Spiritual growth is self-awareness, and so removing fear and shame (or rather, not holding on to these feelings) from the part of ourselves that is meant to receive and give pleasure is a potent place to start on a spiritual path."

Which should give you plenty to think about next time date night rolls around and nothing on the Tinder menu seems that appealing. And the kicker? Learn to feel good about giving yourself sexual pleasure, and waiting for "the one" becomes way more bearable. Most men are totally okay with masturbation, after all, and, as we're pretty well aware, they also don't appear to expend nearly so much energy as women angsting over their currently single status. Um . . . coincidence?!

### Self-Love Is . . . Holding Yourself

And for the nights when you just need to "cuddle"? You can do that for yourself, too. When Elyssa got real about her desire to meet a life partner, she designed a self-love meditation practice to help cultivate the feelings of unconditional love in her self that she knew would in turn attract the kind of relationship she wanted. It goes something like this: "Before you go to bed, go into a meditation and embody your higher Self. Now ask to see, feel, or hear, the higher Self of your Soul Mate, and then invite them to hold you as you sleep."

When Elyssa practiced this for a period of months, she says it helped her to know and *feel* that she was completely worthy of love. She paused the practice when she began dating somebody, but says, "I was so glad to return to the idea of my Soul Mate when that relationship ended." And although she was cultivating a valuable self-love tool that meant finding a partner actually became less important, there's a fairy-tale ending to this story too. Shortly after we spoke, Elyssa embarked on a journey of self-discovery in the Pacific Northwest, where she met the guy she calls "my person" during the very first week—using a popular dating app, no less. The last I heard, they were engaged to be married.

## Self-Love Is . . . a Holistic Self-Care Practice

And I repeat: I'm not just talking about rose-scented Epsom salt baths (these are a given!). I want you to think back to the way the shamans approach healing, taking into account the needs of all four bodies— physical, mental, emotional, and spiritual—and adjust your approach to self-care accordingly. For me, this looks a lot like . . .

PHYSICAL: the Epsom salt baths, a regular deep tissue massage, yoga, minimal alcohol, regular vegan ice cream consumption

MENTAL: no e-mails or social media before 9 A.M. and after 9 P.M., and not comparing my self, my life, my achievements, and my desires to others'

EMOTIONAL: a commitment to feeling all my feelings, sharing how I really feel, and allowing myself to cry—a LOT

SPIRITUAL: TM meditation; my dream diary; regular visits with my astrologers, healers, and shamans; honoring my intuition; and rituals to connect to the phases of the Moon

Then you have to actually prioritize this stuff. Which means setting BOUNDARIES—which can also be described as "sacred me time and space"—and which I see as a self-care practice in itself. With the Capricorn, for example, I had no boundaries whatsoever. He steamrolled into my life and hijacked all four of my bodies before I even saw him coming. And sadly, this happens all the time in our relationships: romantic, at work, and with our families. Especially since being so connected by technology means there's even more pressure for us to be available, to everybody, all the time. But to truly be available in your relationships, you must first be available to your Self.

## Self-Love Is . . . Loving Self-Talk

Under "mental" (above) I also want to add the practice of "monitoring self-talk," since being overly critical and mean to our selves is probably one of the biggest and most common stumbling blocks when it comes to cultivating self-love. This is because most of us don't even know we're doing it, which brings me back to meditation, as always, as the essential component in learning to hear the ego / monkey mind gossiping away.

Once you're able to listen in, you can gently steer the conversation in a more loving/forgiving direction. Ask yourself: Would I ever talk to my best friend that way? Or my child? As Elyssa puts it, it's about "almost treating myself like this delicate little girl that needs understanding and nurturing." This is particularly effective in practicing *body-love,* she adds. "The second we decide to talk to our bodies this way, it's like we've been waiting for it our whole lives. Like a plant that just needed water."

Which is not the same as sugarcoating life's less palatable truths, by the way. For example, when you inform your best friend she's dating an asshole, or taking too many drugs, or maybe should not have dyed her hair that color, you only have her very best interests at heart, right? A sign you really *don't* care would be to just let it slide. But would you detonate this truth bomb while also reminding her that she's an idiot? Exactly.

Self-Love Is . . . Doing the Right Thing

Getting real with yourself is actually an intuition practice—since, as discussed, I equate the feeling of a "yes" in my gut with the feeling of *the truth*. Equally, I know I'm ignoring my intuition (higher self, spirit, the Universe, etc.) when it feels like I'm telling a lie. And since telling the truth and acting with integrity is pretty much always the *loving* thing (if not the nice thing) to do, then self-love requires the same commitment to being truthful with yourself.

Like, don't lie to yourself about how much you're really spending on clothes you never wear, or how bad meaningless sex makes you feel. No more pretending you're only having seven drinks a week when you know it's more like seventeen, or that you're okay with the fact you don't really talk to your mom.

This piece is about building self-esteem (which is really just another term for self-love), since being truthful with your self, following through on your promises, and taking actions in alignment with what you're really feeling is a message that you're *listening* and that you *value* what your higher Self is telling you it *needs*. Or, as Jennifer Kass puts it, "finally being the heroine of your own story, pulling out your sword, and saving your self."

Which also means not needing a relationship, the classic knight in shining armor, to slay the dragon for you.

# 9.

# YOUR PERIOD AS SACRED GODDESS CODE

I can't remember exactly what sparked it, but at some point on my numinous journey, synching my menstrual cycle with the Moon became one of my witchier lifestyle goals. One that developed out of an ongoing crusade to regulate things "down there," period.

My cycle had been patchy for as long as I could remember—or at least going back to when it disappeared completely during my teenage anorexic phase. Matters had been further complicated by the impact of various methods of birth control I'd tried over the years, the hormones having either given me "fake" periods (the pill) or wiped them out completely (an IUD).

Decades healed of my eating disorder and several years "clean" of hormonal intervention, however, and my cycle had still never settled down. And as well as the inconvenience of my bleeding being wildly different from month to month, the more invested I became in the concept of mind, body, and soul operating as one, the more it had begun to feel as if this was symptomatic of a deeper imbalance in my cosmic operating system.

I mean, think about it. The fact that a twenty-eight/twenty-nine-day cycle exactly mirrors the waxing and waning of the Moon, from New to Full and back again, is the most tangible evidence I can come up with that human life is directly and intimately connected to the planets in our wider solar system.

Throw in the not insignificant detail that a woman's cycle is a physical monthly reminder of THE MAGIC OF LIFE ITSELF, and the more deeply I began to ponder periods, the more intrigued by the mysteries of menstruation I became—fueled by the fact that my own "Moon time" seemed to be more elusive and mysterious than most.

Not that my doctor thought so. When I asked her opinion, as in, *Is this something I should be concerned about?*, she told me it was totally normal to have an irregular cycle. But just because something's "normal" doesn't make it right. After all, one in ten Americans is taking antidepressants, and it's been estimated that by 2050, up to one-third of the U.S. population could have diabetes. These states of affairs could be considered normal—in that they are the "norm"—but they aren't exactly indicative of a population thriving in optimal health.

So I started having acupuncture—commonly acknowledged to be awesome for anything to do with hormones—but several months in, there was no evidence that it was having any impact. I'd also been keeping a period "diary" to try to actually track my cycle, a frustratingly slow process since sometimes six or even eight weeks would go by with no real period, just some confusing "spotting."

Disheartened, I felt my enthusiasm for my project begin to wane. Also, since I wasn't planning on trying to get pregnant any time soon, I began to question why I was so concerned about it anyway. If anything, bleeding less frequently meant less stress and a whole lot less mess, right? Uh, wrong actually. One of the reasons I was so keen to get my flow on was that I actually enjoyed the feeling of physical and emotional release that accompanied my menstruation.

Uh-huh, you read that right: I LOVE getting my period! I actually think of it as sort of like an emotional orgasm. The tension builds and builds, and as soon as I bleed my heart sings, my head clears, and all is right in the world once more (thanks in part to the oxytocin that's released, remember?). Without it, sometimes it felt like the PMS phase would last for weeks.

Then my friend Alexandra Derby, an artist and menstrual wellness expert, mentioned she was going to be leading a Red Tent activation at the natural birthing center in the basement of her Williamsburg brownstone, and a (red) lightbulb went on in my soul.

A daylong ritual designed by a woman named DeAnna L'am, widely regarded as a leading voice in "menstrual empowerment," the basis of a Red Tent ceremony is for participants to share and reclaim the stories of their first period. "It's all about letting go of the judgments and prejudices you took into your precious early teenage self that have kept you from fully accessing your power and creative potential as a goddess Creatrix today!" explained Aly.

The second part of the ritual would involve "enacting the ceremony we never receive in modern society—that of a girl being welcomed into womanhood," she went on, with that wild, excited look she gets whenever we get talking about healing for the greater good. "Ruby, it

DeAnna L'am began her journey as a healer in 1992, after she too embarked on a personal journey to better understand her PMS and attempt to "reverse the curse." Her studies led her to discover the myth of the Red Tent, a place in biblical times where women would retreat while menstruating or giving birth. DeAnna has made it her life's work to reinstate the Red Tent as a ritual to acknowledge the rite of passage of a girl's first period, and she and her facilitators now host Red Tent ceremonies all over the world. There's a full calendar of events as well as information about how to organize a Red Tent activation near you on her website: Womenoftheredtent.com.

is deeply moving to take your place as a woman on the planet with the capacity to birth LIFE—be that children, ideas, businesses, or even a new Earth. Yes, it is that big!"

Whoa. What if *this* was the missing piece of my period puzzle? There was no physical reason for my irregular cycle, after all, and yet I *was* harboring a whole lot of judgment about it. Not to mention frustration, doubt, and disappointment with my body. And what about all this stuff Aly had said about me being a "goddess Creatrix," and women coming together to birth "a new Earth"? I signed up there and then, before left-brain logic had a chance to talk me out of it.

## INTO THE RED TENT

The Red Tent activation itself took place on a Virgo New Moon, when my period was right about due. I woke with hard-core butterflies in my stomach. What the hell had I gotten myself into? We'd been instructed to wear something red, and I was dismayed to discover that I didn't own a single scarlet item of clothing, not even a pair of red knickers—and so I made do with a slash of my trusty, confidence-boosting red lipstick (adding a mental note to invest in some red lingerie, stat. I mean, seriously).

When I arrived, Aly was dressed in a vintage red prom dress and amazingly had transformed the space into an *actual* red tent, using lengths of gauzy red material. I counted six other women in attendance, and one by one we were smudged down with palo santo as we entered the space, having been invited to repeat after Aly: "I enter this circle in perfect love and perfect trust." Since we would be sharing some of our most intimate truths, she explained, setting this intention was essential.

And since I also feel like a proper introduction will further help set the scene here, Aly is terribly British and well-spoken and has a degree in archaeology from Cambridge University (the British equivalent to Harvard). But she also happens to be one of the most magical people I've ever met—think Hermione from *Harry Potter* meets full-fledged fairy queen. In other words, exactly the kind of woman you want as your guide on a journey to connect with your Divinely Feminine self.

Once seated inside, we were invited to place items on an altar strewn with red roses, and then the ritual began. With Aly, we called in the energies of the different elements, before acknowledging the women in our ancestral lineage. And over the following four hours, there would be layers and layers of similarly heady ritual—which Aly describes as the language of the soul, since "the only way the soul can speak to us is through symbols, metaphor, and ceremony."

But most relevant to this story is what came up for me when we got to the part where we spoke about the first time we got our period. Mainly because I hadn't been aware of this being awkward or problematic for me—hell, I'd even been looking forward to it! But turns out this in itself was deeply interwoven with feelings of inadequacy and shame. Looking back, I could see how the fact that I was so desperate to get my period was because I wanted so badly to be seen as more grown-up, sophisticated, and cool (the same motivations, at heart, for me pursuing a career in fashion). After all, the most popular girls were essentially the most "developed," and I already hated my body for remaining stubbornly childlike. I'd bought a sports bra waaaay before there was anything to fill it, and even practiced inserting tampons (ouch!) long before my first period.

And sharing the *truth* of my story with the group, which I realized I hadn't even shared with *myself* until that moment, I could suddenly see oh so clearly how this mirrored the battle I was *still* having with my body every month, willing my period to come on as physical proof that I was a "normal" functioning sexual woman. Also, how the conversation I began having with my body at age fourteen was essentially setting up all the insecurities that snowballed into me starving myself for six years—not to mention the feelings of not being "enough" that I know so SO many women struggle with in their lives.

Yes, I cried buckets speaking these truths, also deeply saddened by the fact that I'd been too emotionally distant from my mother to share any of this with her at the time. We finished that part of the ceremony by washing our hands with lavender water, to cleanse the negative feelings associated with our first blood, and by the end of the day, I felt

> "The only way the soul can speak to us is through symbols, metaphor, and ceremony."
>
> —ALEXANDRA DERBY

vulnerable but curiously relieved. But would my participation make any difference to my cycle?

I got my answer two weeks later. As I mentioned, my period was "due" (going by a twenty-eight-day cycle) the day after the Red Tent—but in this case it held out for another fourteen days, until the next Full Moon. An *Aries Blood Moon Eclipse,* no less, which I also happened to be able to watch up close, since I was on a delayed flight back to NYC from Montreal that night. A cosmic coincidence? Or evidence that my soul had been listening, and my body was ready to embrace my need to bleed.

## MAIDEN, MOTHER, CRONE . . . AND THE SCARLET WOMAN

The Red Tent ceremony had ended with us going around the circle and welcoming each participant as "a new woman," reenacting the ancient feminine rite of passage, from girl to woman, that Aly described as having been scratched from modern society. Without it, she believes the soul becomes confused about what life stage a woman is at, leading to all kinds of karmic confusion around everything from our relationships to our life purpose. Allow me to explain.

In pagan traditions, "womanhood" is defined by the triple Goddess archetype of "Maiden, Mother, and Crone"—referring to a woman's role in society before, during, and following her menstruating years.

As a girl, or Maiden, she is completely in her own world, free to use her creative and spiritual energy purely for her own personal development, to discover and learn about herself and the world. During her menstruating years, she moves into the Mother phase, using these discoveries to nurture the life she now has the capacity to birth, be that actual children, creative projects, or business ventures, as Aly reminded us.

And what happens when we don't properly acknowledge this transition? The Maiden gets pissed and begins acting out to get attention—fixating on her appearance by obsessively playing dress-up (hello, shopping addiction), choosing partying as her pastime of choice, and picking partners who are more interested in games of kiss-chase than a mature and mutually respectful relationship. Basically, your classic late teen-to-thirtysomething hot mess, and not at all unfamiliar to me.

Further down the line, the Crone, or Wise Woman phase, is when she takes her place as a tribal elder, menopause having relieved her of the responsibilities of motherhood, and she has amassed enough wisdom and experience by now to lead and mentor on a broader scale.

The Crone is the matriarch figure—think Arianna Huffington or Oprah Winfrey. The fact that neither of these powerful and inspiring women would likely be thrilled to be described as a "crone," however, not to mention that the word itself is also negatively associated with witchcraft, speaks volumes to me about how our female cycles have been disenfranchised under the dominant *patriarchy*.

In fact, the more I learn about the history of women and menstruation, the more I am coming to see how this is a deeply feminist issue, steeped in centuries of gender equality bloodshed—and more on the wider ramifications of that later. But in relation to the triple Goddess archetype, Aly has pinpointed a missing "fourth player" in this saga, one who relates directly to your sex life, and with whom the dominant patriarchal society is far from comfortable.

"It's almost like she's been deliberately written out, but what about the Scarlet Woman?" Aly is talking about the phase *between* Maiden and Mother, "when a woman gets to bleed, and enjoy and use all the gifts that come with this, before she has to sacrifice part of herself to being a mother."

To get just a little bit biblical on your ass, Aly identifies the Scarlet Woman as Mary Magdalene, a follower of Jesus who traveled with him and hung out with the other disciples, and who was also the first person to see him alive following the Resurrection. But during the Middle Ages, Western Christianity began to paint her as a prostitute or an "unpure" woman—the menstruating yet childless and freely sexual woman Aly believes is missing from the collective mythology of womankind.

Cue mass paranoia about women fully owning their sexuality, a.k.a. slut shaming, the perversion of female desire in pornography, and the sanitized, patriarchy-friendly "celebration" of female sexuality known as the Victoria's Secret fashion show.

## THE BLOOD MYSTERIES

Aly also talked about "the Blood Mysteries," ancient myths around women and menstruation that speak directly to the "gift" of our monthly cycle. Also, how this gift came to be rebranded as "the curse."

So let's go back, way back, to when humans are living in tribes. When the women bear children and the men, wombless and generally faster and more muscular, go hunt for food. And since women spend the majority of their time running the village (i.e., *in government*), they develop a "sixth sense" about what's best for the community—an inner knowing it appears is heightened when they bleed.

Since they also all live in such close proximity to one another, the women get their periods at the same time (a phenomenon we're all familiar with). And without the intervention of alarm clocks, electric lighting, international travel, and other inventions that have allowed humans to operate "as normal" outside the cycles of our natural habitat, this happens at the same time every month, in the dark of the New Moon.

Enter the *original* Red Tent. Relieved of their regular tribal duties, women went to this sacred space to bleed and *dream* together, all the better to receive cosmic downloads from the Universe in answer to the most pressing questions being faced by the tribe at the time. Like, y'know, what herbs are good for an outbreak of fever, and what days are best for hunting this month. Ha—I love the way we assume our ancient ancestors were only concerned with bare survival. They were probably asking stuff about who was having sex with whom, and what to wear for the Solstice celebrations, too.

Anyway, along with the fact that they got to do all the birthing of life, women's mystical connection, through menstruation, to the oneness,

God, the Universe, and so on, obviously gave the females of the tribe pretty much all the power. Coupled with the fact that they would bleed freely and copiously for days at a time, *and not die,* women must have seemed nothing short of superhuman to the menfolk.

So at some point in history, right around the time agriculture kicked in and organized religion began trying to put some logic around the messy and mystical story of human evolution, the more insecure among the males decided to use the brute force they were no longer using to hunt to redress the balance. And the rest, so they say, is the history of the patriarchy.

Which is certainly *one* theory as to why menstruating women came to be seen as impure, and periods in general a messy inconvenience to be medicated out of existence or shamefully hidden away. Also, as society began to revolve around more and more masculine ideologies— competitive, goal driven, and linear, versus collaborative, cyclical, and intuitively led—the wisdom we receive at our Moon time basically got labeled "crazy-ass PMS."

I don't know about you, but I generally go around apologizing for the fact that I get super super sensitive right before my period (like, I really don't want to socialize and could cry over a burst tea bag). The fact that it's so hard to contain my emotions at this time feels like a weakness of character, as if I'm being held hostage by my own body.

But what if that was the whole point? What if we're *supposed* to retreat from society when we bleed, and use this time to feel deeply into the wisdom of our subconscious, or intuition? In astrology, our menstrual running buddy the Moon represents our most fundamental yet often deeply buried needs and desires, after all.

In which case, what if the "anger and frustration" part of PMS (any- body?) is actually a genuine response to all the subtle ways our needs are not being met, not to mention the injustice that says we (woman- kind) are being too demanding or needy or are just plain loopy if we kick up a fuss about it. And as for the chocolate cravings? Seen in this context, the overwhelming premenstrual urge to gorge on raw cacao fudge brownies looks to me like a case of self-medication at its finest.

## KNOW YOUR CYCLE, KNOW YOURSELF

Embodying the cyclical nature of ALL LIFE, Now Age thinking
women's menstrual cycles are designed by nature to move us th
the phases of "Maiden, Scarlet Woman, Mother, Crone," each
every month, our hormonal fluctuations inviting in the energies of our
most creative, sexual, nurturing, and knowing selves. And that when
we actually bleed, this is symbolic of us being "reborn."

For example, in Chinese medicine it's believed that the spirit, or *shen,*
lives in the heart and travels in the blood—and that when women bleed,
our spirit is being "cleansed" of psychic gunk that builds up throughout
the month. As an aside to this, I've even heard that the Native American
sweat lodge—an intense outdoor sauna situation known to induce a
trancelike state—was actually designed to help men purge in the same
way and keep pace spiritually with women!

One of my favorite writers on the subject of women and cycles is
another British witch, named Lisa Lister, who believes that some of
our greatest spiritual work as women lies in realigning ourselves with
the rhythm and rhyme of our Moon time. "Getting to know your
cycle is like a master key to your monthly superpowers," she told me
recently. Even if I had to wait three days for her e-mail, since when I
first reached out she was on Day 1 of her cycle and had just begun to
bleed. "Retreating from the outside world on Day 1 is sacred and a
total nonnegotiable for me. I have said no to TV appearances because
I was on Day 1," she explained.

According to Lisa's research (which became her life's work after she
was diagnosed with endometriosis at age twenty-five and told she needed
a hysterectomy), the four distinct phases of our cycles can be mapped,
and therefore utilized, as outlined on the next page.

The issue is that what Lisa terms the "dude-centric" systems we live
by don't allow for these fluctuations. Week in, week out, we're expected to
show up in the world and perform in the same way. Considering society
celebrates confident, productive, sexy women, this makes phases 1 and 2
easier to navigate. But when the expectations of society go against where

# THE MOON CYCLE

This is a guideline based on a twenty-eight-day cycle and may be slightly different for you, if your cycle is longer or shorter.

Preovulation (days 7–13)
High energy, risk taking and expansive vision, getting shit done

Ovulation (days 14–21)
"The queen of freaking everything," sexy, social, wanting to be seen

Premenstruation (days 22–28)
No time for BS, a shift from "doing" to "being," letting it all hang out

Menstruation (days 1–6)
Deep intuition, retreat and forgiveness, a reconnection to our inner truth

we're at in our cycle (see phases 3 and 4), frustration—along with major chocolate cravings—sets in.

"But if we actually listened to our bodies during the second two phases, we'd unlock some extremely powerful ways to access our inner wild woman—intuition, rage, truth, alchemy—and that's where the real MAGIC happens," Lisa goes on. Magic, just maybe, like listening to your highest Self and allowing it to guide you toward your most magnificent and significant life purpose.

All of which I got pretty darned excited about when I was first introduced to Lisa's work—the idea being that once you come to know your cycle intimately, you can begin to plan your life around it—all the better to capitalize on the energy and gifts of each different phase. This is easier if you're in a position to make your own schedule, granted. But if you do have the kind of job where you have to show up to a cubicle at the same time every day, you can at least go easy on yourself if you "underperform" because a big pitch happens to fall on Day 1 of your cycle.

But wait a minute: What if you have an irregular cycle like me? Which Lisa also thinks is very common BTW, if not exactly "normal." Her theory? "It's another symptom of working against our cyclic nature and trying to live in a linear, dude-centric way." Considering my whole career has meant being creative on demand to hit weekly if not daily deadlines, phase 3 or no phase 3, it's not exactly a huge leap to see how this alone could have affected my flow. Many, many of *our* flows.

Lisa's advice to me as I continue to work on finding mine? Keep diligently mapping my cycle, like literally taking daily notes on everything from my mood and energy levels to how I'm feeling about my appearance, until I begin to understand where my unique phases begin and end. This is something I encourage you to try too, whether it means making daily notes in your diary or on your phone, or downloading an app (I've started using one called Luna) to keep track of where you're at. "The more you chart, the more your cycle will start to find her groove, since generally she'll be 'irregular' because you're not paying attention and are working against her, opposed to with her natural rhythm," she told me, adding that actually the length of each phase will be different for everyone.

In my case: "You may notice that your preovulation is superlong because your body needs it to be that way so that you CAN get more done. This is how freakin' incredible it is!" And never mind my own cycle—when it comes to what I've been learning about periods in general, freakin' incredible sounds about right.

## PERIOD PRIDE AND THE MENSTRUAL REVOLUTION

At the time of writing this, there's a T-shirt doing the rounds among the Now Age crowd, bearing the slogan THE FUTURE IS FEMALE. I think the reason it's struck such a chord is not because we're all "angry feminists" demanding "our turn" at running things, but rather that it speaks to a collective and mystical understanding around the next wave of feminism. Namely, that this goes *beyond* equality between biological men and women in the material world (granted, a campaign that's far from won), and that actually it's time to step into a whole new *feminine* paradigm.

The new feminine model includes collaboration over competition, nurturing versus oppression, building relationships not empires. In matters of business, politics, the environment . . . in the Now Age (the *full-fledged* Age of Aquarius, the astrological era we began shifting into in the 1960s and which is all about the toppling of hierarchical structures), it is increasingly evident that what the world needs is a whole lot more of the knowing feminine energy of our tribal ancestry injected into what now feel like dangerously outplayed modern human systems.

I'm hearing a lot of talk about a return to the Divine Feminine (which we'll dive into in chapter 11), which essentially is about connecting to the idea of God(dess), the Universe, the cosmic oneness, and so on, as a feminine versus a masculine force. And I am most definitely not the only woman (or man!) waking up to our periods as secret Goddess code, and embracing menstruation as a magical symbol of each and every woman's embodiment of Her.

I recently got to meet Miki Agrawal, the amazing entrepreneur behind Thinx—stylish panties with built-in period protection, designed to "eliminate shame" around periods (along with the need for panty liners and the majority of other disposable period products we use, which are one of the major contributors, along with disposable diapers, to landfill sites).

It speaks volumes to me that when I first heard about the brand, back in 2013, not one of the editors I pitched the Thinx story to would touch it—"too icky," being the general response. Fast-forward to fall 2015, and Miki's first chic and sexy ad campaign has gone viral, not least because the MTA (the governing body for New York's public transport system) tried to ban the ads from the NYC subway for using the word *period*. #WTF

For part of the Thinx campaign, Miki reached out to her customers and asked them to complete the sentence: "Thinx is _____." Here are a few of my favorite responses:

"Thinx is a connection to the Goddess within."

"Thinx is the key to my fluid existence."

"Thinx is strength, dignity, and freedom for all women."

The last one in particular speaks to what Miki calls "period pride." As she puts it, period pride is "the importance of experiencing our periods as a time of cleansing every month, as our connection to the moon, and to each other as women." And for me the story of Thinx—from "too icky" for women's magazines (!) to being named one of *TIME* magazine's best inventions of 2015—proves that the time for period pride is now.

# 10.

# THE UNIVERSAL MOTHER

Confession. I once used my media connections to jump the line to get a hug from Amma. Okay twice, actually. Both times, I did not have to endure the average eight-hour wait for an audience with the woman they call the Hugging Saint. What can I say? PR guru Kelly Cutrone, a longtime mentor and supporter of The Numinous, also reps Amma the guru—a little pro bono work for the woman she says saved her life (in a spiritual sense). And even in matters of holy pilgrimage, it would appear that guest list privileges apply.

For the uninitiated, Amma is an Indian spiritual leader who mainly spends her time traveling the world dishing out, yes, hugs. All-enveloping, all-loving hugs that people literally line up for days to receive. To her devotees, this is an act of *darshan*—the opportunity to visit with a holy person, or deity. The ultimate, and very personal, *puja,* or expression of ceremonial worship.

Born Mātā Amrtānandamayī Devī in Kerala, India, in the early 1950s, the story goes that even as a very young child Mātā was compelled to do everything she could to ease the suffering of others. She would take food and clothing from her own home to people in her village who were living in poverty, often spontaneously embracing them to ease their sorrows. Before long, little Mātā had earned herself the nickname Amma, Hindi for "Mother."

Of course word got out, and soon spiritual seekers were traveling from all over India to get a hug, often in the hope of becoming Amma's devotees. Meanwhile, her parents weren't *at all* sure about the whole guru jam and repeatedly tried to marry their daughter off. But Amma was having none of it. The way she saw it, "the duty of a doctor is to treat patients. In the same way, my duty is to console those who are suffering." Or, rather, her *dharma*.

The rest is a similarly mixed bag of fantastical folklore and factual history. Amma broadened her reach by establishing an international humanitarian charity; she performed miracles, such as diverting storms and feeding multitudes from a single tiny pot of rice; and in 1987 she began traveling the world dishing out hugs, millions and millions to date, as a means of spreading her message that what the world needs is LOVE. And that we'd better all be loving one another, since "all of our children are all of our children."

Of course, there's one major element missing from the story of a woman named Amma: children of her own. Not that "saints" are traditionally expected to produce mini-me saints (most of them are men after all), and anyway, when is she supposed to have found the time? Amma hugs and she hugs, often around the clock, forsaking food, sleep, and bathroom breaks (which will no doubt sound familiar to any actual mothers out there).

But children or no children, to me Amma represents a *Universal* mother energy. Her life is one of utter selflessness (see hugging and hugging around the clock, forsaking food, sleep, and bathroom breaks), and she sees it as her Goddess-given duty to deliver comfort to those in need. Not to mention the fact she's also the mother of all multitaskers.

I know this because I also got to interview Amma once, and it took place during darshan (the hugging). Since darshan can often go on for twenty-three, twenty-four, or even twenty-eight hours straight, "all my meetings happen during darshan," she said, laughing. Let me paint a picture of what this looks like. We're at the Javits Center in NYC (an expo hall the size of an aircraft hangar), where Amma is set up on a stage to do the hugging. At least half the floor space is filled with rows of chairs, where people sit and patiently wait their turn, while the rest of the center has been transformed into a sort of mini bazaar, with people selling clothes and devotional trinkets, and some of the best curry you've ever eaten for about $2 a dish.

As your turn for a hug draws nearer, you are moved to a chair closer to the stage, then a chair on the stage, and then a chair closer to Amma on the stage. There's music playing and people singing, incense and garlands everywhere, and by now it's all getting pretty intense. When the hug finally happens, it smells of roses and everything else disappears, with Amma herself whispering "my daughter, my daughter, my daughter," in your ear. While simultaneously taking phone calls, making decisions to do with the running of her foundation, instructing an army of helpers, and doing interviews, via translator, with the likes of me.

So here are my questions to you. Does not being a mother to any biological children make Amma any less of a woman? Does it make her, since she hasn't experienced the mortal intensity of growing and giving birth to a new life, any less of a spiritual person? And does it suggest that she's emotionally stunted or has in any way shied away from the full burden of adult responsibility?

As somebody who has chosen to remain "childless by choice" myself, I really would like to know, since I've asked these questions, and more, of myself on a fairly regular basis since around age twenty-five. Then there was the therapist who only wanted to talk about the fact that I didn't want kids; the (male) shaman who told me I'd only be taken seriously as a voice in the spiritual community once I became a mother; and, of course, the multiple magazine editors who have asked me to write about my "unconventional" decision. Editors, and by extension their readers I guess, who simply could not get their heads around the fact that an apparently healthy and happily married woman could quite so resolutely declare that being a mom was just not for her. Of course I have my reasons, which fall into two categories:

A. There are too many people in the world already; I'm petrified of childbirth; I'm too much of a career woman; I feel
   like I would love my baby so much I would end up sacri-
   ficing my career; I am a very private person and need lots
   of alone time to stay sane; my marriage would suffer; the
   planet is dying, and the situation does not look particularly
   forgiving for future generations.

B. I've just always known I never wanted to be a mom.

Obviously reason B is the only one worth focusing on, since all
the reasons in category A are basically fear-based future-tripping and
therefore not real. So let's focus on B.

I have a very distinct memory of me at age five asking my mum
why people were so obsessed with babies. And since we were on the
subject, how come baby animals were so cute, when most *human* babies
I had encountered were wrinkly little worms who screamed all the time?
Granted, this maybe had something to do with my baby brother arriv-
ing on the scene and taking all the attention off me. But there's also a
picture of me aged about nine holding our neighbor's baby. The look
on my face (fear, confusion, please-somebody-take-this-away-NOW)
pretty much tells the whole story.

Wow, even writing that makes me feel like there must be something
wrong with me. Like, did I miss something about what it means to be a
woman? Or "womb-man," as Dori Varga, founder of Now Age female
empowerment movement Tribe de Mama, likes to call it? So ingrained
is the societal message that women and babies are like chips 'n' dips,
you can't have one without the other. And sticking to my guns—or
rather my *gut*—on this one has been a practice of tuning in, again and
again, to my intuition.

Because periodically, I'll decide that actually *of course* I want kids.
It's an integral, if not THE integral, part of being human, the ultimate
life and death adventure. And because when you strip it all away, family
is the only thing that really matters. Right? But when it comes to the

crunch, a.k.a. actual unprotected, baby-making sex, the message from my gut is always *Hold up, wait a minute, WTF*. And in the words of business impresario Marie Forleo, "If it's not a HELL yes, it's a hell no."

None of which, by the way, is meant to come across as bitter or defensive. And neither am I comparing myself to Amma, who—I think we've already established—has led quite an exceptional life when it comes to being of service in the world.

But I've used her as an example here, because for me Amma and what she stands for are an invitation to investigate *all* the ways women (and men, why not!) can embody a *Universal* mother energy in their lives, whether they choose to become "parents" or not. A Universal mother energy, it feels to me, that is the underpinning of all Now Age thinking, feeling, and being.

Even if actual babies are a "hell no" for me, I'm still very much aware that I am currently in the prime of my mothering years. But besides the fact that I have a womb and have not yet entered menopause, what does that even mean? And without any kids in the frame, what is "mother energy" anyway? The way I've come to see it, there are three key pillars to Universal mother energy.

## PRINCIPLE NO. 1: CREATION AND BIRTHING

In Hinduism, the energy of Mother Earth flows through all beings as the primordial creative energy of the Universe and is referred to as *Shakti,* which translates as "power" or "empowerment." Also "the great divine mother," as Shakti is understood as the embodiment of *love* and as the seed of all *creation*. And creativity is the first piece of the mother puzzle for me—because a mother, by her very definition, *gives birth* to something, right?

When I met the founders of theSkimm, the crazy popular current affairs newsletter, they told me how during their first year in business they basically didn't sleep. They lived together and would do shifts, getting up at all hours to check the newswires before pressing send on the most up-to-date version of their newsletter at 6 A.M.

## THE THREE PILLARS OF
## UNIVERSAL MOTHER ENERGY

Creation and Birthing: meaning the willingness to acknowledge whatever manifestation of spirit wants to come into being *through you* (actual children, businesses, charitable initiatives, works of art, etc.), and then dedicating the necessary time and energy to bringing it to fruition.

Nurturing and Protection: which speaks to both the tender care and attention, as well as the fiercely uncompromising "I know what's best for you" stance our "babies" need in order to thrive.

Unconditional Love: simply choosing to see your creations, your community, and your own life through the eyes of love. Meaning without judgment or expectation, and with due respect and appreciation for all the frustrating, annoying quirks that make us uniquely and beautifully human.

"So kind of like having a newborn?" I suggested. At which they'd smirked and replied they'd had to stop using that analogy since several mothers of actual newborns had expressed their displeasure at the comparison. But their tired eyes (they were three years in) told a different story: basically like a newborn, yes. Just without the crying, the cuddles, or the dirty diapers.

A woman's business being her baby is a bit of a cliché, but for good reason—especially when it's a business or creative project that's "born" of her "passionate desire" to bring "something of herself" into the world. You'll lose sleep over a business like that, sacrifice friendships for it, and give it money you haven't got when it's hungry. You'll also fight for what you believe is best for it, turning away suitors you don't like the look of no matter how fat their checkbook is.

I'm speaking from experience, obviously, since The Numinous is *my* business baby. If I thought I loved my magazine career, then conceiving, birthing, and nurturing a creative venture of my own has opened up my being to a whole other level of fulfillment. Not to mention anguish, financial worries, and sleepless nights. Since bringing my idea for The Numinous into the world, I have experienced some of my highest highs, and my most heart-wrenching lows. And like any loving parent will tell you, the highs are worth the lows and then some.

In *Big Magic,* her book on creativity, Liz Gilbert describes inspiration thus: "Ideas are a disembodied, energetic life-form. . . . Ideas have no material body, but they do have consciousness, and they most certainly have will. Ideas are driven by a single impulse: to be made manifest. And the only way an idea can be made manifest in our world is through collaboration with a human partner." So basically, when a brilliant idea just shows up and won't leave you alone—it's the Universe trying to have sex with/impregnate you.

She goes on to describe how these idea spirits are constantly swirling around us in the ether, searching for available and willing human partners. Which also sounds to me a lot like popular beliefs about human spirits; astrologers believing we choose our parents, for example. The Numinous came to me as a name first, which planted itself in my consciousness and simply refused to be ignored. *But I'm too busy with my career,* I told it. And: *I'm afraid I won't be any good at it* and *I don't want to do this on my own.* But evidently The Numinous wanted to collaborate with me and only me, *wanted me to be its mother,* since this back-and-forth went on for about two years before I finally succumbed. Although it knows and I know that it was a "hell yes" from the get-go.

And this book, which was conceived two more years down the line, feels like baby number two. Writing/birthing it has been a period of intense soul-searching (I joked to a friend the other day that it would definitely go down as "one of those agonizing seventy-two-hour childbirth stories"). It has also meant abstaining from alcohol for the health of my child, pretty much kissing my social life good-bye, and recruiting professional childcare for baby number one in the form of some brilliant interns (cue major separation anxiety!).

Which reminds me of one of my favorite Amma quotes: "Where there is love, there is no effort." Because has any of this felt like *work*? Hell no! It feels like life.

It's interesting, actually, how many of my favorite female writers don't have children: Lionel Shriver, Candace Bushnell, and, yes, Liz Gilbert. I know this, by the way, because my ego likes nothing better than to go on a Wikipedia spree comparing my life and "achievements" to famous women of a similar age. (I know, I know, SO low vibe and generally to be avoided, but also completely addictive.)

Of the above, Liz has commented the most extensively about her kid-free status, describing it as reflecting "my own choice, my own desires, my own destiny." In another one of her books, *Committed,* she also describes how her grandmother (a mother to seven) once told her how she'd prayed Liz wouldn't have any children of her own and would instead dedicate her life to writing books and traveling.

And if the future really is going to be female, or *more feminine* in attitude at least (just wait for the next chapter for plenty more on this!), then the way I see it we're going to need more women to dedicate their lives to shaping thoughts, opinions, and events outside the family unit. To dedicate their lives to our wider *human* family.

But I do also appreciate that book babies and business babies are not flesh and blood. Nobody will die or become orphaned if I just decide to stop writing tomorrow (you should have seen *my* mum's face when I tried to make the comparison), and I could totally sell The Numinous to another family (like some big media conglomerate) and nobody would bat an eyelid. Actual motherhood IS life and death, and my decision not to participate is still something I'll always question (along with my therapists). In the meantime though, I continue to focus on ways to express my own nurturing mother energy in other ways.

## PRINCIPLE NO. 2: NURTURING AND PROTECTION

One woman who absolutely embodies this idea for me is Lisa Levine, a former jewelry designer turned Reiki master and acupuncturist, who now runs my very favorite place to get healed, Brooklyn's Maha Rose Center for the Healing Arts. She's also an actual devotee of Amma, meaning that in 2010 she officially renounced all other gurus and spiritual teachers and was given an Amma mantra to use in her meditation practice. Subsequently, she once felt moved to ask Amma to "let me do your work" during darshan.

The result is Maha Rose, which Lisa set up in her home a couple of years later, and which is one of the most nurturing spaces I've come across on my numinous travels. You just feel *held* (yes, hugged!) by the energy there. There's no other way to describe it, and discovering the center and meeting Lisa, just a couple of years after leaving my own mother behind in the UK, was incredibly comforting to me.

There's also an altar to Amma at Maha Rose, and when I last met Lisa for lunch (with her actual, human, newborn bouncing on her hip), she described her guru as "the overarching protectress, the matriarch, and the mother of it all." She also told me there are two main aspects to how she herself sees Universal mother energy.

First "there's the loving, nurturing mother that holds you and loves you and gives her breasts to you, gives her everything to you; everything, everything, everything. Utter selflessness."

On the flip side, meanwhile, "is the fierce mother, the mother who's like, 'you are NOT going out dressed like that.' She's being protective, but can be quite severe."

And Amma embodies both, says Lisa. One the one hand, "there's not one moment of her day that she's not involved in doing something to help us." But also, "when I first began to follow Amma, all the messages from my higher Self that came through as a result of the light her work shone on the way I'd been living my life were about letting go of stuff that wasn't really doing me any good. It was a very scary and painful process."

If there's a celebrity who embodies mother energy for me, it's Angelina Jolie Pitt. Everything about her suggests this same fierce-yet-loving vibe: from the way the entire Jolie-Pitt tribe traveled together to be on location whenever she and Brad made a movie (Brangelina, RIP), to her preventative operations to remove both breasts along with her ovaries and fallopian tubes, resulting in her entering menopause at age forty. Shown to have a high risk of both breast and ovarian cancer, *as a mother* it was an easy decision, she has said. She needs to stick around, because she needs to be here for them.

And lucky for you, the Universe conveniently arranged for me to interview Angie for a glossy Sunday supplement just as I was beginning to work on this chapter! So I got to ask her about mother energy too.

Considering she has adopted three kids and also has three biological children with Brad Pitt, my head spun when she told me she actually never thought she'd be a mom. As in she never babysat or played with dolls growing up and never thought of herself as a "maternal" person.

She adopted her oldest son, Pax, after she began to experience overwhelming compassion for all the kids in the world who don't have a mother of their own. And then she met Brad, and I guess you can understand her wanting to make the most of those genes.

Since her character in the movie I was interviewing her for (a movie she also wrote) suffers a nervous breakdown following a miscarriage that has left her barren, I also had to ask: Having unearthed her own maternal instincts after all, did she believe that any woman who didn't become a mother, for whatever reason, was destined for a bitter and lonely old age? (Read: Please, Angie, tell me, am *I* destined for a bitter and lonely old age?!)

Oh NO, she assured me. By no means. (Phew). "But I do think it's important for a woman to be able to *nurture* something. To nurture— that's a woman's nature."

Which to me speaks to both aspects of Lisa's Universal mother: the idea of "mothering" as lovingly tending to something that is very dear to us, because it feels like our duty to nourish and protect it so that it can thrive. Like, you know, our *planet* maybe?

Which brings me to Mother Earth, a.k.a. Gaia, or Pachamama, as I have heard her referred to in Now Age circles. When I first launched The Numinous, the fit between all things mystical and the environmental movement wasn't immediately evident to me. If anything, I wanted to distance my platform from the crusty connotations of the Greenpeace crew. But, oh MAN, has my perspective shifted on this one. Getting connected to the cosmos is *all about* accepting nature as the ultimate creator, the strict yet life-sustaining mother of our *every*thing. And I think it's pretty evident to most of us that Mama Earth could kind of use some loving back.

There comes a time in every human's personal evolution when we become aware that our own mother, despite the fact that she gave us life, is not in fact immortal, and that actually it's our turn to mother *her*. (You may not be there yet, but trust me it will happen.)

And the way I see it, in the face of what even very sensible scientists have got to say these days about impending environmental Armageddon, it could be argued that perhaps we've also reached this point as a human race. All the more reason for us all—women *and* men, maybe especially the men who mainly get to make the big decisions about this kind of stuff—to channel some mother energy when it comes to taking care of our planet.

## PRINCIPLE NO. 3: UNCONDITIONAL LOVE

Besides my rapidly developing awareness about environmental issues, one of the most surprising things to happen after I finally said yes and accepted my role as mother to The Numinous was the e-mails I began to get about the site. Usually from young women, most said something like: "Thank you for creating this; I feel like I've finally found my tribe." And that's a word I use a lot—*tribe*—to describe what feels like The Numinous family I've created.

Now would I die for my Numi tribe? Probably not. But do I feel unconditional love for them? Yes, because in my book (this book) *unconditional love*—the mother's love that doesn't require anything in return, and only wants what is best for her child's ultimate happiness and fulfillment—is simply a choice. This for me is the final piece of the Universal mother energy puzzle, and I challenge you to watch your world transform any time you take a step back and choose to see your

# 10 COMMANDMENTS FOR EMBODYING THE UNIVERSAL MOTHER

**1.** Thou shall open yourself to the Shakti flow, allowing life to happen through you.

**2.** Thou shall investigate what planets are in Cancer in your birth chart (for clues to your personal Universal mothering style).

**3.** Thou shall practice the art of selflessness.

**4.** But thou shall channel the growling mama bear when it comes to protecting yourself, your "family," and your entrepreneurial/ creative interests.

**5.** Thou shall be willing to give all you can when you encounter a soul in need.

**6.** But thou shall also create healthy boundaries, so as to conserve your own energy.

**7.** Thou shall remember that even your boss from hell was a helpless baby once, and that his or her temper tantrums are actually a cry for help/love.

**8.** Thou shall remember the nurturing and protection your *own* mother showed you, that felt so annoying when you were fourteen, and remember to thank her for it.

**9.** Thou shall show due respect to the Universal great-great-great-great-*grand*mother Earth.

**10.** Thou shall give freely and deeply of your hugs.

situation (any situation) through the eyes of a loving yet protective mother.

Like, how would you respond differently to the megabitch boss you're convinced is out to get you if you choose to see her through the lens of unconditional, Universal, mother love? How would your food choices differ, viewing yourself and your body this way, not to mention each and every one of the beings involved in *producing* what you're about to eat? Would you still be holding out for that guy or girl who only texts you back when they're drunk and horny?

After I got my second hug from Amma, I wrote about how "the effect of the hug can last all day, all night. The whole of the next week. You've been embraced by a real life saint, by *the Universal mother* herself. You want to pass the feeling on, and you'll be a nicer person until it wears off."

And so I invite you to make it your mission, in everything you do, to make people feel that way, too. Whether they're your kids, your nieces and nephews, your coworkers, your employees, your customers, your parents, your friends, or even complete strangers. Whether it's yourself. If Amma is here to remind us that "all of our children are all of our children," then in the Now Age, let's all be each other's mother, too.

# 11.

# FINDING MY DIVINE FEMININE

"Yay, the real Ruby's back!" It's the last day of our vacation in Hawaii, and the Pisces is referring to the fact that I've blown my hair out into a sleek and shiny curtain of blond for the journey home—having pretty much let it do its own thing for the past two weeks. "Its own thing" being an utterly unruly mess of curls and frizz. Three decades of experimentation with different products and methods of air-drying have failed miserably at coaxing my natural mop into anything I deem passable for public consumption. My solution? Flatten the fuck out of it with an arsenal of high-powered heated instruments. But put me anywhere remotely "tropical," and this becomes a losing battle. The elements and my curls conspire, and it's easier to just . . . go with the flow.

He didn't mean any offense—I prefer my hair without the kinks also. It actually makes me physically uncomfortable to wear it "natural." And I can tell by his use of the word *yay* that he also thinks it's cute, this ongoing standoff with my hair. But something about his comment strikes a nerve this time. "No," I correct him. "The *curly* hair is the *real* me. This is how I have to wear it to feel beautiful in the eyes of society . . ." Which is maybe getting a little deep as we navigate our way past the hotel valet, Starbucks in hand, and into our rental car to head for the airport. But then this trip has been the backdrop to some pretty deep realizations about the nature of *the Divine Feminine*.

It's a subject that's been coming up more and more lately among my Numinous crew—the reframing of the Universal creative energy as a feminine as opposed to a masculine force. A connection to the notion of the Goddess and a reclaiming of the passage of human evolution as not just history, but also *her*story. And everybody knows that Hawaii is, like, Goddess central.

Pele, Hina, Kapo, Haumea . . . goddesses of the volcanoes, of the earth and sky, of the South Pacific, and of birth itself, these are the names given to the most elemental forces of creation in ancient Hawaiian narratives—among hundreds for all the different deities that were once worshipped on the islands. I'd read all about them in an old book I found during our trip, how a different god or goddess was believed to govern every part of life—from fishing to music, and the waxing and waning of the Moon. And how sadly, the author noted, information on the female idols was often harder to find—due to the fact that most historical record keepers had likely been male.

Also perhaps, I couldn't help thinking, because the feminine Goddess energy I was reading about seemed to speak to the wilder and more unpredictable forces that impacted human life—as opposed to the gods, who ruled over specific plants, animals, and *man*-made concepts such as carpentry, agriculture, and war. Wild and unpredictable *feminine* forces that pretty much the whole history of civilization has been about striving to suppress. For our survival, of course—but also in the name of proving and maintaining our place at the top of the food chain.

Could it be that the legendary power of the goddesses had *also* been suppressed along the way? Had been written out of *his*tory, as the systems of modern civilization took hold?

Whoa—see what I mean about deep?! Well, these are the kinds of thoughts I began having after two weeks away from e-mail and social media. (Just sayin'.) And as for what my theory had to do with my *hair*? Well, I've kind of always seen my need to tame my curls as a metaphor for wanting to tame the perhaps "messier" aspects of my *self*. A nice, neat blowout makes me feel put together and in control, after all. Not to mention "prettier" (read: more palatable to polite society). But running alongside this train of thought had always been another, somewhat exciting, thread—if the curls also represented my *true* nature, then perhaps in my soul I was *wilder* than even I knew.

All of this had begun to come into deeper relief as we bid farewell to the volcanoes and lush green vistas of Hawaii and boarded our plane back to JFK. Back to New York City, and civilization as we knew it.

## THE DIVINE FEMININE AS A FEMINIST ISSUE

Like, what if women *in general* are wilder, more dangerous, more demanding, and more unpredictable than we believe we're allowed to be? And what if this *wildness* has been suppressed because, like the forces of Mother Nature *her*self, the feminine principle can't really be fully understood, and therefore harnessed? Is truly, awe-inspiringly, *numinous*?

To me, it seems like these questions are at the crux of the Divine Feminine conversation I keep bumping up against on my Now Age path. And, as such, it's a conversation that speaks loud and clear to the next wave—or "contraction" as I like to think of it—of the female empowerment movement. Contraction, since the wider implication of women becoming more and more empowered in the full expression of our wildness, is, quite literally, the *birth* of a whole new paradigm (as Aly suggested in chapter 9).

Interviewed in Michael Moore's brilliant 2015 documentary *Where to Invade Next* (in which he visits various European countries to compare how they live, work, play, and govern versus American systems), Vigdís Finnbogadóttir, former president of Iceland and the first female president in Europe, has this to say on the subject: "My conviction, my belief in women and the intelligence of women, is that if the world can be saved, it will be women who do that. And they do not do it with war, they do it with words. Women, if they are running society, they are looking for peace. They want to save humanity. They want to save their children."

And the contractions are coming closer together—following the suffragettes of the late 1800s and the bra-burning of the 1970s, this decade alone has given us Lean In, Lena freaking Dunham, and the 2017 Women's March on Washington. That "the future is female" T-shirt? A symbol of exactly how confident the next generation to call ourselves "feminist" is that sweet equality might finally be within our grasp (despite Donald fucking Trump).

Because then you look the other way—at the women living under Taliban rule, at female circumcision, at the fact that only 30 percent of rape victims in the United States even bother to report the crime—and it becomes clearly evident that the fight is far from won. And interesting, isn't it, how all the examples I've listed of the ways women are still repressed are directly related to the expression of female *sexuality*? (Oh, and you can add the issue of equal pay, since this often comes down to the fact it's women who bear and nurture children.)

As for the Divine Feminine and how it relates to women's empowerment, a conversation with my editor went something like this: "Why is feminism necessary? Because patriarchal society has subjugated women and stripped us of our equal rights and thus our POWER, especially our power over ourselves. Why? The answer to that seems to be: fear. Fear of what? Fear of the Divine Feminine."

Not fear of the loving, nurturing, collaborative feminine qualities that color Vigdís Finnbogadóttir's warm and fuzzy vision of a more female-forward future. The patriarchy doesn't have a problem with women being "nice." But fear of our unpredictable moods and emotions; fear of our intuition; fear of our connection, through our menstrual cycles, to the workings of the cosmos; fear of our invisible, enigmatic orgasms; and, ultimately, fear of our sexual power—since this manifests in the ALL-POWERFUL ability to create and nurture life itself.

Which is why this chapter is in the section "Love, Sex & Relationships," y'all! Because the ultimate goal of moving beyond this fear and embracing the Divinely Feminine aspects of our human nature, male *and* female? Better relationships (and better sex) between men and women; a sense of true sisterhood among females; a better understanding of and connection to, our higher Selves; and perhaps above all, a more respectful relationship with the ultimate Divinely Feminine force—Mother Nature herself.

## ENTER THE WITCH

Between the fifteenth and eighteenth centuries, the witch trials of Europe and the colonial United States saw thousands of women accused of "devil worship" and executed in punishment. This "officially" came to an end with the introduction in Great Britain of the Witchcraft Act in 1732 but continued in sporadic outbursts until as recently as the last recorded prosecution, in Tennessee in 1833.

But as anybody who's been persecuted for acting, dressing, or expressing views outside the societal norm will know, the modern-day "witch hunt" is alive and well. See also slut shaming, body fascism, and gay bashing. And it's an interesting aside that the overarching astrological climate of the early twenty-first century actually harks back to the time of the original witch trials.

As author and mystic Sarah Durham Wilson writes in her memoir, *The Do-It Girl Diaries: Awakening the Divine Feminine*, "A woman was tried as a witch if she: spoke her truth, lived alone, owned land the govt. wanted, worked with the earth, was too beautiful/ugly/sexy/smart/powerful, didn't fit in, believed in magic, loved the wrong man or woman." Further, she states: "These were your ancient sisters."

Meaning that no matter how emancipated our lives might feel on the surface today, we all—*men and women*—carry the ancestral wounds of these injustices.

Want a chilling and heartbreaking example of how this might play out? Then read *Luckiest Girl Alive* by Jessica Knoll (a former editor at *Cosmopolitan* magazine)—a rabid page-turner of a novel I also happened to read in Hawaii. It tells the story of TifAni FaNelli, who, gang-raped at age fifteen after the boy she likes (and his wealthy, popular friends) get her blind drunk at a party, is subsequently cast out and branded as the school slut by students and teachers alike. And so, y'know, WITCH HUNT.

The kicker is that TifAni's story is based on Knoll's real-life rape, a teeny-tiny detail she only revealed after the hardback had sold half a million copies and the film rights had been snapped up by Reese Witherspoon. After all, she told me when I got to ask her about "coming out" (which she did in an essay for Lena Dunham's Lenny Letter website): "There's still a stigma against women not shielding uncomfortable truths from people."

TifAni's story ends with her taking the first steps to reclaim her identity and sense of self-worth, and, in a similar vein, factions of the Divine Feminine movement are seeking to reclaim the word *witch*. Women like Bri Luna, a.k.a. The Hoodwitch, whose website peddles "everyday magic for the modern mystic" (along with some badass crystals). When we interviewed her for The Numinous, she defined a witch thus:

"There is no 'one size fits all' answer. Every woman is a Witch. She may not know it, or maybe she does. But to me, being a Witch means more than spells and candles. To me, it means the power to boldly and unapologetically embrace nature, to heal yourself, and heal your community. To respect the seen and unseen realms. And it means the freedom to be your most authentic self. To embrace ALL aspects of whoever that may be, and fiercely. That is the Witch."

To me, this description is a battle cry for crusaders of the Divine Feminine. And it's been incredible to begin to notice just how conditioned I am, and we as women are, when it comes to denying the less fragrant, say, aspects of the feminine. My obsessive taming of my naturally curly hair being a particularly fluffy (pun intended) case in point. My allowing the Capricorn to take what he wanted from me sexually, year after year, with little or no regard for my needs or desires—*which I agreed to because I thought this was normal*—a less palatable example.

After all, as Jessica Knoll reminded me: "As women, it's ingrained in us to be people pleasers. And that's something that has far-reaching tentacles . . ." Like, as far as "you're always clean and thin and pretty" (something women's magazines love to remind us on rotation—an industry that interestingly, like me, Knoll found herself drawn to as a

"There is no 'one size fits all' answer. Every woman is a Witch. She may not know it, or maybe she does. But to me, being a Witch means more than spells and candles. To me, it means the power to boldly and unapologetically embrace nature, to heal yourself, and heal your community. To respect the seen and unseen realms. And it means the freedom to be your most authentic self. To embrace ALL aspects of whoever that may be, and fiercely. That is the Witch."

—BRI LUNA

way of papering over the cracks). But also, of course, as far as bedrooms and boudoirs the world over, where I have next to no doubt I'm not the only woman to have "given" more than I got.

## THE DIVINE FEMININE . . . IN BED

So let's get right to the nitty-gritty. Embracing the Divine Feminine means demanding that your sexual needs are met. As in, demanding this of your partner—and of yourself. Why? Well, there's what I said about cultivating self-love being about acknowledging your deepest needs for starters. But if it could also be said that sexual desire is the most basic human instinct (the species will survive without food and shelter so long as we can just keep on procreating, right?), then learning to identify and own our desire, and to then ensure it is fulfilled, is at the root of learning to claim and satisfy *all* our needs as women—as well as our rightful place beside men as cocreators of the Universe.

All this is what came up when I did a follow-up session with Aly after my Red Tent experience. Not that I went to her to talk about my sex life (which, let's just say, has been the exact *opposite* with the Pisces). Rather, I was feeling generally "stuck" and figured this lack of "flow" might be linked to my irregular periods. I had identified that this "stuck-ness" often manifested in me feeling let down by people, who failed to deliver what I had told them I needed. Or . . . had I?! Aly suggested that perhaps I wasn't being as clear or up front as I thought, for fear of seeming too *demanding* (a Divine Feminine biggie). Her solution? "Well, Ruby, you're just going to have to get really sexy!" (Spoken, don't forget, in her terribly posh British accent.)

My homework was to spend the next few weeks identifying all the "fantasies" I had about what it meant to be a sexual woman (look this way, act that way), and to then perform a private ritual to give this conditioning back to the Universe (or rather, to the patriarchy). The idea was that this would help me get back in touch with my own individual and utterly unique needs and desires.

A big one that came up for me? The belief that we should only have sex when *he* wanted it—to the point that I had become so afraid of being "rejected," I was scared to initiate sex when *I* wanted it! No prizes for guessing where that one came from—not to mention the influence of our collective understanding about what happens to women who are "asking for it." Yes, I faced the (slut) shame and shared this revelation with the Pisces. Yes, we've been having a lot more sex. And YES, I have seen the ripple effect in my life as the fear around "telling people what I really need" has begun to melt away like snow on a spring day.

## THE DIVINE FEMININE . . . IN BUSINESS

And how can you run a business, or rise up the ranks in your chosen profession, without making a few demands? More than a few, actually! When it comes to getting the assistance, the pay, and the (self) respect you need to make it happen, I've learned that you pretty much have to ask for / demand these things on a daily basis—a.k.a. get reallllly comfortable with potentially coming over like a bit of a bitch (which actually sounds kind of like a "badass witch," doesn't it?).

I've learned this the hard way: by repeatedly burning out because it just feels "easier to do it myself" than instruct somebody else; by finding myself working seven-day weeks and still earning less than I need to feel financially secure; and by shying away from reaching out to people I deem to be "above me" for mentoring and advice.

The "getting sexy" has definitely helped with this, but it's a work in progress. And one way I've been able to embrace making these "unreasonable" demands is to keep coming back to the concept of *dharma*. To tapping back in (using the self-awareness generated by tools such as meditation and astrology) to the fact that in fulfilling my business/career goals I am also serving in my role as an active participant in the fabric of humanity. Which makes it way easier to get fierce about what needs to get done!

After all, if the Divine Feminine is our human expression of the laws of nature, it's the energy that says: I seek abundance, so that it can be shared among my tribe. So that I can create new life (also projects, products, jobs). So that I have "enough" to nourish others (babies, contributors, staff).

And here's another interesting thing I'm learning. My friend Chloe Kerman, a former fashion stylist who now works as a Divine Feminine energy healer, told me: "The key is realizing that this abundance (of money, assistance, respect) may not come in the same form you gave it. It's not about, 'Well, I did this for you, now give me this in return.' Rather, the feminine way is about recognizing that the flow of abundance is *around us always,* and simply being open to receive."

It's what life coach and "possibilitarian" Cherie Healey described to me once as: "allowing life to happen *through* you"—whereas the masculine approach is to make life happen "*by* you" (through sheer will and effort). And it's definitely not the easiest to master—especially when there's rent and staff to be paid, and the "flow" of abundance appears to have stalled in your client's accounts payable department.

But again, we can tap into this *idea* at least by taking a cue from nature. By meditating on the idea that we can give and give and give of ourselves and our creative gifts in the image of the Divine Mother, of creation HERSELF, and not *expect* anything in return—secure in our trust that we will receive all we could ever need from our connection to the all-abundant Universe, to Source.

## THE DIVINE FEMININE . . . AS SISTERHOOD

But also: collaboration. One of the saddest outcomes of our disconnection from the Divine Feminine is competition among women, which it seems to me is born of the fear that there's simply not *enough* (love, acceptance, decent salaries, Instagram followers) to go around. But what's the fastest way to get the support we need to manifest our deepest, most heartfelt desires? To team up with each other. After all: there is POWER in numbers.

Fear of not being accepted for who we are is a HUGE one here, and one that's born of deeply ingrained conditioning about what it means to be a woman. As Sarah Durham Wilson puts it: "I was frightened of her, me, it. I knew what was in me was big, unfamiliar, wild, voracious. You have been deeply programmed (by the patriarchy) to fear yourself." Also, when we see another woman being big, wild, voracious, to fear *each other*. And what do we do when we're afraid of something? We fight it, or we compete in an attempt to win whatever (love, acceptance, salary, Instagram followers) is available.

But, because it believes that we are all connected, the Divine Feminine says, her success is *your* success. Taryn Longo is another prominent voice in this field, and she told me how, having come of age in "a bitchy party scene," "I came to this work seeking a woman who was strong enough to have another woman's back without it being self-investing. Who could look at her success and let it make her feel successful, opposed to being threatened, jealous, or envious."

Two women who personify this for me with every atom of their beings are Ellen DeGeneres and Oprah Winfrey. Daytime talk-show rivals? HELL NO, they don't have time for that; they're too busy spreading peace, love, and positivity—and building gigantic empires on the side. And it's an interesting aside that neither of these incredible women have children—an observation that builds on my conclusions in the previous chapter.

And speaking of mothers . . . Since mother-daughter rivalry is beyond common (some might even say instinctual, to which I say: sup, psychoanalysts of the patriarchy), your relationship with your mom is the first opportunity you get to practice the art of sisterhood. Getting to this place will look different for everyone (maybe you're there already!), but, by *Goddess,* is it worth it. I actually believe that healing my relationship with my mum has been the key to my ultimate self-acceptance, and therefore my ability to accept all women as my sisters.

And speaking of the Goddess . . . Since your mother is the first and only true creator you know, for the formative years of your life she IS Goddess—your source of all nourishment, of all protection. Also, since it is within her terrible power to take it all away at any moment, she is also the one who first asks that you *just trust* that the Universe WILL provide. As such, if you find yourself experiencing an extra helping of skepticism in the "all flowing abundance" arena—then it is my humble suggestion you make your next bout of self-inquiry and healing about her. Not to mention your mother's mother, too.

## THE DIVINE FEMININE . . . IS GENDERLESS

This chapter was originally going to be called "Divine Feminine Meets Empowered Masculine." Because if the future really does need to be more "female," I think this is about cultivating a more *feminine* mindset in our relationships with each other and the planet—regardless of biological sex. After all, this is also about finally laying the battle of the sexes to rest. As Vigdís Finnbogadóttir surmises in *Where to Invade Next:* "When men open up to women's way of seeing things, and add it to their way of seeing things, then we will get a better world."

That is, a world that's more collaborative, more nurturing, more willing to talk, more ready to listen, and more in tune with the natural rhythms of nature. Also keep in mind that as a model for the expression of the Divine Feminine in us, as well as our unconditional source of love and support, Mother Nature is our fiercest and most brutal teacher. And if "feminine" qualities have been painted by *his*tory as weak, um, you might wanna consult the legend of Kali—Hindu Goddess of transformation, power, and time—when it comes to reframing that one (more on her in the chapter on spiritual style icons).

Taryn Longo's husband, David Wagner, a coach and author specializing in men's spiritual work, spoke to this in an interview for The Numinous: "The average person, when they hear that I'm doing a spiritual book for men, they're like, 'Oh, good. You're going to teach them to open their hearts.' It's like, 'Yeah, I'm going to teach them to open their hearts, but the book is really about growing a backbone and balls.'"

Because actually? It takes some serious guts to be in touch with your emotions and operate from this vulnerable, heart-centered, Divinely Feminine place. Emotions are scary and unpredictable and they have the power—like the scary unpredictable forces of nature, of our mothers when we are small—to utterly blindside us. But it's also our job to invite this in our men—be they our partners or our bosses, our fathers, sons, and brothers.

After all, as Taryn puts it, "A lot of women have not 100 percent gotten on board with seeing men in their empowered masculine, meaning with men showing their emotions. But why would you want to be in a situation with somebody who is afraid of any part of themselves?" Afraid of their emotional self, she means.

The way to finally face down this fear? The only way out is THROUGH, which means being ready and willing to embrace the Divine Feminine, inner wilderness and all.

## THE DIVINE FEMININE . . . IN PRACTICE

PRACTICE MAGICAL SELF-CARE. The same way our neglected planet acts out in wild and unpredictable ways (see: extreme weather episodes caused by climate change), self-neglect (physical, emotional, mental, and spiritual) causes our Divine Feminine to get out of balance. Address this by making utmost care for your whole self your number one priority. And get witchy with it.

"I like to take very long beautiful baths—my daily ritual to connect me to the Goddess within. I enjoy being surrounded by candles, while listening to soft music. Depending on the purpose of the bath, be it for attracting or self-love, aura cleansing, or just simply relaxation I'll add in ingredients that are reflective of those purposes. Essential oils, milk, salts, or flower petals. I just enjoy the beauty of it."

—DEBORAH HANEKAMP

SPEND TIME IN NATURE. City life means we're often utterly divorced from the rhythms of nature—and since we fear what we don't understand, learning to welcome the Divine Feminine into our lives means reconnecting to the wilderness as our ultimate mother and the source of all life.

"When I'm walking the earth, when I'm drinking or washing with water, or feeling the wind in my face, I am able to see and feel the spirit that is around me in every moment, and how my life is full of magic and miracles."

—CHLOE KERMAN

SUPPORT OTHER WOMEN. Pitting women against each other ("Who wore it best?" "Beyoncé versus Rihanna!") is one way the patriarchy has kept us fearful of the Divine Feminine, in ourselves and each other. Plus, infighting is the fastest way for any army to give away its power!

"Being in the company of other empowered women is really important. Find people in your world or online who you feel are connected to themselves, and who represent the feminine in a way that resonates with you."

—TARYN LONGO

KNOW YOURSELF. But like ALL parts of yourself. Use astrology. Meditation. Journaling. Make a vision board of YOU. All ways to access and explore the memories, experiences, impulses, and emotions that make up your Divinely Feminine self—especially the ones the

patriarchy / polite society would rather you kept wrapped up in a pretty pink bow.

> "Peeling off layers of self and healing WOUNDS and facing stuff. Allowing it to be very hard. I mean it is not easy."
>
> —TARYN LONGO

GIVE YOURSELF UNCONDITIONAL SELF-LOVE. A.k.a. self-awareness, self-forgiveness, self-acceptance.

> "'Chloe, I'll love you today if you look like this, Chloe, I'll love you today if you feel like this.' Coming out of the fashion industry, my self-love and self-worth were pretty, pretty low. I didn't even realize how deeply conditioned I was."
>
> —CHLOE KERMAN

SHARE STORY MEDICINE. The Numi term for coming together to share our difficult, painful, Divinely Feminine truths, and in turn offering the gift of deep, compassionate listening, as a way to connect and heal each other's shame.

> "Beneath the character names and places and timing of events, we share similar stories of shame, exile, self abandonment, fear, healing, and love. This communion, of coming into union with your sisters and recognizing yourself in their stories, brings us into wholeness, and oneness, moves us from isolation into community, and from a feeling of being alone to the understanding that we are all one."
>
> —SARAH DURHAM WILSON

FORGE A CONNECTION TO THE GODDESS. Meaning the archetypes that have existed throughout history as symbols for the different expressions of the Divine Feminine. In a world that's still sadly bereft of diverse female and feminine role models, make your Goddess oracle deck your study book.

"Goddess Venus teaches us to be accepting of all facets of our womanhood and sexuality. In fact, one of the qualities that separates Venus from the Aphrodite myth is that Venus was also the goddess of prostitutes. She allows for sexuality to be fluid, to exist in a space without judgment."

—ELYSSA JAKIM

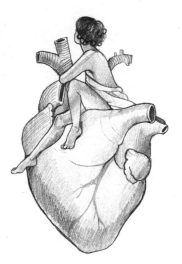

LIVE FROM THE HEART. Faced with each and every decision, ask yourself, *How does this feel?* It's human nature to know right from wrong, and what feels right, what feels like *the truth,* is the Divinely Feminine path.

"In the masculine world everything is very mind oriented, whereas the Divine Feminine is a deep expression of your heart's longing. So you're living from your heart, making decisions from your heart all the time."

—CHLOE KERMAN

HEAL YOUR WOMB. As the crucible of life itself, your womb space is the seat of all Divine Feminine power. So become vigilant to her wounds and tend lovingly to her well-being and her needs. (Step #1—more orgasms!)

"The birth of the Divine Feminine is the birth of new life, new creativity, new projects, your soul's purpose, your heart's desire, and it's what we came here to do. It means rediscovering who you really, truly are, and what your purpose on this Earth is."

—CHLOE KERMAN

BE WARM, NURTURING, COLLABORATIVE. Finally, please definitely DO keep on expressing all the warm and fuzzy attributes of your Divinely Feminine self. But fiercely.

# SOUL MATE OR TWIN FLAME?
# (AND HOW TO TELL THE DIFFERENCE)

Ah, the infamous Twin Flame versus Soul Mate dilemma. How do you know if your partner is the one, or the ONE; the one for *this* life, or the one for *each* life? Although some soul-searching and a lot of getting real will be necessary in discovering the true answer, here's a quiz to help you figure it out. Definitely can't hurt.

1.  WHEN YOU MET YOUR SIGNIFICANT OTHER, THE FIRST THING YOU FELT WAS . . .

    a.  An instant connection. I intuitively knew things would never be the same.
    b.  I felt a connection, but it took a while for me to know they were the one.

2.  LET'S TALK CHAKRAS—HOW DO YOU AND YOUR PARTNER ALIGN?

    a.  Completely and utterly. If my sacral chakra's out, they know the key is to work on unlocking my heart. It's spooky.
    b.  We're balanced. We give and take and we feed off each other (spiritually, you know!).

3.  YOU CAN'T DENY YOU MET IN A PAST LIFE, BUT IN WHAT CAPACITY?

    a.  We've been lovers in many, many lives. This connection transcends anything else.
    b.  We've definitely incarnated together before, but our relationship is more multifaceted than that. We've loved each other before, but we've also learned from each other, you know?

4.  HAVE YOU EVER FELT THIS SENSE OF CONNECTION WITH ANYONE ELSE?

    a.  I don't think that would even be possible.
    b.  Yes and no—I have friends I feel this strong of a bond with, but not in a romantic way.

5. OKAY, SO YOUR PARTNER ISN'T PERFECT, DON'T SWEAT IT!
   BUT WHAT HAPPENS AFTER YOU ARGUE?
   a. Since there's no ego in our relationship, it's no biggie if we argue—
      nothing a little cooling-off time can't fix.
   b. Things can get "passionate," but there's always a sense of growth
      and we end up closer than when we began. It's like I can't get away.

6. WHAT WORDS BEST DESCRIBE YOUR RELATIONSHIP?
   a. Beautiful, important, peaceful, complete. I needed them in my life,
      it's like there's a sense of wholeness when I'm with them.
   b. Otherworldly, meaningful, deep, passionate. It's changed the way in
      which I view the world.

## MOSTLY A'S: SOUL MATES

This is IT. This is your true love, the one soul you're meant
to be with in this life. You have definitely journeyed with
your Soul Mate in past lives, and there's a really similar, and
intimate, energy between you as a result. You may not have
been lovers from life to life, but the lessons you've taught
each other in each incarnation have been essential to your
soul's evolution. There's no ego in your relationship, since
your Soul Mate is incarnated with you to help you learn; you
literally need each other, and you both respect this. You may
have also found a Soul Mate in your best friend or sister, but
the romantic Soul Mate takes the bonding to the next level.

## MOSTLY B'S: TWIN FLAMES

You have a love that transcends lifetimes—but the thing with this kind of
bond is that it can take courage to commit, and you both have to be ready

to accept it. Hooking up with your Twin Flame, or Twin
Soul, is #relationshipgoals to the $n$th degree. This person
probably set your life on a new path, one that transcends
every expectation you had of love. Lucky you! Twin Flames
are rare and not promised in each incarnation. So are you
ready for this deep a connection? The union may not feel
easy at times, but by working *with* your Twin Flame you can
help each other become whole within yourselves. This kind
of love is the best teacher you'll have in this life.

# PART IV

# FASHION & BEAUTY

# 12

# SPIRITUAL STYLE ICONS (A NUMINOUS BEST-DRESSED LIST)

For a while there, I wanted to be a fashion designer when I grew up. From the age of about eight, I would draw outfits for hours, filling sketchbook after sketchbook with images of "models" in my creations. I can't remember what I was most inspired by, but it was likely a combo of old movies, my Sweet Valley High collection, and Madonna.

In retrospect, I think I was actually drawing versions of the woman I couldn't wait to grow up into, as I would spend equal amounts of time getting my model's hair and face and figure right, paying extra special attention to how her boobs looked in her dress. After all, not only did grown women get all the best clothes, they also got to have men fall hopelessly in love with them.

Considering my dad had apparently fallen out of love with my mum (and by proxy out of love with *me*), making sure I looked like the kind of woman this would never happen to again had evidently inched quite close to the top of my priority list. The story of my parents' breakup is obviously way more complex, and *of course* I wasn't consciously aware of the effect it had on me back then, but if reading and writing had always been my comfort and my joy, there came a point when I decided that, actually, fashion was my "thing."

Fast-forward twenty years and I'm working a six-month contract covering maternity leave for the style editor on the British celebrity gossip magazine *Heat*. Not exactly the glittering career as a designer eight-year-old me had in mind, but close enough since I still got to write and think and talk about clothes all day. More specifically, in this particular role, who'd gotten it right and who'd gotten it oh-so-wrong on the red carpet.

*Heat* was right there at the beginning of the whole "celebrity fashion" thing, the first magazine in the UK to run a regular "Steal Her Style" page (showing us civilians how to copy celebrity outfits on the cheap) and pit A-listers against each other in the battle of "who wore it best?" Yes, anybody under the age of thirty-two, there was a time in history— before the likes of *Heat, People,* and Instagram—when not ALL our fashion inspiration apparently came from celebrities and "influencers."

And since it was still a fun new game in 2006, when I worked at *Heat,* even the highbrow catwalk crowd had decided they were allowed to obsess over Jennifer Lopez versus Geri Halliwell in the green Versace in an *ironic* sense. How hilarious. But let's face it, also how addictive— since it's a game that feeds one of the ego's favorite pastimes, comparing *ourselves* to others.

My favorite part of the job was picking through the paparazzi images that piled up on the picture desk each day (the agencies still sent bundles of actual prints!), selecting candidates for our weekly "best-dressed" list. Which, like all best-dressed lists in the history of the Universe, was actually a "best-looking," "best legs," and "least likely to scare the children" list. In other words, pure, unadulterated, comparison-making poison.

But obviously, with perspective, every inch of my numinous soul can now see how fundamentally WRONG this was. Yes, it may be human (ego) nature to compare how we measure up against our "rivals" for survival—and for women, at the most basic level, this tends to come down to how we look (i.e., how lovable/fuckable) we are. Since a lot of it is about dressing to impress, it seems to me that fashion will always play a pivotal role in our collective neuroses around this.

But it doesn't have to be this way. In the chapter titled "Calling in Number 1," I wrote about how, for me, self-love is essentially about cultivating self-knowledge, self-acceptance, and self-forgiveness. And actually our wardrobes can be a great place to practice this. How?

*Self-knowledge* because your ideal closet will be filled with clothes that reflect the real you, and make the real you feel amazing.

*Self-acceptance* since this may mean getting *really real* about where you're at *right now,* versus dressing (or spending large amounts of cash on unworn outfits) for an "ideal" past or future version of yourself.

*And self-forgiveness,* which basically goes hand in hand with self-acceptance; for example, forgiving yourself for the extra ten pounds or the extra ten years that mean you're probably never going to rock those denim microshorts again (soz).

Thinking back, I can pinpoint numerous occasions when I was *not* dressing from a place of self-love, when what my friend Annmarie O'Connor, a fashion stylist and author of the book *The Happy Closet,* describes as "the mean girl in your closet" was calling all the shots. "She's also the one who tells you to hold on to that pair of size 2 jeans because you're going to diet back into them," Annmarie told me. "She might frame it as 'motivation,' but it's actually a rejection of the person in the mirror right now. It's a mockery and a reminder of our perceived failures."

I met Annmarie when I was editing a special Irish edition of *Style* magazine, and she was essentially the fiercest fashionista in Dublin. Every time I saw her, she was decked out in another killer look: Louboutins and a vintage kimono one week, cropped leather jacket and a Westwood kilt the next. And topped off with a perfectly coiffed rockabilly quiff. *Wow, she must live and breathe fashion,* I always thought to myself, in awe of her Bradshaw-like ability to "Carrie" off (haha) a look.

So you can imagine my surprise when we Skyped recently and she told me, "Any time Fashion Week rolled around, I had a next-level meltdown about what to wear. I always felt like I was some sort of circus performer, you know? Like I had to dress for the shutterbugs." It reminded me of Chloe Kerman talking about her experiences at Fashion Week—how it would leave her feeling utterly drained of her own life force—and I began to wonder how many people in the fashion industry were secretly feeling the same way. I can see now that fear of being judged for my outfits, being subjected to an unspoken "best dressed list" I could sense was rolling behind my fellow editors' eyes, was one of the reasons *I'd* always avoided Fashion Week like the plague.

And perhaps you're more highly evolved than me and don't really need reminding of this fact. But when I take even the briefest moment to check out the kind of "style icons" being championed in the mainstream media, it strikes me that we're still pretty much stuck in the Dark Ages with embracing fashion as a path to self-love.

The word *icon* is defined as "a person or thing regarded as a representative symbol of something." But also, "a painting of Jesus Christ or another *holy figure*." And I'm sorry, I see nothing remotely holy in Kim Kardashian's shopping addiction (let's call it like it is), while in no way is she representative of how I have come to view the role fashion plays in my life. But that's also just me, and I can't really comment on Kim's motives for buying out every Christian Louboutin store in existence since I've never actually met her (although an . . . interesting . . . interview I once did with her sisters Kendall and Kylie *did* go a little bit viral—oops).

So what exactly does a *spiritual style icon* look like, then? Simply put, she or he is somebody whose clothing choices and the vision of human expression they represent to you as a result make them worthy of the term "icon"—to YOU. Whose "look" in some way speaks to your soul and inspires you to clothe your physical body in a way that feels like a healthy, genuine, and joyous reflection—or rather projection—of the mind-body-emo-spirit being you know yourself to be.

And so, in the name of diversity, and to kick off the section of this book that will address the ways in which we adorn our exterior being, there follows an alternative Best-Dressed List. To be referred to in times of self-doubt, body-image crises, and "help I've got nothing to wear" moments.

## KALI

SPIRITUAL STYLING TIP: Make your outfit mean something.

Okay, so the full blue body paint is a strong look, and I'm not suggesting that you might literally want to dress like Kali, Hindu goddess of time, change, power, creation, and destruction. But as far as fierce

feminine figureheads from ancient mythology go, she's pretty much up there.

The "destroyer of evil forces," Kali is usually depicted as having wild, matted hair and raging bloodshot eyes, her hot pink tongue panting from the exertion of, y'know, creating and destroying whole worlds. She is also naked from the waist up, #freethenipple, usually dressed in a skirt made of human arms, and with a garland of heads dangling from her neck. Dripping in gold jewelry, she also wields a trident, a severed head, and a bloodied sword. Gruesome!

Again, there is no scenario in which I envisage you stealing Kali's *actual* style, but what I love about her—and all the Hindu goddesses for that matter—is that she is dressed in *symbols*. For example, the severed head is said to depict the ego; the sword, "divine knowledge," its destroyer. The wild hairstyle, meanwhile, is a symbol of nature's freedom from civilization (yes, Divine Feminine icon!). Therefore, to channel the spirit of Kali is to make fashion choices that actually mean something to you and to drape yourself in talismans that amp up your sense of personal power.

Sure, I could have picked a less aggressive goddess to depict this idea, like Lakshmi, goddess of abundance, sitting pretty in her pink lotus blossom. But Kali's name comes up time and again as the deity whose energy women most wish to channel when feeling in any way "less than," which is maybe because she's often portrayed dancing over the prostrate body of her husband, the great god Shiva. Kali's soundtrack? It's gotta be "Caught Out There" by Kelis.

## THE QUEEN OF PENTACLES

SPIRITUAL STYLING TIP: Shop for what you REALLY love.

As discussed elsewhere, in the tarot the Pentacles represent the Earth element, which in turn speaks to all things concerning the material world. Root chakra stuff—like food, shelter, money, and physical comfort. Oh yeah, and fashion! And the Queen of the suit embodies the emotional part of Earth, our intuitive and passionate connection to our stuff.

When I asked my friend the New Age Hipster to write about the Queen of Pentacles for The Numinous, she likened her to Beyoncé. "Powerful, strong, determined, and super hot, she can basically get paid for just breathing," she wrote. "On top of that she's actually just really cool. Everyone wants to be her friend, not only because of her money but because she totally *works it*."

Interestingly, she is also associated with the energy of Capricorn, the sign of so many regular old-style icons: see David Bowie, Kate Moss, and Michelle Obama. Capricorn energy might be kinda practical, but Capricorns certainly know how to get dressed. No Capricorn could ever be accused of not wearing the (rhinestone-encrusted Versace) trousers, and with the Queen of Pentacles there's absolutely a sense of mastery over the material, of ruling, as opposed to being ruled by, life's luxuries.

So what I'm suggesting is that you make her your default personal shopper. Like maybe even carry her card when you hit the shops, or prop it up next to your computer the next time you decide to indulge in a late-night Nasty Gal shop-a-thon. Her message is one of empowering indulgence, and she will guide you toward fashion choices that make you *feel* like a million dollars—versus splurging for the sake of it and ending up with a closet full of designer swag you never wear. Oh, and since she also governs over seriously good food, she's kind of the ultimate lady who lunches. Why would you not want to shop with this bae by your side?

## DAME VIVIENNE WESTWOOD

SPIRITUAL STYLING TIP: Dress for the character you want to play today.

I never get tired of telling people how I share my birthday with Vivienne Westwood. Because this like totally makes us soul sisters, right? It means I also like to think of this absolute badass of a designer, the woman responsible for bringing punk to the mainstream in the 1970s and who remains a major disrupter well into her seventies, as kind of my fashion spirit animal. But as a complete confrontation avoider myself, I actually find Viv equal parts inspiring and intimidating—which is also her appeal as a spiritual style icon.

While some (most) fashion designers are all about creating trends in the name of selling as many units as possible, Vivienne Westwood seems more concerned with telling a story with her creations. Specifically, a properly scary fairy tale, involving pixies, pirates, lost little boys, plenty of gender fluidity, and at least one evil stepmother. She's also a total Peter Pan figure herself, absolutely and resolutely refusing to allow age to dampen her personal style—or her sex life (see hot Austrian husband, also her former student, also twenty-five years her junior).

What I like about Vivienne's approach is that she's all about creating characters, which is what we're all doing every time we get dressed anyway. She also recognizes that some of those characters will be "good," and some of them will be "bad," just like the many selves that reside within us. The best fairy tales and myths depict exactly this, the multifaceted nature of being human and the moral dilemmas we're faced with as a result.

Vivienne Westwood says: don't you dare deny your dark side. Because we all know the upshot of this: your less attractive impulses will find another, often self-destructive, outlet. As a designer and with her personal style, Vivienne is a champion of celebrating your *whole* self, and playing with the many aspects of your personality, all the better for getting to truly know, love, and accept yourself. Also why it feels so liberating to dress up in costume, and something kids do naturally. Maybe let's not be in such a hurry to grow out of it.

## VENUS

SPIRITUAL STYLING TIP: Dress for a body you love.

When Vivienne Westwood went to collect her OBE (Order of the British Empire) from Buckingham Palace, she wasn't wearing any knickers. The world knows this because when Viv did a twirl to "show off my outfit," the paparazzi got a lens-full of her lady parts—and Venus, goddess of love, sex, beauty, and abundance, would no doubt have approved wholeheartedly. Wherever she's been depicted throughout history, the most she has to preserve her "modesty" is a wisp of diaphanous drapery.

Personally I'm not big into nudity. If, as my mum tells it, I refused to wear any clothes for the first six months of my life, it's because the year I was born the UK experienced one of the hottest summers on record—nothing to do with me feeling innately more comfortable unclothed. I did not grow up in a naked household, and the one time I stripped on a nudist beach in Ibiza my bikini went back on as soon as I needed to stand up and find a bathroom.

But I do think overall it serves us humans well to get comfortable with what we look like naked, and how it feels to simply exist beyond the "boundaries" of clothes. Comfortable as in "accepting." What makes Venus sexy is her total lack of self-consciousness—you definitely don't get the impression she's stressing over the diameter of her thighs, sucking in her stomach, or trying to hide her cellulite.

Rather, she looks like a woman who knows that her body is hers to be *enjoyed*.

How does this make her style icon material? The years I spent trying to get my body to be a certain shape, a lot of the time it was so I could wear certain clothes. And, okay, I might have taken it to extremes, but I know I'm not alone on this one. For me, Venus is a reminder that your body kind of got there first, and so the clothes should fit *it*. See the day I decided it was okay to buy something in a size 8 because it just looked—and felt—better on me than the 6.

## MAN REPELLER

SPIRITUAL STYLING TIP: Self-expression is the best accessory.

Yes, Leandra Medine, the brains behind megablog Man Repeller, is deeply in the pocket of the same mainstream fashion industry I basically just took a shot at in the beginning of this chapter.

*But.*

What I (and her gazillions of followers) like about Leandra is that she uses fashion as a means of pure self-expression and creative play. The name of her brand is also a reference to the fact that in its highest expression as an art form, fashion is actually nothing to do with looking "hot" and making it onto any-body's best-dressed/best-body list. Her outfits tend to be a crazy mishmash of colors, textures, and styles that just somehow seem to work, while her whole shtick is a subtle poke in the ribs at anybody who takes it all too seriously (i.e., has bought into the idea that the only way to be a credible human being is if your outfit is sufficiently on-trend).

This bit could also have been about Carrie Bradshaw, who embraced a similar disregard for the "rules" of fashion. But Carrie was always way too hung up on designer labels (not to mention bagging Mr. Big) for my liking, which are essentially Girl Scout badges for the ego, particularly later in the series and in the SATC movies. When she was seduced by the glamour of the megabucks brands, her early playful experimentation was replaced with OTT peacocking.

Not so the Man Repeller, who clearly *never* grew out of her five-year-old fancy dress phase and has, in fact, managed to make a career out of it. I don't know about you, but I LOVED my five-year-old fancy dress phase, which for any little girl (or boy) is also about discovering the transcendent power of clothes. In the same way one of my old editors used to don a jade green trilby when she was suffering a creative block, sometimes a simple outfit change can shift our whole perspective on life. Something else that helps me understand how everything, including the clothes we wear, carries its own energy.

THIS, as the Man Repeller reminds me time and again, is the power of fashion as fancy dress.

## JOHN LENNON

SPIRITUAL STYLING TIP: You don't have to get dressed to impress.

Our honorary dude, John, makes it onto the list because his beautiful Libra soul did some of his most numinous work in his pajamas, a.k.a. the infamous Bed-Ins for Peace that he and Yoko Ono staged following their marriage in 1969.

With the conflict in Vietnam at its bloodiest, the bed-ins were a publicity stunt designed to redirect the media attention around their nuptials to the antiwar effort, and the iconic images of

John and Yoko receiving the press from their marital bed have always rocked my world. This to me is an example of activism at its finest—I'm a huge proponent of the peaceful protest (what Mahatma Gandhi termed "Satyagrapha")—and is also the kind of exploit I believe any celebrity worth their social media following should be embracing in the Now Age.

Like, if you've already got a million eyes on your feed to check out what you're wearing (ahem, a certain famous family obsessed with K names again), I see it as kind of your duty to throw a few consciousness-raising nuggets into the mix. And no need to get all heavy on anybody's ass! As John himself put it, "It's part of our policy not to be taken seriously. Our opposition, whoever they may be, in all manifest forms, don't know how to handle humor. And we are humorous." To embrace hu*mor* is to recognize that we hu*mans* are all in this together, after all.

Plus, the PJs themselves. Since my working day tends to begin with me rolling out of bed and onto the chair in front of my computer, I also do a lot of my best work in my pajamas. In fact, I'm wearing a version of pajamas right now (it's 6:47 A.M.), and I can't tell you how liberating it's been not to have to begin my day putting together an "outfit"—and one that I felt needed to in some way "impress" my colleagues at that.

In one of my old magazine jobs, a coworker once mused that I was "a funny little dresser." Which basically was him picking up on two essential truths: (1) I am very much in touch with my multiple selves and never really grew out of *my* five-year-old fashion-as-fancy-dress phase either, and (2) ideally I need a good few hours in my PJs each morning before deciding who I'm going to dress up as that day.

## DONNA KARAN

SPIRITUAL STYLING TIP: Yoga pants every damn day.

You might not think it considering she's known for her love of beige, plus the fact she has a whole line called Urban Zen, but Donna Karan is a bona fide, one-hundred-mile-per-hour human hurricane. At least that's how she came across when I interviewed her a few years back. There are certain women who truly embody the phrase "force of nature," and Donna, all click-clacking wooden bangles, gravelly voice, and deep Haitian suntan (from a recent humanitarian mission), is one of them.

A native and typically high-strung New Yorker, it's no wonder Donna is also a person who just NEEDS yoga in her life. Plus, she's a Libra, so it totally makes sense that she's into the concept of the "work-chill" balance. A regular practitioner for almost forty years, she once said, "To me, yoga is a way of life. It is meditation; it is consciousness; it isn't just wrapping your leg around your head. It's about connecting on a spiritual level—opening and bringing the heart out."

OMG, now that I think about it, is Donna actually the original Material Girl, Mystical World?! It was her need for clothes she could wear to yoga *and* to work (creating some of the most directional collections of the 1980s) that shaped her original signature look: leggings + body-conscious layers of cashmere-jersey. Clothes that are designed for a holistic, mind-body-spirit way of life, and basically the way I, and many of the Numinati, dress the majority of the time.

And then there's the fact that she's dedicated the latter part of her career to turning the mainstream medical establishment onto yoga and meditation, as well as other alternative healing practices, not to mention donating her time and money to the survivors of natural disasters. But never, ever at the expense of looking fierce in a pair of thousand-dollar yoga pants. It's what she calls "dressing and addressing."

Just to get a teeny bit political here too, Donna's Urban Zen line was actually founded to fund her wellness education initiatives, and the further removed I am from the mainstream fashion industry, the crazier it seems to me that more big brands aren't actively invested in "giving back." After all, after oil, the fashion industry is the second-largest polluter on the planet.

## THE SPIRIT WEAVERS .

SPIRITUAL STYLING TIP: Craft is not dead.

For the uninitiated, the Spirit Weavers Gathering is a five-day, all-female immersive retreat dedicated to the traditions of cultures past, which takes place each summer at Camp Navarro, deep in the redwood forests of Mendocino County, California. According to Instagram (I've never actually attended), the festival mainly attracts properly witchy women who live 80 percent off the grid, home-birth babies for breakfast, and would rather go naked than wear man-made fibers. But who also left their hot filmmaker husbands holding down the eco-friendly fort back in L.A.

As the organizers describe it, Spirit Weavers is "a place to re-skill, re-wild, and remember." There are workshops *for days* on ancient dying, beading, textile making, and, yes, weaving techniques; the "look" of the festival could be described as "tie-dye tribeswoman meets Venice beach vintage." Talk about fashion and clothes-making as a vehicle for creative self-expression, and Earth-felt connection.

I love how in *Big Magic,* Liz Gilbert draws attention to the fact that "the earliest evidence of recognizable human art is forty thousand years old. The earliest evidence of human agriculture, by contrast, is only ten thousand years old. Which means that somewhere in our collective evolutionary story, we decided it was way more important to make attractive, superfluous items than it was to learn how to regularly feed ourselves."

And what are clothes that offer anything more than the most basic protection from the elements, if not attractive, superfluous items? But in modern society, our addiction to trends and fast fashion are just another example of our collective *root chakra problems*—and a major contributor to our polluting of the Earth to boot.

You know me, I'm still, like, "yay, Alexander Wang"—and by including the Spirit Weavers here, I'm not suggesting you cut up your Barneys store card and commit to sewing all your own clothes from here on out. Rather, I see this colorful tribe as a reminder that the desire to adorn ourselves is deeply human, and that on some level, choosing artisanal anything is choosing a connection to the Creator. And not to mention the human hand that crafted it.

## MADONNA

SPIRITUAL STYLING TIP: You are every woman.

My favorite teaching from the tarot is that all life is a process of evolution, and that as such, incarnating in a human suit is essentially signing up for a never-ending cycle of transformation. And for me, nobody has embodied this concept more spectacularly than Madonna.

Madonna was my first bona fide style crush. The *Like a Virgin* video came out when I was eight (that tutu!), followed by *Desperately Seeking Susan* a year later (which I probably didn't get to see until a year after that, since you had to wait forever for films to come out on VHS in the 1980s). So let's say, then, I must have been ten years old when I dragged my stepmother to Camden Market in search of a bag like the giant hatbox the Susan character essentially lives out of in the film. (Ah, the psychology of handbags—that could be, and probably is, a whole book unto itself.)

Something about her East Village thrift store style in that movie evidently spoke loud and clear to the fledgling #rebelspirit in ME, while simultaneously opening the door to a world of exciting possibilities about what it meant to be an autonomous, free-spirited woman, like her character in the film.

Moving on from her club kid punk phase, Madonna has gone on to embody pretty much every subculture, trend, and feminine archetype going with her wardrobe choices—from Voguing transvestite, to rhinestone cowgirl. Clever marketing, yada yada, but also done from a place of such authentic self-expression (true to her Leo Sun sign) that you can't help but be inspired by her perpetual use of fashion as a way to transform and explore all the different ways of being human.

Which is not to say I've been motivated to rush out and copy any one of Madonna's looks since the *Susan* hatbox. But Madonna, self-proclaimed, Divinely Feminine, "unapologetic bitch," makes me feel better about my own fashion "mistakes," which I might also read as playful experimentation. Because, as I've also learned from the tarot, there is no such thing as a wrong decision—only never-ending opportunities to evolve and learn, on the journey to becoming more and more ourselves. Going forward, may the same please apply to how we get dressed.

# 13

# THE INNER BEAUTY V. BOTOX DEBATE

I was thirty-six when I first got Botox, and it coincided with a time I was feeling pretty fearful about life. On the surface, things could not have looked more glamorous. It was the year I moved to New York, and having taken a summer job editing a magazine in Ibiza, I was commuting back and forth between Manhattan and the Med, spending two weeks in each location. Living the dream, right? Except the reality was probably the closest I've ever come to having a nervous breakdown (and not in the "spiritual awakening" sense).

The move stateside had absolutely been the most incredible adventure, and one the Pisces and I had been actively manifesting for quite some time. As in, after he got a job in the London office of a company based out of NYC, I gave him his morning cup of tea in an "I ♥ NY" mug—and continued to do so, every day, for the next two years. A rudimentary approach, but Spirit had apparently been listening and now here we were.

The thing is, the move had also meant leaving behind everything that gave me a sense of security. I'd traded my beautiful home in East London for a $4K-a-month shoebox infested with roaches and vermin in a building where random workmen would come into the apartment, uninvited, around the clock. Instead of cozy friendships nurtured over decades, my social life had become an endless round of blind "friend dates" with similarly rootless souls.

Not from a particularly close-knit family, my clan now felt further away than ever. But perhaps most unsettling of all (which also says so much about my shaky foundations at the time), I'd given up my job at *Style* magazine. A position I'd coveted my entire career, which also came with a regular salary and glittering piles of freebies and lifestyle perks, the role had finally bestowed on me the industry status and respect (i.e., sense of belonging) I'd always craved. Walking away had left me feeling supervulnerable—talk about first-world, root chakra problems!

So when my friend Ben offered me the summer job in Ibiza, I grasped at the opportunity to regain some lost ground in the financial/status stakes. But with no direct flights the commute was brutal, and I was constantly jet-lagged. There were also some gnarly politics going down at the magazine, which translated as a major lack of editorial support. Two months in, I was already running on way below empty. And yep, you guessed it, self-medicating with alcohol to bridge the "isn't my life fabulous" gap.

Which is about exactly when I met Raj, a Botox "guru" who was doing a summer residency (only in Ibiza) at the island's most chichi spa hotel. When he offered me a freebie, I didn't hesitate to accept. Because what do lots of women do when we're feeling insecure, vulnerable, and in any way "less than"? We fixate on our appearance. Look "perfect," we'll be accepted/loved, and everything will be okay.

At age sixteen this translated as me developing an eating disorder, as I waged war on the very first dimples of cellulite that dared to invade my thighs. Now, the "wrong side" of thirty-five, my wrinkles had become enemy number one.

The thing is, the whole Botox situation didn't go too well. I wanted Raj to zap the (teeny tiny) fine lines that had begun to show on my forehead, having read that it wasn't advisable to use Botox around the eyes. I figured my smile lines could stay. But he managed to convince me otherwise, and lying back on his couch, feeling relaxed and "special" (journalist freebies always brought out my inner princess) for the first time all summer, I figured *why the hell not?* It wasn't until a few days later, once the toxin had kicked in, that I got my answer.

Yes, my forehead was blessedly smooth, and even the nasty scar between my eyebrows (the one I got when I bashed my head at age five *right* on the spot above my third eye—talk about "awakening"!)—was less pronounced, making the top part of my face appear more relaxed. But where the Botox had frozen my crow's-feet, it had created saggy little pouches of skin, with nowhere else to go, underneath my eyes. In other words, I now had the eye bags to match how utterly depleted I was feeling inside.

So this is where I'm supposed to tell you how my numinous journey has helped me see the light—that *true beauty* is all about how you feel on the inside, and that no amount of pampering, products, and procedures can substitute for the glow that comes from perfect health. And I apologize in advance if that's what you want to hear. Because while I absolutely, 100 percent subscribe to this warm and fuzzy human truth, I also came of age in a society where what's on the outside counts. Not to mention I pursued a career in an industry that's dedicated to reinforcing this message.

To pretend I'm not a product of this environment would be utterly inauthentic, and so I won't insult your trust in me as a reliable narrator by even going there. What I can say is that the more time and attention I bring to the things you can't necessarily *see* about me, to my *numinous nature,* the less time and energy I have to spend fretting in front of the mirror.

But, MAN, is it a work in progress. Unpacking decades, no . . . generations, no, wait . . . a whole *civilization's* worth of conditioning around female beauty does not happen overnight. Here, I will share with you the wisdom and the tools I've learned along my numinous way that are helping me bridge the inner versus outer beauty divide, as well as attempt to redefine what it means to be beautiful in the Now Age. Some of it warm and fuzzy, some not so much.

## MIND THE COMPARISON TRAP

When I was working at *Style,* some beauty brand sent out a press release declaring that a woman began to "lose her looks" at age 35.09. It was official; they'd done the math. On receiving this, I was not nearly as mad at the fact the company's PR department thought it was okay to be peddling such a fear-based missive as a valid "news" story as I should have been, since this is the language of the mainstream beauty industry. And in my old magazine life, it was a language I'd become fluent in.

But it did make me depressed, not least since I had just turned thirty-five—my imminent descent into old hagdom also coinciding neatly with the introduction of a new social media tool called Instagram. It would be another three years until 2014 was officially declared the Year of the Selfie, but already you could feel the shift. If appearance had always mattered on some level, it was surely only a matter of time before image was everything.

Social media, and Instagram in particular, has created a culture in which we're hyperaware of how we look. It's a minute-by-minute rolling news channel inviting the opportunity to compare ourselves to others—what Brené Brown cites as one of the key drivers of our shame-ridden "never enough" society (never pretty enough, never thin enough, never cool enough).

Step number one in avoiding this comparison trap? Cultivate the awareness to recognize when it's happening. This is what your meditation practice is for. Also, learning to notice and act on the physical sensation that is your intuition telling you to "just put the iPhone away." Meaning, when you notice yourself obsessing over a feed that triggers feelings of anything less than self-appreciation and sacred sisterhood, UNFOLLOW (I've also been known to sage my phone if it gets really bad!). Which is easier said than done, since that "less than" feeling can actually be highly addictive.

Why? Every time we tell ourselves we're not pretty enough, not thin enough, or not cool enough to put ourselves out there, we're writing ourselves a permission slip to keep playing small; that is, to choose to ignore the awe-inspiring magnificence of our true nature and step down from venturing bravely forth *into the path of our dharma.*

## A NEW DEFINITION OF BEAUTY

Old media is based on (as in literally financially supported by) mainstream advertising, and so the representation of beauty we see in magazines must always conform to the Mad Men school of selling. Which basically boils down to: make people feel "less than," and then offer up the antidote. But the *great* thing about social media is that, used mindfully, it allows us to curate our own unique worldview—which also creates an opportunity for us to redefine what beauty looks like on our own terms.

Aesthetician and Reiki practitioner Rhea Horvath runs a company called Psychic Beauty and is dedicated to what she names "awakening (women's) ability to see the beauty in yourself and all things." And she thinks a huge shift is occurring around the perception of beauty, based largely on abolishing the idea that to be beautiful means to look a certain way.

Ask her about this, and it becomes clear that truly living this is deeply rooted in cultivating a connection to your spirit, higher Self, the Universe, and so on. "We know not every soul finds the same things beautiful. For example, the song that makes me cry may not move you at all, and the painting that I moon over for hours could bore you to tears," she says.

What about physical beauty? "When we dig in and embrace the aesthetics that truly inspire *us,* and also stop to acknowledge the pieces of the world that make us feel whole and connected (*the feeling which true beauty creates*), then we become willing to shine out as our own truly authentic Self, too, without fearing our individuality." In other words, without fearing that what makes us different will also make us weird and therefore unlovable.

But again, this can take a whole lot of discipline (see: unfollowing IG feeds that make you feel less than), and even more undoing of social conditioning. So DO NOT expect to read this and wake up tomorrow with a whole new appreciation for your wonky eyebrows and dimpled thighs. What you can do in the meantime, though, is keep cultivating practices that connect you again and again to your higher self, while being extremely choosy with the company you keep. Every relationship is *a mirror,* remember? And you have every right to surround yourself with people who reflect the most beautiful you.

## Beauty as Self-Love (a.k.a. Self-Awareness, Self-Acceptance, Self-Forgiveness)

It's important to acknowledge that redefining beauty doesn't automatically mean throwing out our favorite products with our vanilla-scented bathwater, or stopping wearing makeup altogether in the name of honoring our Goddess-given natural self (unless that's what's beautiful to you!). Rather, for me, it's about tweaking our beauty rituals so that we're primping and preening from a place of self-love and self-respect, as opposed to fear of not being good enough.

I once went for a series of "energetic facials" (meaning she did Reiki on me and had me hold quartz crystals during the treatment) with a wonderful woman named Maureen Dodd, and it was Maureen who helped me understand the difference between "vanity" and "narcissism." Yes, the dictionary definition of vanity is "excessive pride in one's appearance or achievements"—but Maureen also believes that vanity, stemming from a desire to present our most beautiful self to the world, is actually an act of *gratitude,* for our physical body, and for the gift of being alive. *An act of self-love.* Narcissism, on the other hand, is a fear-based obsession with being "the most beautiful of them all" (since "most beautiful" equals "most lovable").

Viewed this way, I believe our beauty practice and our spiritual practice can actually become interchangeable. And as always, it's about intention. Two of my favorite women walking the Now Age beauty talk are Cindy DiPrima and Kerrilynn Pamer of natural beauty apothecary

CAP Beauty. And Kerrilynn gave me a brilliant example of how she'd recently experienced this shift around using makeup: "In high school, I would use makeup to cover up what I saw as my imperfections," she says. "But using some of the products from our store the other day, I realized I was actually using them to highlight what I found beautiful about myself."

I think this was an example of Kerrilynn connecting to her *inner* self—or spirit—in the mirror, and using her beauty tools to *reveal more* of this divinely beautiful self. And she says this simple shift in perspective about putting on her morning "face" blew her mind. "Like, I used to be so hard on myself, and I wasn't even aware of it."

It's like physically, nothing changes. Your face is your face. But as they say, beauty is in the eye of the beholder (in this case, you). And the same way your best friend, or your child, or your lover could never be anything less than perfectly beautiful to you, I believe that cultivating the same unconditional love for your inner self is how you can begin to see your *outer* self as the very definition of beauty. After all—the times I think I look most beautiful? After a good sleep, after a good shag, and after a good cry, times it could be argued I have been most closely connected to my spirit.

As for the self-acceptance and self-forgiveness piece, yes, this has also meant accepting and forgiving my Material Girl self for using Botox as a quick fix. I may well be a perfectly beautiful creature of the cosmos, but when it comes to feeling vulnerable about getting older, I am still very much an earthly, *im*perfect human.

## Beauty Equals Vitality

At CAP meanwhile, Cindy and Kerrilynn define beauty thus: "Beauty is wellness, wellness is beauty." This means they are dedicated to furthering the philosophy that "beauty is actually taking such good care of yourself, and having such a good time doing it, that no matter what age you are, you always look like a really beautiful version of that age."

They framed it this way since we were talking about different approaches to aging at the time, but the same mind-set can be applied whether you're fifteen or fifty. In her book on veganism, *The Good Karma Diet,* Victoria Moran quotes from the business card of an acupuncturist she once visited, who promised "insightful care of the precious physical envelope and the spirit within." And I love this poetic description of well-being, which also speaks to a holistic approach to beauty.

And speaking of veganism, "we approach beauty a lot like diet," says Cindy, explaining how lots of the products they stock at CAP, both topical and ingestible, are often "really rich in healthful, nutrient-dense vitamins, minerals, antioxidants, and probiotics." Ironically, it's also Kerrilynn who reminds me that Botox, a drug made from the bacteria that causes botulism, is actually a "natural" product. But the new breed of *superbeauty* products (think *superfoods*) on sale in her store is designed to support other healthy lifestyle choices—lifestyle choices that are often rooted in wanting to look better on the outside, but which lead to a deeper connection to spirit by default. And which also look a lot like Marika Messager's shamanic self-care regime.

If they're honest about it, when most people give up eating sugar or dairy and begin with a dedicated exercise regime, nine times out of ten it's to address something they don't like about their physical appearance. The thing is, it often triggers a positive chain reaction in which the purging of toxins and the increase in happy endorphins create an overall feel-good factor on the *inside* that then contributes to you looking more radiant on the outside.

And that "feel-good factor"? I believe that's your spirit operating at optimum default settings, at a higher vibration, without having to fight its way through a toxic soup of processed food and *un*processed negative emotions. It's the vitality you were given a physical body to express. Seen this way, you could say "beauty" is your birthright.

## "WHAT DOES NOT LOOK GOOD IS STRESS"

Cindy and Kerrilynn, who I assume are around the same age as me, are a living, glowing testament to the philosophy of *beauty as self-care*. I first met them when they were in the very early planning stages for

---

# 5 NOW AGE
# BEAUTY BRANDS TO LOVE

BENSHEN. Handcrafted in Brooklyn, New York, Benshen founder Desiree Pais created the line based on the findings of her own healing journey—and following extensive studies with the big names in Chinese medicine, acupuncture, and Kundalini yoga.

JUICE BEAUTY. Most famous (to date) for a fab collab with Gwyneth Paltrow for Goop, who elected to work with the brand on her own line after she was stunned by the "efficiency" of these all-organic products.

NUCIFERA. At the time of writing this, this Venice Beach-based brand only has one product on the market—a do-it-all wonder balm named simply The Balm. You can use it everywhere—skin, feet, face, hair—and it's scented with palo santo, the patchouli for the Now Age.

SUN POTION. Beauty in the Now Age is as much about what you put in your face as what you slather on it, and the potions and powders from this "transformational foods" brand (think medicinal mushrooms and high-grade raw cacao) are all about that glow.

CEREMONIE. Straight outta Vancouver . . . it's skin care blessed by a shaman! And not only that, founder Mimi Young creates her formulas based on "suggestions" from her plant spirits, before her suppliers bless their raw ingredients too.

CAP, and a year after launching their brand, they both appear to have been aging backward.

Now I know from experience that choosing the entrepreneurial path is by no means a cakewalk. You're always "on," money is scarce, and there's no one else to blame when things go wrong. Anxiety and sleepless nights are a given. I believe the reason the CAP ladies look so good on their business/dharma path is because (a) they've got access to the most incredible "pantry" of next-generation high-vibe products and (b) taking better care of yourself becomes nonnegotiable once you begin doing your dharma.

It's no coincidence that Virgo, the sign governing diet and healthy habits, also rules over the ways in which we are of service. And just like a woman starts taking her vitamins and cleaning up her diet the minute she becomes pregnant, the responsibility that comes with birthing your soul project (whatever that might be) can *also* be the catalyst for making the kinds of positive, vitality-boosting lifestyle choices that just happen to enhance your physical radiance too.

And anyhow, consider this from Cindy: "I really believe that the people I know with the deepest meditation practice are winning the aging battle. Like, shockingly. What does not look good is stress." So from a beauty perspective? The job you hate, the soul-sapping relationship, the unresolved emotional issues with your mom—if it's making you feel like shit, chances are it's making you look like shit too.

## THE ART OF SACRED ADORNMENT

And YES, the mainstream beauty industry has come up with a plethora of products and procedures to act as a Band-Aid and make you look like a million dollars even when the circumstances of your life are crushing your spirit and dulling your vitality on the daily. They've even co-opted the language of self-love to sell them to us: *"because you're worth it."*

But like I said, just because you're doing the work of honoring your uniquely beautiful spirit, and are beginning to view your perfectly beautiful self through the lens of *true* self-worth, there's no reason not to have some fun with the beautifying tricks and tools that remain at our disposal. It brings me back to that idea of our beauty routine as an act of self-love, and vanity as an expression of gratitude for our "precious physical envelope." Which includes not judging the beauty choices we make.

Spiritual seduction expert Kitty Cavalier wrote a brilliant piece for The Numinous on the art of sacred adornment, citing how, for ancient civilizations, "ceremonial beauty rituals included things like bathing

## BEAUTY AS CEREMONY

Here are a few examples of how the chicest Now Age seekers I know are bringing a sense of ceremony to their beauty practice:

CHOOSING HIGH-VIBE NAIL ART TO CREATE A MINI-ALTAR WITH A MANICURE. The rule of thumb? Images and symbolism of what you want to *call in* go on the right hand; what you want to *release* goes on the left. For example, if you want to call in protection and good luck, how about getting a hamsa, a four-leaf clover, or a black cat painted on your right index finger? Having a hard time with your Saturn return? Then a depiction of the ringed planet could go on the left. But since symbolism is the language of the soul—be sure to pick imagery that resonates with YOU.

HAIR COLOR AS COLOR THERAPY. Whether you're going to get your roots done or are opting for an entire color overhaul, take the opportunity to *feel into* the transformative sensations this creates in your body and your life. Like, acknowledging the positive physical sensations that come with going peroxide blond—and actually using them to propel you forward on your path (à la Miley Cyrus, for example, whose infamous 2012 hair transformation opened up a whole new chapter in her soul journey).

RUNNING A RITUAL BATH. And filling it with salts and herbs, oils, flower essences, and crystals that have special significance to where you're at on your journey, and even choosing a mantra to recite while you soak.

for days, massaging oneself with fragranced oil and herbal salves, face painting, and ornamenting the entire body with glittering shells and earth gems." After all, she went on, "when the Gods themselves are your Friday night date, you'd better damn well get your glow on."

Meanwhile, Kitty had this to say about ritualizing your morning makeup routine: "As you line your eyes or mascara your lashes, remember you are drawing well-deserved attention to the portals of your soul. When you rouge your lips, be aware that you are bringing red, the color of passion and power, to every word you speak. As you paint your fingernails, remember that every stroke of the polish is a prayer of adornment for the magic your hands create every day."

Your mantra for creating a beauty practice that feeds your spirit and honors your unique journey? "Intention, intention, intention."

## GOING AU NATUREL

One of my favorite things about magazine land was the endless stream of beauty freebies. Being the recipient of a $170 jar of Crème de la Mer can make a girl's ego feel majorly special, after all (just like when Raj offered me the free Botox). I also loved to raid the "beauty cupboard," literally a whole room stacked with boxes of products we'd been sent in the hope they'd be featured, and would often go home with bulging bags of beauty booty.

In fact (how crazy is this!), one of my major fears about leaving *Style* was that the supply of free products would dry up—and there was no way I'd actually pay that kind of money for a cream, no matter how seductive the antiaging/life-transforming message. Deep down, this was because I knew they didn't really work anyway. But still, the myth of mainstream beauty was so deeply rooted in my psyche that before my move to New York, I panic-stockpiled and lugged what was probably thousands of dollars' worth of products across the Atlantic with me.

But slowly, I found myself throwing a lot of them away. And this was mainly because I began paying as much attention to the part of the label that listed the ingredients as the part selling the "miraculous" beauty claims.

Let's go back to what Cindy said about the correlation between beauty and diet. The same way cultivating a more mindful approach to food *automatically* leads to you giving a shit about what's in the food you're eating, becoming more aware of what you're putting *in* your body also makes you more aware of what you're slathering *on* it. Moreover, cleaning up your diet often means you "need" fewer products like concealer, foundation, and blush anyway!

As Cindy points out: "You read all these celebrity profiles where by 10 A.M. there's been meditation, green juice, a private yoga session, all these wellness-driven things. And then you get to the bathroom, and it gets really out of sync with all the things this person is doing to support their inner being."

Thing is, until only recently, "natural" beauty products just couldn't and didn't cut it in the performance stakes—and when I talk about "performance," I really mean they didn't smell, feel, and look as good as mainstream luxury products. Though I truly believe that a lot of why these products appear to "work" is a perception game, often fueled by the advertising message, the lack of certain chemicals in the natural alternatives *did* lead to inconsistencies in quality and application.

But YAY, times they are a-changing, and companies like CAP are leading the charge in showcasing the equally seductive array of beautiful, aspirational products and brands that are beginning to fill out the natural beauty space. And slowly but surely, these products have crowded out my mainstream beauty faves.

Slowly because, yes, the good stuff is expensive! There's no way I could afford to revamp my entire bathroom cabinet overnight. But the brands I covet now are expensive because you're often talking about small batches of handmade products, using only the highest-vibe ingredients—versus expensive because the company has a lab full of white-coated scientists and a billion-dollar celebrity-fronted ad campaign to fund. And often all in the name of selling you the "antiaging" dream.

# A RITUAL BATH FOR BEAUTY
# BY DEBORAH HANEKAMP

In esoteric spiritual practices all over the world, bath rituals are used as a way to unify with the sacred waters for detoxification, regeneration, clarity, and blessing. As we bathe we are taking a moment to reflect, set intention, and wash away old habits and patterns that no longer serve our highest good, all while making our skin sing from the inside out!

I learned about healing ritual baths from the native women of the Peruvian Amazon while apprenticing there. These women use baths to heal almost any spiritual, emotional, mental, or physical illness. From receiving these baths myself, I experienced complete inner balance and as a result began to feel more beautiful on the outside.

My studies in the Amazon, combined with my experience with herbal medicine, yoga, crystals, and sound healing, have since led me to develop my own ritual baths—like this one, for inner and outer radiance. I recommend practicing this ritual once a week, as a way to honor yourself and your own unique beauty.

## For Your Altar

Make a small altar near the tub. Include a candle, a rose quartz crystal, a flower, and any other personal power items that represent beauty and truth to you.

## For Your Bath

- Pink Himalayan salt 2 cups

- Red wine 1 cup

- Calendula flowers (dried) 2 cups

- Pink rose petals (fresh or dried) 2 cups

- Oatstraw

- Cacao powder 1 cup

- Rose quartz crystal

- A carton of milk (I prefer raw goat's milk, but hemp or any other will work)

For Your Ritual

• Raw local honey

• Cinnamon stick

• Selenite wand

Method

• Set up your altar.

• Run a tub of hot water, and throw all the bath ingredients in.

• Cover yourself head to toe in the raw local honey—you can even get the honey in your hair!

• Light a cinnamon stick with the flame from the candle from your altar, and burn it around your entire body, including under the soles of the feet.

• As you stand there naked, covered in honey and scented with cinnamon, take a moment to ask yourself if you are holding any outdated, untrue, and unkind beliefs about your appearance. Check to see where your current level of self-worth is.

• Clean your aura with the selenite wand.

• Look into your own eyes and ask your self if there are any truths she'd like to share.

• After letting the honey set into the skin for seven minutes, step into the bath.

• Practice Kapalabhati (shining skull breath) by exhaling from the nostrils, inhaling three-fourths of capacity, and then making at least eight quick, sharp forceful exhales through the nose. Repeat three times.

• Repeat the mantra "I can feel the light in me, I'm gonna set my spirit free" at least three times.

• Now close your eyes, and soak in the powerful energy you have created.

• When you are done with the bath, blow out the candle on the altar to signify the closing of the ritual.

## A FINAL WORD ON OUR FEAR OF AGING

That word: "Antiaging." Flicking through a magazine recently, it struck me just how ridiculous this concept is. Every living organism gets older—and so surely to be "anti" this process is to be anti life itself! But I might as well come right out with it. Despite having integrated all the above into my beauty regime, yes, I still, on occasion, get Botox. Call me a hypocrite if you like, but as I said at the beginning of this chapter, bridging the inner versus outer beauty divide is a major work in progress for me.

For example, by the time this book comes out I'll be forty—and you should hear my ego freaking *out* about it! Not least since it's the first time I'm putting myself out there in a majorly *visible* way. Fortunately, my higher Self interrupts my ego's tantrum, like: *Whoa, sister. This isn't about your freaking author photo, it's about the message!* One step forward. Then my ego chips in again: *Totally. And thank fuck for Photoshop.* Two steps back.

When I was deciding whether or not to have Botox again after my disastrous first attempt, I had lengthy conversations on the subject with Maureen, my energetic aesthetician. Her overall philosophy? "The whole Botox question becomes so silly when we realize there's a way of seeing ourselves (as energetic beings) where we don't even notice the little lines. Honest to God, what is wrong with us? Maybe it's actually a calling to a higher level of consciousness . . ." And maybe I'm not quite there yet . . . and maybe that's also TOTALLY okay.

If getting Botox is ultimately about striving for an unattainable mirage of "perfection"—then isn't beating ourselves up for "succumbing" to its allure actually stemming from the same place? Like, if I was a "perfectly" spiritual person, I would be able to transcend the desire to "fix" my face. If Botox had existed in Cleopatra's day, I have no doubt she'd have been doing it. And anyhow, the more I've learned to love, appreciate, and operate in honor of my internal self, the more and more I'm aware how the physical stuff is all just cosmetic. Meaning, my choice to have Botox feels like it has very little bearing on who I am on the inside.

But on a deeper level, our conversation also got me thinking about why we're so fearful of aging in the first place. It's obvious, as Maureen says, that "fear of aging is because most people are afraid of getting sick and dying." But to get a little more numinous on this subject, perhaps this is rooted in the fear that our time will be up before we've found and lived our true calling. In other words, before our soul has fulfilled its karmic mission in this lifetime.

Think about it. At the other end of the line, babies are *so* perfect and *so* beautiful to us because they represent the unlimited potential we're all born with. The *innocence* of our faith in this potential. And, as this faith becomes diminished with every setback and put-down and with every year that passes, as demarcated by the lines that appear on our face, what if this creates a sense of time running out on our highest hopes and aspirations *at soul level*.

What if the antiaging creams, the Botox, and the facelifts are all just signs we wish we could suspend the passing of time and buy ourselves a little longer to get back to that innocent faith in our potential and our journey. My message for you if this is the case? DO NOT WAIT ANOTHER MINUTE to begin reimagining your life in line with the instructions of your highest Self. And also, with this intention *firmly* in place, do what the hell you like to look and feel your best while you're at it.

# 14.

# GET YOUR ROCKS ON: CRYSTALS AS WEARABLE HEALING

Chatting to Kerrilynn at CAP Beauty about different healing modalities once, she mentioned that flower essences—tinctures formulated with the energetic imprint of different flowers—required the biggest leap of faith for her. And, well, for me that honor had always gone to crystals.

The flowers I could get my head around—mainly, I think, since they're ingestible. And even if it was the placebo effect at work, I'd also experienced tangible results firsthand from using them. Then with Reiki, for example, there was a laying on of "healing hands." With acupuncture, I could feel the energy zinging through my body, and it was the all-over body chills that told me a healing gong bath was having a physical effect.

Even something as seemingly abstract as astrology made sense to me through the lens of psychoanalysis, plus, as I mentioned, the way the tides (not to mention women's menstrual cycles) move with the

Moon seemed like "proof" enough that life on Earth is linked to the movements of the celestial bodies. But crystals? How could being in close proximity to an inanimate object that just happened to look pretty have any kind of healing effect?

As I wandered further down my numinous path, however, it became evident that crystals played a very special role in the healing arsenal of

# CRYSTALS: A STARTER KIT

QUARTZ. The most diverse stone in the crystal kingdom, quartz appears in many variations and is known to be a potent conductor of energy. For this reason it is known as the "master healer," and clear quartz can be used to amplify any healing intention it's programmed with.

ROSE QUARTZ. The "love" stone—amplifies compassion, peace, tenderness, nurturing, and comfort. Can be used for attracting new love and repairing existing relationships.

SMOKY QUARTZ. The "survival" stone—facilitates connection to the energies of the natural world, cultivating stability and grounding.

BLACK TOURMALINE. A.k.a. "the protection stone," black tourmaline is said to offer a psychic shield against negative energy, while also guarding against environmental pollutants. It also aids in transmuting negative thoughts to positive intentions, an essential for modern city dwellers.

CITRINE. A stone of manifestation and success, citrine amplifies creativity and imagination, while helping cultivate the personal will it takes to make our hopes and dreams a physical reality.

AMETHYST. Once classified a "precious" stone, along with diamonds, emeralds, sapphires, and rubies, amethyst is known for its calming properties, helping soothe the mind and the emotions. For this reason, it's also known as the "sobriety" stone—since it helps quell addictive compulsions (e.g., for booze, food, shopping, boys).

most modern mystics. On the Material Girl side of the coin, meanwhile, a hip new breed of crystal enthusiasts was also creating some seriously badass jewelry collections using these ancient, mysterious rocks. And so I decided to investigate further.

Cut to the afternoon I spent at "crystal school," an in-depth intro to the healing stones led by Luke Simon, healer and cofounder of Maha Rose Center for the Healing Arts (not to mention, without doubt, a direct descendant of the pixie kingdom). Class would cover how crystals were formed, theories about their healing properties, an introduction to the different stones, and how to use and care for them. Time permitting, we'd also have the opportunity to practice mini crystal healing sessions on one another.

Luke kicked off the session by telling us: "I started working with crystals when I first moved to New York and realized I needed some serious juju to wear ON my body." As in, being plunged into the swirling energetic soup that is New York City, he felt in need of some *talismans* to keep about his person—symbolic items that were the physical embodiment of his connection to his intentions, to his inner strength, and to his higher Self (spirit, God, the Universe, etc.). It was this moment, when Luke explained the origin of his journey with crystals, that their role in our modern mystical lives really clicked for me.

Perhaps the reason his story resonated so strongly was because I'd had a similar experience myself. Like him, my own move to New York had felt like the emotional and energetic equivalent to being shot out of the ejector seat in the Batmobile. But as chance would have it, that first vermin-infested apartment in Manhattan's West Village was right up the street from Stick, Stone and Bone, one of the city's most beloved esoteric supplies stores.

Investigating my new 'hood and with my idea for The Numinous beginning to take shape in my mind, I'd often find myself there, perusing the incense and smudge sticks and oracle decks. And then there were the crystals, arranged on shelves and piled in little dishes, with handwritten cards listing their "magical" healing properties. I still didn't really see the point in just having loose stones rolling around my desk or in my bag, but I *was* drawn to the rings made of tiger's eye and black tourmaline that sat on the counter by the register—both of which promised grounding, protection, and relief from anxiety.

Well, I ended up wearing those rings all summer, the same summer I was doing the crazy commute between New York and Ibiza, and in need of some serious . . . grounding, protection, and relief from anxiety. Who knew if they'd "work," I thought, but what did I have to lose? Just seeing them every day became a visual reminder that on some level *I was willing to believe the Universe had got my back.* They had become *my* talismans.

But weirdly, the rings kept breaking. Like suddenly, they'd just snap in half and fall off my finger for no apparent reason. I freaked out a little bit every time this happened, and one time when I was in Stick, Stone and Bone buying yet another replacement, I finally asked the girl behind the register what was up. She told me: "Oh, they must be working too hard. You need to remember to charge them."

Whoa . . . what? Charge them like . . . my phone? Well, yes, actually, which we'll get into a little later on. But since I'd definitely been navigating one of the least grounded, most vulnerable, and most anxiety-inducing periods of my life, her theory made total sense to me. Those babies had undoubtedly been working *overtime*.

It's safe to say that I was going from crystal curious to becoming a bona fide convert. That fall I bought a few actual stones I just felt drawn to, which I lined up on the windowsills of my funny little apartment and which seemed to bring a sense of calm and lightness to the space. And then there were the new designers I kept discovering, who were producing some seriously covetable crystal creations. My protection rings were one thing: simple bands of polished stone. Now I found myself lusting over chic, sophisticated pieces that ran into the thousands of dollars. When it came to how the crystals actually "worked," however, I still didn't have a clue.

## FORM AND FUNCTION

Because I want to get into the fun stuff about how to choose, use, and care for your crystals, I'll keep the science part fairly brief, but I am going to include it, since (a) I felt like *I* needed it so I'm assuming you will too, and (b) it's actually kind of fascinating. (N.B. And I should probably preface this section by adding that the following information is based on conversations with the Numinati, and not the result of extensive scientific research on my part.)

Essentially, crystals grow from molten rock, or magma, and are formed over millions of years as the magma cools and solidifies. Different chemical compounds in the magma are what create different types of crystals. But what makes all crystals so special (including what we know as the "precious" stones)   and what is also the key to their healing properties—is that unlike other rocks, the atomic particles in crystals form intricate and perfectly symmetrical shapes. And, like plants, they only stop growing once they've been cut out of the earth. Not such inanimate objects after all.

Let me hand over the reins here to my friend Victoria Keen, my favorite witchy science geek. VK makes her own line of high-vibrational yoga clothing and also practices a form of sound healing known as "biofield tuning," which is based on the theory that our physical body is surrounded by a biomagnetic field of energy (which you may also have heard described as the "aura"). Victoria believes that perfect "health" is the unencumbered flow of this energy, which in turn helps the particles of our aura or "energetic blueprint" retain their own perfectly symmetrical pattern, *similar to the patterns found in the structures of crystals*. Disease, on the other hand, is the result of blockages in our energetic flow leading to these particle structures becoming compromised and scattered.

In her medicine practice, Victoria manipulates sound waves (also uniquely and perfectly structured at an atomic level) in order to adjust the biofield and return the energetic blueprint to a state of symmetry and coherence. This is because: "According to what's called the *law of entrainment* in physics, the structure with the more overall coherent pattern—and thus a higher vibration—will bring what is of a lower and less coherent vibration into its pattern," she explains. And she believes that crystals work in a similar way, the theory being that when we're in close proximity to crystals, any kinks (due to past emotional traumas, say) in our biofield will *entrain* to the perfect symmetry of the stones.

Which is right about where my brain begins to ache. But it's actually the same theory behind all "vibrational" healing, which includes homeopathy and flower essences—and if you're interested in diving deeper into the subject, Victoria can never rave enough about a book called *The Holographic Universe,* which she says breaks it all down beautifully.

## CHOOSING THE STONES FOR YOU

For now, though, let's talk about how to shop for some beautiful rocks! As well as how to use and wear them to maximize their healing potential.

The general rule of thumb is to allow your crystals to find you. "FEEL it out," says Victoria. "What you are immediately drawn to is most likely what you need in your life at that moment. Then close your eyes and hold the crystal, (using) your nondominant hand to feel the subtle vibrations of the stone more clearly. Is it warm, cool, tingly? Does it bring you an 'up' or 'down' sensation?" she asks.

Here's an example of how this might also work "in reverse." Say you go shopping for a piece of rose quartz, widely recognized as "the love stone," since you're having a hard time attracting the kind of relationship you want. But there you are in the store, and all you can do is gaze longingly at the rainbow hues of a hunk of chalcopyrite (a.k.a. peacock ore).

Well, the peacock stone is said to release stagnant energy and soothe the pain of old wounds, so perhaps the *real* reason you're still single is that you've got some more work to do getting over an ex—and the chalcopyrite is letting you know it's here to help with that.

Likewise, as Luke pointed out at crystal school, "if you feel repelled by a certain stone, it could be an invitation to look at anything you might be deliberately avoiding in your life." For example, I used to think amethyst was really "boring" and be put off by the woo-woo purple color. Um, think this might have had something to do with it being known as "the sobriety stone"? As my feelings about drinking less alcohol have shifted (i.e., that far from boring, this is actually key to a fully intentional, connected, and creative life), so have my feelings about the stone—and who knows if it's a coincidence, but since investing in a gorgeous amethyst cluster for my nightstand I've found myself more and more appreciative of what I have even come to term "high sobriety!"

Meanwhile, being repeatedly drawn to the same stones is an indication you may have worked with them in a past life.

In my experience, another reason to just go with your gut is that it can be really hard to remember the properties of all the different stones—the lists are often extensive, and there can be lots of overlap. It's also way more fun to select your stone first and *then* look up the meanings, since there'll likely be an element of serendipity in your choice.

Like what happened to Jill Urwin, a London-based designer who makes some of my favorite crystal pieces. When she left her job as a fashion buyer to start her own line, the first stone she was drawn to was a smoky quartz: "I was going purely for aesthetics, but I discovered later on that it's a root chakra stone and activates your survival instincts—perfect for starting and running your own business!" she told me.

She wears smoky quartz to this day, along with regular clear quartz and an especially rare form of quartz called a "Herkimer diamond"—named for the place they're mined in upstate New York, and which grow already perfectly faceted by nature with a symmetry that can't be replicated by man ("which makes them more precious than diamonds in my mind," says Jill). And as luck / the Universe would have it, Jill's favorite stones also suit her personal style to a tee.

As for me? I've always been a bit of a "magpie," and I tend to go for anything gold and shiny. Pyrite (for action, vitality, and will), gold stone (the stone of ambition), and citrine (the "success" stone) are some of my favorites—a lineup that's also befitting all the Aries and Sagittarius fire in my astrology chart. And then, of course, there's *ruby* . . . my namesake stone. Strangely, I never felt drawn to it until very recently, but when the Pisces offered to buy me a piece of jewelry this past Christmas, the delicate ring with the tiny, rich pink ruby from Brooklyn's Dirty Hands Jewelry was really the only choice.

And looking up the properties of my ruby, it makes sense that it's come into my life now. Ruby is POWERFUL. Ruby is a regal, root chakra rock, the stone of kings and queens. Crystalvaults.com (a great resource for stones and their meanings) describes its properties and powers as promoting "a clear mind, increased concentration and motivation" and bringing "a sense of power to the wearer, a self-confidence and determination that overcomes timidity and propels one toward prosperity and achievement." Wow!

Exactly the energy I needed to write this book. Also, my namesake stone carries the kind of *leadership* vibes I've shied away from my whole life—but which creating The Numinous, and the sense of coming into my own *wholeness* that I've experienced as a result, has helped me acknowledge and step into as part of my dharma. In fact, I can hardly believe I even just wrote that! My ruby must be working hard today.

## WHY EVERYONE NEEDS A TALISMAN

In short, my ruby is my current favorite talisman—what Kirstie Gibbs, a former jewelry buyer for Harrods department store in London and founder of high-vibe crystal line The Alkemistry, describes as "worn treasures used for a higher purpose and energetic attraction."

In a piece for The Numinous, she wrote: "In our world of over-stimulation I believe it's even more important that we stay tuned in to our own purpose and carry a personal, sacred object of our choosing," going on to add that "when a woman wears her own talisman she charges herself with the energy of what she wants to attract and/or harness, be that protection, a successful date, or a flow of creative ideas in her work life." To which I could only respond with a resounding (virtual) high five.

Thinking about it, for many of us our smartphones seem to have taken the place of traditional talismans—shiny objects we keep on or about our person at all times, which we often decorate to make more beautiful. Our phones are where we keep apps to track our projects, our pilgrimages, our social life, even our periods. They're how we access social media, and are a tool to record our ideas, hopes, and desires. As for offering us protection? I'm surely not the only one who feels less "safe" if I accidentally leave the house for an appointment and forget to bring my phone. And with the advent of wearable tech, we're only being encouraged to merge our lives more intimately with our machines.

So how about investing in some *wearable healing* in the form of crystals instead—talismans to charge up your connection to your higher Self (spirit, God, the Universe, etc.), and to the planet that birthed these mystical rocks?

Jill Urwin told me that when she created her line, "having worked as a buyer in fast fashion, where everything felt so disposable, I felt compelled to create pieces with meaning." And for me this speaks to what Luke Simon describes as crystals embodying "the Tinker Bell effect": the fact that using crystals is also an invitation to *believe,* in ourselves, in our journey, and in the all-loving oneness of our Universe. The same way Peter Pan only believed he could fly once he'd been doused in fairy (a.k.a. crystal) dust—or "star stuff," as J. M. Barrie called it in his original story (which, by the way, was published in 1904, seventy years before cosmologist Carl Sagan's famous quote: "We are all made of star stuff").

As Victoria Keen puts it, "intention is everything" when working with crystals, since *our thoughts carry their own vibration too*. In this respect, it also becomes possible to "program" our crystal talismans with our own sense of meaning and purpose—which we're naturally inclined to do with our most special pieces of jewelry anyway, a traditional diamond engagement ring being a classic case in point.

## WHERE TO WEAR YOUR CRYSTALS

So having said all that about not liking having loose stones just rolling around . . . I have loose stones rolling around *everywhere*. My desk, my different bags, my altar, my nightstand . . . which I am actually seeking to address by investing in a special shelf for them in my home office. It's time I started treating them with a little more respect!

But the more I'm delving into my crystal studies—and the more my numinous path sensitizes me to their subtle healing energies—the more I feel called to wear them on my person. Not to mention the fact that, as I mentioned, crystal jewelry has become a whole different beast in recent years.

Some of my favorite designers totally rocking it right now, and which you might wanna check out, are Jill Urwin; Unearthern; The Alkemistry; Rock & Raw; Vega Jewelry; Communion by Joy; Jacquie Aiche; Pound Jewelry; and it-girl Audrey Kitching's line Crystal Cactus.

Chatting to Jill, I got to thinking about how different types of jewelry are also designed to place your crystals near the different chakras—worth taking into account when picking your piece. Like a pendant necklace will totally line your stone up with your heart chakra, a choker the throat, and a belly chain or stud your solar plexus. Which led me to consider the origins, say, of the classical "diamond tiara," beloved of fairy princesses, Victoria's Secret stylists, and royalty throughout history. Any coincidence, d'you think, that the diamond is said to be a symbol of perfection and illumination—activating the *crown* and etheric (third eye) chakras when worn this way?

Speaking of being a bit of a magpie, not to mention princesses, I became kind of obsessed with the crown jewels—a collection of high-bling ceremonial pieces belonging to the British royal family—after we went on a school trip to visit them as a kid. And having looked up the pieces again while writing this, almost every crown boasts a GIGANTIC (like 300+ carats) diamond right in the center of the forehead—or above the third eye. It seems like one of the most powerful families in the history of modern civilization was *very* well aware of the diamond's ability to enhance the powers of perception—and how to use this to their advantage. Um, hello #illuminati conspiracy theories. But seriously—google "British crown jewels" and tell me these are not ancient pieces of technology designed for accessing higher planes of consciousness/communication with life on other planets!

And when it comes to activating your chakras, you can also choose stones based on their color correspondence with particular chakras: for example, ruby for the root, citrine for the sacral, gold stone for the solar plexus, emerald for the heart, turquoise for the throat, sapphire for the third eye, and amethyst for the crown.

In Vedic astrology, meanwhile, different fingers relate to the different planets and elements—useful when choosing which finger to wear a ring. Although, again, your crystal will likely have its own ideas about this.

Many of the jewelers I mentioned above also make custom pieces, so you can always have your favorite stone set into your talisman of choice. Victoria Keen even sewed subtle pieces of citrine into a beautiful custom scarf she made me once, but you can also go way more low-fi with it. I love the little leather pouches you can buy for carrying crystals around your neck, and a quick straw poll of my Instagram tribe revealed the bra as a particularly popular place to stash stones! Totally up to you how you explain this to your next Tinder date.

## MORE WAYS TO WORK WITH YOUR STONES

Beyond wearing or simply keeping your stones in close proximity, there are all kinds of other ways to tap their healing energies.

### In a Tincture

Like flower essences, gem essences are formulated as a way of ingesting the vibrational properties of different stones, and it's actually pretty simple to make your own. Look for "recipes" online and use them as spritzes and add a few drops to your bathwater. You can also buy a special water bottle designed to safely charge your drinking water with your crystal tinctures. **(Beware: not all crystals are ingestible).**

### In a Healing Session

Laying crystals directly on the skin—called a "layout"—is the best way to maximize their healing potential, and they can be placed on the body during treatments such as Reiki or sound healing. Consult with your therapist first, but you could bring to your session a stone you feel particularly connected to. Or maybe your massage therapist can even incorporate the stones into your next treatment? Don't be shy about experimenting with this technique at home too—as always, be mindful with your intentions and allow yourself to be guided by your intuition. And it's worth adding that smooth stones are most comfortable for using directly on the skin!

### In a Crystal Grid

Luke Simon describes crystal "grids"—where you place several stones in a geometric pattern, on an altar, for example—as "like a recipe for merging the properties of different stones to heal on a more potent level." For example, placing quartz in a grid with black tourmaline, the quartz will amplify the protective properties of the tourmaline. Again, use your intuition about what stones to use in your grid. Victoria sometimes creates grids to place under the treatment table during a sound healing session and creates her own grids for her altar at home. "They're a way to really focus my intention and energy around a particular issue or desire," she says, adding, "I also like to light a new candle with each grid, as when it's burned down, which could be over a period of weeks, I will disassemble the grid and work with a new intention."

### During Meditation

Any stones can be used during meditation (just hold them loosely in your hand while you meditate), but blue, purple, and clear crystals, relating to the third eye and crown chakras, are said to be most effective in helping clear the mind and access higher states of consciousness.

You can select a stone that relates to a particular concern and program it with a specific intention before you sit. "I've experimented with meditating with many different stones, and it's interesting to feel how different each one feels when you're in the zone," says Victoria Keen. "I've had them pulsate in my hand, get tingly and warm, and felt a flow of energy come from them."

### In a Ritual Bath

My friend Deborah Hanekamp is the queen of the "ritual bath," and her "recipes" for these baths (like the one on page 220) always include a crystal or two, along with different herbs, salts, and mantras. Since water entrains (remember?) very quickly to the perfect symmetry of crystals, it acts as a conductor for their energy. Again, you can use your intuition to experiment with this technique yourself, remembering as always to set a clear intention first. And also keep in mind that some crystals don't do so well in water. If in doubt, you can put them in a clear glass jar and take that into the bath with you instead.

### Keep a Crystal Journal

I love this suggestion from Luke Simon—the idea of charting your progress over a period of time when working with a specific stone. Useful, since this is some *subtle* healing, people, and the "results" may not be immediately obvious. But guess what, since written words have their own vibration too, the more you can *crystallize* (so to speak) your intention for your healing journey with the stones, the better.

## CARING FOR YOUR CRYSTALS

So now you've selected your stones and begun incorporating them into your wardrobe and your life; please remember that since these are *not such inanimate objects,* their vibrational nature means they're constantly interacting with the energy around them. As such, you'll obviously want to cleanse them of any low-vibe nastiness they may have sucked up along the way.

There are various different ways to do this, such as:

- Smudging them with the smoke from burning sage or other cleansing herbs, such as palo santo, cedar leaves, sweetgrass, or lavender (try imagining the smoke as water).

- Submerging them in natural spring water (unless they're a kind that dissolves in water—check online), anywhere from one to twenty-four hours.

- Burying them in salt (for more intense cleansing), for several hours, overnight, or up to a few days.

- Burying them in earth, either outdoors (remembering to place a marker in the ground!) or in a plant pot, for three days to one week.

Because of the programmable nature of both water and crystals, Jill Urwin says it's also safe to cleanse them under the tap—so long as you do so with a superstrong intention.

As I discovered with my tourmaline and tiger's eye crystal rings, it's also important to *charge* any crystals that have been working over-time—or any time your stones begin to look or feel "dull" to you. You can do this by placing them in direct sun or moonlight, for anything from a couple of hours to overnight.

And as your collection develops, Luke has one final thing to add: "never have more crystals than you have time to love." So how, as he puts it, to "close the chapter" with a particular stone, if and when you feel like your work together is done?

One way is to return them to nature. "When crystals break, when what they were programmed for has come to manifestation, or when you are called to let them go, returning them to the wild is a charged ritual in itself. It feels like putting stars back into the sky," he says. He suggests leaving them in the nook of a tree, or burying them, but adds,

"It also feels beautiful for them to just be in silence, at the base of a river or ocean."

The other option is to simply give them away, he says. "If you intuitively feel you are meant to gift them to others, listen! Receiving crystals in this way is so fun too, when a friend says, 'This called to me and wants to be with you.'"

And so I rest my case. Crystal healing might win my "most numinous, verging on the totally woo-woo" award, but as time goes by I'm becoming more convinced the stones have a consciousness of their own. Or perhaps I'm just more willing to believe. Are you feeling the Tinker Bell effect yet?

# PART V

# PEOPLE
# & PARTIES

# 15

# HEALING IS
# THE NEW NIGHTLIFE

I signed up for the breathwork session because my friend Sophie said it was the best natural high of her life.

It's a Friday night in Williamsburg, Brooklyn—epicenter of New York's hipster music scene, and land of the ironic dive bar—and I'm sobbing my heart and soul out in a tepee in Havemeyer Park, the location for a summer series of high-vibe healing events and workshops. Breathwork is an active pranayama meditation designed to quickly move any stagnant or heavy energy out of the body—and "a super-fast way to emotionally detox," as Erin Telford, the facilitator, put it. What this looks like is me on my back on a blanket, pinned to the floor as if by some cosmic force, my whole body convulsing as the tears just come, and come, and come (in future breathwork scenarios, I have been known to refer to this phenomenon as a "multiple cry-gasm").

The lights are dim, and Björk's "Big Time Sensuality" is being pumped into the air on a cloud of sage and sweetgrass, mingling with wails, whoops, and even what sounds like hysterical laughter. By now the group, about twenty of us, have been maintaining a fairly fast three-part breath into the abdomen, up to the heart chakra, and out through the mouth for I don't exactly know how long. In my altered state, time is an abstract concept.

My eyes are closed, and at one point, I feel my forehead being anointed with some kind of oil or tincture. Somebody places a crystal into each of my upturned palms, which have cramped up into what feel like hard little claws. In fact, the physical sensations I'm experiencing—overall tingles, a kind of underwater pressure on my limbs—are overwhelming. It's like being on that fairground ride, when the floor drops away twenty feet in the air and somehow you remain pinned to the wall, spinning to what should be your death but what actually feels like flying.

But just as I think I might either internally combust or begin to levitate over the Williamsburg Bridge, Erin instructs us to slow down our breathing. The music becomes an ambient soundscape, and the buzzing in my bones begins to settle. By the time we're breathing normally again, I feel a deep sense of calm begin to trickle through my body. I let out a giggle, the tears still damp on my face.

Okay, so WTF just happened? When I push myself into a seated position, it feels as though my body is made of bubbles and my head wants to float off into the cosmos. It's also like I'm connected by a golden thread of pure love and compassion to each and every person in that tepee, and I can tell from the curious smile making its way around the circle like people doing the wave at a stadium that I'm not the only one.

Erin then invites us to begin an openhearted sharing of our experiences, which range from simple feelings of physical release, to processing deep-seated memories and realizations about ourselves and our lives that surfaced during the breathing. Some people have a hard time even articulating what went down for them, since the connection between their brain and what's coming out of their mouth appears to have been warped. A bit like after three tequila shots, but without the slurring.

When it comes to my turn, I say something like, "Is everybody else as high as me right now?" Because every cell of my body feels buoyantly awake and full of love, which is translating into a strong desire to hug everyone and share with them the most intimate details of my emotional life. Erin explains that this is because the breathwork raises your vibration so high, your aura extends three feet out of your body in every direction.

Floating home through the streets of Williamsburg later, the streetlights seem extra bright as I take in the Friday night bar scene spilling out into the night. The sultry summer air is laced with cigarette smoke and gossip. Later, no doubt, there will be declarations of love, hysterical laughter, and tears. Followed by the inevitable morning-after questioning if any of it was real, while simultaneously popping painkillers and carb-loading to fill the emotional void the vodka left behind.

Of which, of course, I speak from many, many years' experience.

And yes, my all natural, 100 percent organic breathwork high felt more sustainable and had a more positive impact on my life going forward than the vast majority of factory-processed substance highs I've experienced in my life.

An observation I most definitely do NOT make from a position of any kind of moral superiority, by the way.

What I'm not here to do is be the judge of how anyone spends their Friday nights—or any night of the week they might be seeking some kind of emotional release, a different perspective on their current situation, or a feeling of connection to others, for that matter. Rather, the simple truth I would like to share in this chapter is that my numinous journey has introduced me to oh-so-many alternative ways to experience all of the above—without the hangover. From healing circles, to Moon rituals, ceremonial dance parties, and sober raves, socializing with positive intention and conscious awareness *as the focus* has altered forever the way I see my social life.

I think Brooklyn yoga teacher Amanda Capobianco coined it best, when she began using #healingisthenewnightlife.

Allow me to explain . . .

## DUTCH COURAGE VERSUS DIVINE COURAGE

At a recent numerology reading, the dude calculating my numbers declared, "Aha, a popular loner." In other words, I'm what I like to refer to as an extroverted introvert; I like people, a lot, but I tend to get really overwhelmed and tongue-tied in situations where there are lots of people to interface with at once. Like, let's say, parties.

In fact, I actively dislike parties. They are perfect for certain personality types (like extroverted extroverts), and really kind of difficult for intense communicators like me. And yet parties by their very definition are the default, socially accepted way humans celebrate life and one another, regardless of whether "partying" comes naturally to us.

I didn't do a lot of teenage partying, since choosing the Capricorn meant smoking copious amounts of weed, and spending most of my nights counting calories and obsessing over my thigh gap. I also abstained completely from alcohol while we were together, since he was one of those stoners who likened it to the devil's brew. But in the end it was booze that gave me the Dutch courage to finally leave him. Namely, some very strong cocktails on a girls' holiday to Greece that danced me into bed with a tall, dark stranger. Exactly the confidence boost I needed (plus the fact I'd just graduated from college with a kick-ass degree) to finally walk.

So right off the bat alcohol represented *freedom* to me, and I spent the next six months high on life, as well as making up some serious lost time in the tequila-slamming stakes. And then I met the Pisces. A party promoter. And who knew, with a by-now trusty cocktail in my hand, parties became my favorite thing *ever*. I even went on to promote my own club nights and would spend all my summers in Ibiza, party capital of Europe. Talk about a 360 turnaround!

So what was the problem with parties that alcohol solved for me? Buzzed on booze, I basically forgot that "I can't do small talk" and discovered it was okay to just, y'know, talk. To say whatever was on my mind, and to stop assuming I was being judged for whatever came out of my mouth (or judging myself for whatever came out of my mouth). It also made the small talk feel more important, and there's nothing I hate more than wasted words (with my Mercury in Aries, what can I say except please let's be direct).

And the popularity of alcohol at parties suggests that I'm by no means the only one who feels this way. Maybe *none of us* can really do small talk, and perhaps we're *all* petrified of putting our foot in our mouth or telling a joke that nobody laughs at. What if we're all extroverted introverts (or introverted extroverts), all craving social acceptance and with a need to feel connected to others, but with too few occasions to do so in which we feel safe as our authentic, sober (as in not-drunk but also as in serious) self?

Yes, there are many times when a dose of "truth serum" can be useful to fast-forward through the getting-to-know-you part and into the sharing-my-life-story good stuff. But in my experience the window of opportunity for this is pitifully small, and before you know it you've veered into not so high-vibe territory. Let's get real—what comes out while under the influence generally cannot be trusted (or remembered in much detail, for that matter). Cue drunken bust-ups with your beloved, bouts of pinot-fueled psychosis, and morning-after texting shame.

So it's safe to say I've fallen out of love with booze again. I've just become way too familiar with the same old cycle of oh-so-short-lived high, followed by self-doubting, stomach-churning low to even really enjoy the fun part. I interviewed a fortysomething nightclub owner once, who put it thus: "When I started partying, there was so much excitement because you never knew where the night would take you. These days I know exactly where things will end up." The implication being that the final destination was never very pretty.

And yes, this absolutely has a lot to do with getting older myself and just "growing out of it"—but which in my case can also be read as "growing more accepting of myself and therefore embracing my inner nerd, who would really rather spend her Saturday night studying her new nephew's astrology chart."

## THE FEEL-GOOD FACTOR

But, of course, I still want to "get buzzed" and connect with my tribe— and that's where "healing as nightlife" comes in. Amanda Capobianco coined the phrase after she moved to Williamsburg expecting music shows and dive bars and instead found an endless round of gong baths and breathwork sessions. And her saying resonated with me the moment I heard it, since it spoke exactly to a revelation I was having about the healing circles and workshops I'd also begun attending on a regular basis—the fact that they were FUN.

Typically, the implication is that if something needs to be "healed," there must be something "wrong" with us, right? And we tend to live in denial of the fact that life is basically equal parts "good" and "bad," or "happy" and "sad"—but humans experience the good *and* the bad on a daily basis. It would be weird if we didn't. And so, for me, "healing" is about simply acknowledging and processing what *feels bad* in order to get to the next *feeling good* bit.

Little kids do this effortlessly when they cry and have tantrums and then seem totally fine five minutes later. And, obviously depending on the intensity of the feelings you're healing, this can happen pretty fast for grown-ups too. Like in the course of any given Friday night.

When it comes to healing as nightlife (which also positions it as a way to meet like-minded people, and maybe even hook up!), yes, there may be some discomfort at first—but that's when the high kicks in! A vibrational high that will remain in your system, to be built on by subsequent highs. When you keep choosing the natural healing highs over the synthetic drugs and alcohol highs, they will begin to crowd out the lows. And before you know it you're generally just living a more high-vibe life.

Moving on, here are some of my favorite Now Age ways to get high on my own supply.

## THE VULNERABILITY HIGH (A.K.A. LEARNING TO LOVE THE SHARING CIRCLE)

So you've decided to try a different kind of socializing this weekend and found your way to some kind of Now Age workshop, Moon circle, or healing gathering. You've raided your closet for something comfortable for sitting cross-legged (I call it "healing circle chic"), and you've staked out a cushion next to the most "normal" looking person in the circle. Because nine times out of ten, there will be a circle.

In fact, "sitting in circle" is a term I've heard used many times to describe the act of coming together for any kind of ritual or ceremony, and there are numerous studies to show that humans connect and collaborate better when positioned in a way that allows unbroken eye-to-eye contact, and an equal stake of the territory. Circles also speak to the Divine Feminine, the unbroken, cyclical flow of life—all the better for sharing where we're at in our journey and our highest intentions for our participation (i.e., our deepest, most vulnerable truths) with the group. GULP.

When I first began to find myself sitting in circles, I would actively dread my turn to share—think sweaty palms, dry mouth, racing pulse. And not least because I had become aware of an uncomfortable fact I shared in the chapter on dharma: vocalize anything remotely close to my heart, sober, and there's a high likelihood of me dissolving into tears. (In fact, the tears probably happen when I'm drunk too, it's just I can't *really feel* them). Not exactly in line with the got-it-all-together, also-got-a-way-with-words, cool-girl image I prefer to present to the world (again, Mercury in egotistical Aries, lol).

But what do you know, the same way parties became my favorite once I discovered booze, these days I can't get enough of sharing circles—"ugly" cries and all (p.s. my Pisces mum read this and wrote me, "no, *beautiful* tears!").

But I've also become addicted to the sense of *relief* that comes from sharing stuff my inner perfectionist (or ego) would rather people didn't know. Like the fact I think I have a "cool-girl" image to maintain. Or that I can't speak in front of a group without tearing up! Because guess what, I say it, I cry a bit, and then it's the next person's turn. No drama. Nobody sneers or doesn't want to talk to me after. In fact, in a high-vibe setting it's usually the opposite.

Baring all in a sharing circle (and yes, I *have* been in some circles where people actually got naked—a step too far for me) is physical, human proof that it's okay to be every ugly/beautiful part of ME. In other words, social acceptance at its realest. No shots required.

## THE CRYING-WHILE-
## EVERYBODY'S-WATCHING HIGH

When Erin Telford, who has since become a friend and Numinous col-
laborator, first experienced breathwork, she was on a retreat in Nicaragua,
and the breathing happened in a forest, at night, right before a storm.
Um, AMAZING. She says she had no idea what to expect, but that
when the emotions started to move through her, she had no choice but
to succumb to the multiple cry-gasm.

"And I had never done that in front of a group of people before," she
told me. "When you need to cry like a child, you do that by yourself.
You do it in your bedroom. You do it on your bathroom floor. And
actually how heartbreaking that we hide ourselves away when we need
each other the most."

What happened next is what made Erin get on a plane to meet her
teacher David Elliott and learn how to lead breathwork circles herself:
"My chest broke open, and I felt so much love and bliss. Riding that
wave of pain and getting out the other side to a place of such profound
gratitude was the biggest heart-opening I've ever had."

From babyhood, we basically learn that expressing our emotions
with tears (happy, sad, snotty, whatever, they're all made in the same
factory) makes people around us pretty darned uncomfortable. So it
makes a lot of sense that we learn to shut the faucet off when in polite
company. But Erin believes that the scarcity of what she calls "emotional
witnessing" in our society is a crime—because allowing our emotions to
physically *be seen* is part of the healing process. After all, as our mutual
friend Victoria Keen puts it: "Emotions buried alive never die." No. They
become like zombie emotions that end up trying to eat your brain alive.

Having now had multiple experiences of crying openly in healing
circles, to the point where I no longer feel ashamed, or pathetic, or
embarrassed about it, has been similarly heart opening and vulnerability
high inducing for me, to the point where I'm actually *thankful* when it
happens now. After all, the fact I feel *so good* after an unashamed public
cry is how I know the healing is happening. So no wonder unashamed

public crying often goes with the boozing territory too! Our body wants to do it, but our ego would really rather we didn't, so waits until we're slammed. *The problem with this? You have to actually feel it to heal it.*

It may be that this is nothing new to you, and you're a totally comfortable crier with no problem letting it all hang out. So this is to all the closet criers out there: do not be ashamed of your tears. In fact, how about next Friday night you actively seek a safe space to allow them to flow forth?

## THE DANCING-WHILE-NOBODY'S-WATCHING HIGH

According to my mum, when I was three I would go around telling anybody who'd listen: "Ruby is truly a dancer!" This after she took me to see the musical *Grease*. And since I loved to dance SO MUCH, when I was old enough she enrolled me in ballet class. Sadly, this was also where I encountered my very first Mean Girls, and soon I was begging not to go back. My dancing "career" was over in a few short weeks.

Since it's no secret that most grown-ups require on average three glasses of pinot to really let loose on the dance floor, I'm guessing I'm not the only one with a story of booty-shaking shaming somewhere in the background. But since the first thing our bodies often want to do once we get them high is dance, I'm also pretty convinced that moving in rhythm to repetitive beats is fundamentally essential to our overall well-being and connection to the cosmic oneness.

This is the thinking behind Gabriel Roth's 5Rhythms, a "dancing meditation" class I decided to check out once, which is essentially two hours of silent, sober, solo dancing in a darkened room, with a hundred or so strangers. Also a regular Wednesday night workshop called Dancorcism that takes place in a church hall near me in Brooklyn, and the booze-free, early morning raves Morning Glory and Daybreaker.

The latter of which sound SO GREAT to me in theory, and which friends have described as verging on a religious experience. Hundreds of humans, jacked on Shakti and espresso drinks, connecting wordlessly through the medium of music. But I have yet to find out for myself based on my experience of the former, which I found to be excruciating. Only for a few fleeting moments did I manage to escape my self-consciousness enough to really get into it. And then, well, the music just really sucked.

Okay, so I'm a MAJOR snob when it comes to music. Not in the "I'll only talk to you if you're into certain bands" way, but based on the fact that even high as a kite my body will only respond if the beats truly speak to my soul. Like how, thanks to the deeply imprinted muscle memories of my early rave days, even stone-cold sober I still get full body tingles from the right mix of bass-heavy, vocal Chicago house music—and not much else. And I'm sorry, but without the tingles, what's the point?

I think dancing is essentially a way to move stuck energy in your body, and that the tingles are this happening. As discussed previously, the Universe knows how to make the things that are good for our body (and our species) feel good after all.

So that cliché about dancing like nobody's watching? Yes, it feels GREAT to lose yourself on a dance floor packed with bodies all grooving together, but there's never any guarantee the DJ will be on my wavelength. So to get my fix these days, I find a great mix on SoundCloud, pump up the volume, and dance around my apartment while nobody, apart from maybe my cat, is *actually* watching.

## THE CREATIVITY HIGH

As well as healing circles, I go to a lot of workshops these days—another great way to socialize with like-minded Now Age seekers, but with way less emo sharing and crying and much more just general chitchat.

The small-talk problem is solved in this scenario by the fact you're there to either make something (say a dream catcher, or high-vibe herbal tincture) or learn something (how to create a crystal grid), and so you basically just talk about whatever that is. Which, invariably when a group of like-minded Now Age seekers get together, turns into talking about where you're at on your spiritual path, a.k.a. sharing your darkest and most vulnerable truths. And maybe some crying.

So there is an element of the Vulnerability High at these gatherings, but the Creativity High itself, the sense of divine flow that comes from actively engaging in the physical process of making or learning something, is well worth pursuing in its own right.

In *Big Magic*, Liz Gilbert describes this sense of flow thus: "Sometimes, when I'm in the midst of writing, I feel like I am suddenly walking on one of those moving sidewalks that you find in a big airport terminal . . . I can feel myself being gently propelled by some exterior force." Which is exactly the way I once described walking through a sunny field at the Glastonbury festival high on Molly. Ha.

But back on Creativity Highs, Liz goes on to link this sensation of *effortless effort* to the ancient Greek word for the highest degree of human happiness, *eudaimonia*, "which basically means 'well-daemoned.' That is, nicely taken care of by some external divine creative spirit guide," she explains.

I've had similar experiences writing, and reading, drawing, cooking, and making other things with my hands. Tingle-inducing experiences, or highs, actually. My dear friend Bethia, a mom of three who is also a brilliant photographer, has another fancy word for this: *forelsket*—a Danish word for the feeling of euphoria when you first fall in love—which she says describes the feeling "of when I am able to re-create in a photograph an image I have in my mind." And because she's so *in love* with photography, spending her Friday night editing pictures is a way more pleasurable "escape" for her than drinking a bottle of wine.

Then there's the fact that getting creative in a social setting also feels kind of like going back to nursery school. And as you know, I'm all in favor of doing things to keep my inner five-year-old happy.

## HIGH-VIBE DRINKING HIGHS

Oh you guys, c'mon, sometimes alcohol can be great! Having said all that stuff about falling out of love with booze, I am not 100 percent teetotal. It's just that I no longer use drinking as my default for getting high—the very opposite in fact. This is largely because compared to all the amazing spiritual highs I've been experiencing, alcohol highs have actually been revealed to me as somewhat flat, and two-dimensional. The McDonald's of highs, if you like. And sometimes cheap and fast is still fun—only these days, I am *extremely* particular about how, when, why, and with whom I choose to imbibe. So to finish up here, following is my four-step, hard-and-fast, high-vibe drinking checklist:

1. HOW AM I FEELING? Alcohol is basically a mood enhancer—and that goes for any kind of mood. Drink when I'm happy, I tend to get happier. Drink when I'm sad, lonely, stressed, frustrated, bored, and so on, and in the moment of being drunk these feelings may be alleviated, but I will bet my bottom dollar that the next morning, if not later that same evening, I will only feel sadder, lonelier, more stressed, frustrated, bored, etc. Boo.

2. WHY AM I DRINKING? This tends to boil down to two options: to enhance how I'm feeling (high-vibe), or to escape how I'm feeling (low-vibe). I could say: *Oh, I'm going to have a drink because I'm seeing X for dinner and I haven't seen them for ages and it'll be FUN.* But behind this statement, I then have to ask myself: *How is the prospect of seeing X making me feel?* Genuinely excited = maybe one! Nervous/anxious *on any level* (in italics 'cos this is the tricky part and can require a full-on discussion with my inner Voice in the time it takes to scan a drinks list) = soda and lime for me, please.

3. WHEN AM I DRINKING? As in what's the occasion and with whom is it taking place (see questions 1 + 2, above), and also what time will the drinking actually be happening? A totally practical consideration, but daytime/afternoon drinking is definitely preferable, since the more time I have to chug water and carb-load *before* I go to sleep, the better. Also, never never NEVER do I drink when I will be requiring a true and clear connection to my highest Self

the following day. Which, having now stepped fully into the path of my dharma, is most if not *all* days. So.

4. WAIT, IS THIS JUST A SUGAR CRAVING? Turns out this is also a very real thing. And feeding the beast with a snack and a kombucha or nonalcoholic beer is currently my favorite way of distracting my taste buds while I work it out.

So there you have it. Feeling good, excited about the occasion and the people I'm drinking with, early enough in the day to get a good restorative sleep in, no tasks for my higher Self on my to-do list the following day, and not just because I'm hungry, and I'm all in. Or in for the first round at least. Having switched out my martini habit for all these natural highs, I've never been a cheaper date.

---

# 5 IDEAS FOR A HEALING HANG DATE

Want an alternative to cocktails and gossip? Try catching up with your friends over . . .

Tarot readings and Kava tea

Shopping for crystals, followed by a sound bath

An astro-themed walking tour of your city (visiting sites that symbolize aspects of your charts)

DIY cacao ceremony, followed by a joint journaling session (as in journaling with your friend, not about or while smoking joints)

Getting your Reiki 1 certificate together

# 16.

# FEELING THE PLANT MEDICINE PEER PRESSURE

Speaking of the ways I like to get high these days, I think I've been fascinated with altered states of consciousness since I discovered, aged around three I'd guess, that by spinning around very fast in circles I could make the world tip on its axis. It's exhilarating, isn't it? The first time you realize that life can literally be viewed from a different perspective. Running across some lawn somewhere *sideways,* giggling and all light in the head with legs that no longer belong to you and can't even keep up anyway. I mean, how cool is that?

Cut to me aged thirteen, teetering on the very brink of becoming a Goddess creatrix of the Universe (the way I saw it anyway), and I am watching an entire generation dance into a Universe of their very own creation, high on a drug they call Ecstasy. It's the summer of 1989, and the media has decided to call it the Second Summer of Love. Because (a) not since the acid-fueled 1969 Summer of Love has a drug exploded into the mainstream consciousness with quite the same *pizzazz.* And (b), whatever these kids are taking, they say it makes them feel like they're in love with the whole world, like the whole world IS love.

And the thing is, they're *my* generation too, if I'd only hurry and grow up already.

Everybody at school is smoking, and I've been sneaking my mom's Dunhills to practice on. I can't go choking to death the first time I do it in front of somebody cool. Meanwhile, my dad also gives me a half glass of wine whenever he and my stepmum have a dinner party, although he's told me I won't like the taste of whiskey or beer until I'm older. But these aren't *drugs,* these are just things that adults do.

Clearly, Ecstasy is a whole different ball game. It's not the kind of drug you do because it looks cool; you do it to get happy and dance all night. And for some reason, people are also going to extreme lengths to do it out in *nature,* chasing down illegal outdoor raves to dance with their feet in the earth and their heads and hands in the cosmos. In all the pictures plastered across all the papers, you can see in their wide open, smiling faces that they think they've found nirvana. By the end of the summer, my curiosity about whatever kind of magical, mystical trip they're on has reached fever pitch.

Talk about peer pressure. Though it's not like there was any one person, or a crew of older, cooler kids, pressing a pill into my hand and making me swallow it down if I wanted to be part of the gang. If anything, I was one of the first in my friendship group on a mission to join the Ecstasy revolution for myself. It seemed to me like there was a tectonic shift in consciousness occurring, as if *everyone* of my generation was embarking on a quest to seek a whole new reality. And I was either going to be a part of it, or I was getting left behind.

That same sense of cultural forward motion returned twenty years later, in—of all places—the living room of my brother's apartment, where I happened to be sitting the night in 2008 that I first heard the phrase "ayahuasca tourism." We were drinking wine with one of his cool DJ friends, who began telling us about this drug you had to go all the way to the Amazon to do—hence the "tourism" part. A drug that was supposedly a bit like LSD, but not, and which people were saying would completely rewire your life.

Having been working as a magazine journalist for some time by then, my sense for the zeitgeist was a finely tuned instrument, and immediately on that piece of information entering my consciousness the indicators that this *ayahuasca* was going to be THE NEXT BIG THING began buzzing. The next thought that surfaced was accompanied by the same dual sensation of extreme curiosity spiked with fear that I felt watching the 1989 Ecstasy ravers on TV: Does this mean *I'll* have to go to the Amazon to do ayahuasca too?

If every social movement has its drug, then the substance fueling the seekers of the Now Age is "plant medicine," the catch-all term for ayahuasca, peyote, San Pedro, and ibogaine—a vine, two kinds of cacti, and an African shrub, respectively. Used throughout history by indigenous shamans, these mind-expanding, heart-opening, and often hallucinogenic plants are thought to bring spiritual healing to whoever imbibes of them—being a fast and effective way to access a deep shamanic trance state. Practitioners believe that this is because the plants themselves have wisdom to share with us, that they are messengers of the cosmic, Universal energy that connects all living things. We can also include marijuana and magic mushrooms here, I guess, since they're also plants, and since you hear about people using them "medicinally" in the Now Age too. Not to mention the medical marijuana lobby gaining more traction year after year. And when considering the overall healing power of plants, it's also worth remembering that the majority of modern prescription drugs also use chemicals derived from plants.

But back to the very specific varieties that come under the Now Age plant medicine umbrella, which, along with the healing, are also said to offer experiences that could be described as downright magical. Of which ayahuasca has emerged as the star player in the plant meds lineup. Maverick philosopher and author Daniel Pinchbeck is credited with being the first person to open up the conversation about plant medicine, ayahuasca in particular, in the West, with the publication of his 2002 book, *Breaking Open the Head: A Psychedelic Journey into the Heart of Contemporary Shamanism.* William Burroughs actually wrote about it in his 1953 *The Yage Letters* ("yage"—pronounced "ya-he"—being another name for ayahuasca), but with the Ecstasy "movement" still in full swing, people's heads were already sufficiently broken open in the early noughties for Pinchbeck's book to have real mainstream appeal. It positioned him as a sort of Now Age Timothy Leary (the psychologist who championed the psychotherapeutic use of LSD in the 1960s) and even landed him a job as "Shaman at Large" for *Dazed & Confused* magazine.

Then there were the memorable scenes of British explorer and documentary maker Bruce Parry taking aya (the slang term) with Peruvian tribespeople for his 2009 series for the BBC, *Amazon,* an experience he subsequently described as "one of the more humbling nights of my life. Remarkably, it seems, my ego decided to take on Mother Ayahuasca in some sort of a battle. Horrified, I watched the whole thing from the sidelines, feeling very annoyed with my ego for putting up such a relentless attack."

If my teenage self had felt instinctively drawn to the late 1990s rave revolution, then for a certain breed of fearless seeker, the stage was now set for a mass awakening to the transformational power of these ancient medicines—and the following decade would see swarms of curious hippies, along with equal numbers of burned-out and disillusioned professionals, and even plenty of celebs, flocking to countries like Peru (swiftly established as the hub for ayahuasca tourism) to try it for themselves. It's a measure of just how mainstream aya has become that even Chelsea Handler took it during an episode of her 2016 Netflix series *Chelsea Does* (this one titled "Chelsea Does Drugs")—claiming to have experienced deeply healing revelations about her relationship with her sister. "I had forgotten that I loved (her)," she later told Stephen Colbert in an interview on *The Late Show.*

For the "plant med curious," both Bruce's and Chelsea's reports provide a fascinating window into what an ayahuasca ceremony looks like—a "ceremony," because unlike with most recreational drugs, these substances are not to be taken lightly. (Although I would argue the same for most recreational drugs, booze included.)

To give you an overview, the aya—actually a combination of two different plants—is brewed into a tea and administered to participants (a ceremony can be for one person or a group) by the shaman leading the session. This tea contains DMT, a chemical that is actually produced in the human body during childbirth and at the time of death, and which is known as "the God molecule" for its ability to open the doors of everyday perception to an utterly cosmic reality. There follows much purging (yes, puking and diarrhea), and vivid hallucinations, during which many people experience deep realizations about themselves, and their lessons in this lifetime. With the shaman and his helpers watching over proceedings all the while, often playing instruments, burning herbs, and singing, to invite the spirit of the plant to get deep and dirty with her work (aya is a Divinely Feminine "she"). In other words, about as far out and otherworldly a healing experience as you can get.

Why has "plant medicine" become so popular in the Now Age? I think there are three main drivers behind the upswell of interest: first, the "natural, straight from Mother Earth" angle fits nicely with our current "all organic, nothing processed" approach to food. Just as we've become well versed in scanning food labels for man-made nasties, why choose lab-manufactured, chemical drugs, for healing or highs, with all the clunky man-made side effects, when there's a natural alternative?

Second, the element of tradition and sacrament. Most plant medicines are taken in a ceremonial setting, like the one described above, and are based on ancient shamanic teachings, creating an atmosphere of reverence and communion that taps the basic human need to connect—both to each other and to something greater than ourselves. The way society is set up now, opportunities to unite with other human beings in a meaningful, tangible way are becoming fewer and further between, and you can't get much more analog than coming together for an ancient ceremony based around a psychedelic herbal tea.

And third, on a more mystical level, it feels to me like the plants *themselves* might just be behind all this. Okay, so bear with me on this one, but *what if,* in a last-ditch attempt to slow down or even halt altogether the unimaginable damage we're doing to our planet, the plants have actually gotten together in their own alternate, leafy reality, had a powwow, and decided that the best way forward was to gain direct access to the hearts and minds of the human populace? (Oh, and p.s., is it a coincidence that I keep writing "planet medicine" instead of "plant medicine" as I'm writing this?!)

Because more often than not, what people report after a ceremony is a feeling of deep connection to nature, a tangible sense of their place in the matrix of all life, and, as a result, a desire to make changes in their day-to-day existence that reflect this new understanding of themselves as children of the cosmos. As in, heal their relationship with themselves and with others, and generally accept responsibility for their place in their community—both local and global.

Taking all this into account, have *I* felt called to drink, smoke, eat, and generally get intimately familiar with these plants? Hell yes. I am a self-proclaimed Now Age adventurer after all, a wannabe pioneer in what I perceive as nothing less than the next phase of an evolutionary shift in global consciousness. Surely it's my duty to join the troops and make my way into the Amazonian trenches.

But will I go there? Probably not.

This is something I sit with on a regular basis, since barely a month goes by without somebody either inviting me to a plant medicine ceremony, or stirring my curiosity yet again with their stories of profoundly cosmic healing and transformation. I couldn't be more intrigued, in fact, and yet something is holding me back. And maybe, after reading this or having had conversations with friends who've dipped a toe (or more) in the world of plant meds, you're in a similarly conflicted place. In which case I invite you to read on for the pros and cons, as I see it, of getting involved.

## PROS

### It's All About the Healing

I asked Deborah Hanekamp, one of the only Western women to have been initiated to lead plant medicine ceremonies by the Peruvian Shipibo tribe (widely recognized as "the masters of ayahuasca"), to describe her first experience with aya ten years ago. As you're going to hear a lot from Deborah in this chapter, please keep in mind that she is also drop-dead gorgeous, was raised Baptist, is a mother, a qualified yoga instructor and Reiki master, a gifted intuitive, and married to *the* hunkiest Dutch male model. In other words, major Numinati girl crush material.

Anyhow, here's what she told me: "It felt like four or five hours of deep, deep, deep healing. All these different people in my life that I love were coming in one after another, and I was sending healing towards them and receiving healing back. I felt like the whole world had been healed after the ceremony, you know?" And seriously, who wouldn't want some of that?

### All the Best People Are Doing It

There's a common perception—true in so, so many cases, especially with alcohol—that people take drugs to get "out of it," to hide from reality, and to run away from their problems. MDMA (and later alcohol and cocaine) definitely became an escape for me. It may have begun with some pretty amazing spiritual epiphanies about the interconnectedness of all beings and our essentially loving nature, but by the time I'd shacked up with the Capricorn and developed an eating disorder, doing Ecstasy was just a way to fake feeling good. Followed by plenty of feeling even worse the morning after.

Conversely, the people I see being drawn to plant medicine are usually in it for exactly the opposite reason—it's not called "medicine" for nothing. I've also heard doing ayahuasca get called "the work," since Deborah's experience is by no means the norm, and in fact all the different plant medicines are known for making you face your most-deep-seated issues in lurid Technicolor. See Bruce Parry's "humbling" nightlong "battle" with his ego mind. For the same reason, aya is known as the "Grandmother" plant, delivering lessons about how to clean up the messes you may have made with your life with an all-loving yet often stern intensity. "She gives you what you need, not what you want," as Deborah puts it.

All of which suggests it takes a certain strength of character to go there, and a fearless commitment to making the changes in your life, however uncomfortable, that may be necessary as you integrate the teachings of the plants. Far from the dropouts of society, the plant med pioneers I've met are often the people making a real difference in their corner of the world, the high-functioning thinkers at the front line of Now Age consciousness.

## An Actual Conversation with God

In all the conversations I've had with dedicated plant med heads, the plants are actually described as having a consciousness all their own, as "beings" that we can interact with, just as we would with other human or animal beings. And of course, the plants communicate using their very own numinous language, one that defies translation and that we can only decipher via psychedelic (or *psychic*) visions and sensations, and the feelings they promote.

How deliciously mystical . . . and how much closer to an actual communion with Source energy itself can you get? If our technology- and progress-obsessed society runs largely on left-brain logic, then we have to give our right brain the stage to hear the wisdom of the plants.

## All Natural, All Organic

Deborah made a really good point when I tried to compare the plant medicine movement with what happened in the 1960s with LSD, or the 1990s with MDMA: "With those kind of substances, there is always a price to pay." Meaning that all man-made drugs, whether they are FDA approved or not, come with a long list of adverse side effects. With LSD and MDMA, these may include panic attacks, flashbacks, psychosis, dehydration, insomnia, heart palpitations, nausea and vomiting, teeth grinding, and depression. Nasty.

Not that there aren't risks involved with taking plant medicines too (see "Cons," below), but the toll they take mentally and physically appears to be minimal. Many of my friends report feeling physically better than ever after taking them, while reports of actual plant medicine *deaths* are rare to nonexistent. Meanwhile, Deborah even told me: "Ayahuasca restores serotonin levels permanently in the brain." This could be one reason plant medicines are said to be particularly effective in treating PTSD and depression, and for healing addictions—as reported by both *National Geographic* and *Scientific American* magazines. As for the problems associated with man-made chemical "solutions" to these emotionally rooted malaises? How long have you got?

## Spiritual Brownie Points

Hello, ego! Part of me, the part that's still desperate to be "one of the gang," feels like a loser, a coward, and a square for not jumping on the plant med bandwagon. This is the same part of me that began smoking weed regularly at age fourteen, despite the fact that it never made me feel good, because I was petrified my perceived lack of sophistication would leave me forever on the outside looking in. A.k.a. feeling the "peer pressure" in the more classical sense of the phrase. You know what I'm talking about, right? It's the reason you say yes when somebody suggests a round of tequila slammers, despite knowing you really need a good head on your shoulders for the presentation you have to give at work the next morning.

Of course, when I asked my French shaman Manex Ibar about this (whose four-day vision quests always end with an optional plant medicine ceremony), he reminded me that the only person putting "pressure" on me to join in—who thought it was "uncool" not to—was me. I know all this, and yet the question remains: *Would people take me more seriously as a spiritual voyager if I did ayahuasca too?*

## I Am Very, Very Afraid

Yes, this makes the "Pros" list. Because as all the greatest spiritual teachers will tell you: that thing that scares you the most? That's *the* thing you need to do.

## CONS

### Psychedelics Are Not My Friend

The world appears to be divided into two camps here—people who love the unpredictability of a psychedelic trip, and those it scares the living bejesus out of. I fall into the latter camp, and I have actually only taken LSD once in my life. It was just me and the Capricorn, in a hut, up a mountain, on a tiny island in Thailand, circa 1995. The trip lasted probably twelve hours, at least eight of which I spent concentrating very hard on not dying. At least that's how it felt to me from the depths of the psychic black hole the acid kept trying to spin me down. Anybody with me on this one?

"Set and setting" was a term first coined by psychoanalyst Norman Zinberg to describe the ideal context for any psychedelic experience—"set" referring to the mental state of the person taking the drugs, "setting" the physical and social environment. Admittedly, I couldn't have gotten these more wrong. I was deep in my anorexia, and allowing myself to be totally mind controlled by my boyfriend (let alone the drug). Looking back, I feel so tenderly toward myself! And so sad that my lack of self-love had left me so darned suggestible. To be clear: I did NOT feel the same pull towards LSD as I had toward Ecstasy, but I did it anyway.

Taking all this into account, you can understand my reluctance to go near anything even *remotely* resembling an acid trip again. And you can repeat all you like how ayahuasca and the other plant meds are, like, a totally different trip (which is something I also hear all the time). But my LSD experience in Thailand is the closest reference point I've got, and that's close enough for me.

## A Ceremony Is Like a Box of Chocolates

As in, you never know what you'll get. Yes, perhaps Grandmother (or Grandfather, as peyote goes by) will take you in her loving embrace and show you the secrets of the Universe. But equally likely, she'll pin you to the ground and give you . . . the most humbling experience of your life. This could go back to the "set and setting" thing, I guess, as well as what Deborah said about the medicine delivering not the message or insight you want, but rather what you *need*.

Call me a control freak (hands up: I am a bit of a control freak), or perhaps I've just done my time and had my fill of "bad trips" (on LSD and other drugs), but I've reached the conclusion that no drug-induced spiritual epiphany is worth risking however many hours in a mental and physical hell of my psyche's own creation. Not to mention the week, or longer, spent regrouping emotionally.

Which is not to say I'm not prepared to face my demons. As I hope I've demonstrated elsewhere in this book, staring down my most painful truths in the name of healing them has become one of my very favorite pastimes! But on my own time, and within the boundaries of my own lovingly constructed comfort zone, thank you very much.

## The Vomit Sitch

They call it "getting well," and for the vast majority of people, throwing up (or physically purging by other, even more potentially embarrassing means) is an integral part of ayahuasca and most other plant medicine ceremonies. I don't know about you, but I hate throwing up. Even worse, feeling like I *need* to throw up, and not being *able* to throw up. The thought of experiencing any and all of the above in a group setting, under the influence of an extremely strong psychedelic, is pretty much enough to close the door on plant meds for me right there.

## Charlatan Shamans

And this is a big one. It might have been that back in the day—2002, say, when *Breaking Open the Head* first came out—you could trip down to Peru and have a safe and authentic experience with the first medicine man to cross your path. But where there is "tourism," there follows exploitation, and common wisdom is that plenty of not-so-well-intentioned "shamans" abound these days.

Most disturbingly, plenty of the stories I hear on this subject center around the sexual manipulation of young women while in a vulnerable, psychedelic state. I've even heard about cases of "spiritual rape," where the shaman leading the ceremony somehow coerces a woman's spirit to leave her body, to be toyed with by him somewhere out in the cosmic realms. Too scary a concept to even contemplate.

According to Deborah, this is partly because it's not unusual, or even particularly frowned upon, for men in Peru to use black magic to cast "love spells" on women—and she told me about the time this happened to her during a ceremony too. How she was given a different bottle to drink from than the rest of the group ("silly girl," you may think—but put yourself in her shoes and see how easy you think it would be to speak up), how during the ceremony the shaman pulled out a bunch of her hair, and she felt "an inch away from being raped." How afterward, she "was in a really bad place for like a month."

Navigating the numinous realms, I can never really state often enough the importance of working with teachers, guides, and practitioners whose credentials and overall vibe you feel one *thousand* percent comfortable with. And when it comes to working with plant meds, as I see it this increases tenfold.

### I'm Very, Very Afraid

See pretty much all of the above.

As you can probably tell, I've really done my research on this one. I've spoken to countless friends about their experiences, interviewed the experts, and read all kinds of reports. And there's something else people always say about plant meds: *when you're ready, the plants will come to you.*

And actually, I believe the spirit of ayahuasca did eventually weave its way into my journey. When we first met, Deborah told me she'd reached out after three different people that week had asked if we knew each other . . . because we *really must.* Having studied with the Shipibo over many years, she proceeded to tell me how she'd actually developed such a strong connection to ayahuasca consciousness, which she described as "pure love consciousness," she was able to channel this outside the ceremonial setting.

She only led one or two ceremonies a year now, having developed a healing modality she called a "Medicine Reading." Incorporating singing the traditional "icaros" (medicine songs) with other sound healing instruments, crystal work, Reiki, and flower essences, it was as close as you could get to a ceremony without actually drinking ayahuasca, she said. Did I want to try it? Well, of course I did!

In the event, the session was incredibly healing, taking me into an ocean-deep trance state where some ancient memories related to issues around *speaking my truths* surfaced from the very depths of my psyche. Getting off her table my body felt leaden, as if I were coming around from surgical-level anesthesia—perhaps related to the level of *psychic* anesthetic needed to allow me to face the painful "truths" I'd witnessed in my mind's eye.

Sure, it may not have been the full plant medicine experience— purging, Peruvian shamans, and all. But it was cosmic enough for me.

# PLAYING WITH PLANT MEDS:
# A HEALTH AND SAFETY CHECKLIST

**Do your research.** Ask around, read up online, watch the docs (there's plenty on Netflix). But also consult the experts. The International Center for Ethnobotanical Education Research & Service (ICEERS) is an amazing resource for information on all aspects of the plant medicine world and also offers a free e-mail support service. www.iceers.org *(N.B. ICEERS does NOT offer sessions or recommend centers/individuals who do.)*

**Be selective with your shaman.** SO IMPORTANT. Ideally, try to get a personal recommendation from somebody you trust, but if this is unavailable, hopefully your own research (see above) will help inform your choice. Some things to consider: Do they provide their own health and safety checklist ahead of the ceremony? How much time have they got for your questions, and how concerned are they with making you feel at ease? Also, if traveling abroad, try to book your ceremony ahead of time. This will give you more time to ask questions, and to investigate the shaman, their ethos, and overall vibe.

**Do the prep.** Getting the most from your plant medicine experience means being in the right space—mentally, emotionally, physically, and spiritually. As such, most shamans will ask participants to do a physical detox for up to ten days ahead of a ceremony—which usually involves abstaining from alcohol and other substances, animal products, and sex! Adhere to these instructions. It's all part of the process.

**Process it properly.** And then there's the aftercare. Any plant medicine ceremony can and will be a deeply emotional and psychologically moving experience, and a proper shaman will include plenty of time to process what's come up for you during the session. Beyond this, definitely DO seek additional professional help if you find yourself having a hard time processing any part of the experience. Again, ICEERS is a great resource for free advice about this.

**If it's not a hell yes . . .** Since every plant medicine encounter can be a wildly different experience, depending on your state of mind, the location, the medicine itself, and the vibe of the group, above all be ready and willing to expect the unexpected. Only YOU will know if this feels like the right step for you. So let your gut be your guide—and if in doubt, don't!

# 17

# LOST AND FOUND
# AT BURNING MAN

I have made it as far as day six at Burning Man without crying, and now here I am, alone in my RV, sobbing my heart out. There's a fuck-off dust storm happening outside, which I rode into on my sparkly pink bike half an hour ago with the rest of my campmates, before realizing this was possibly the worst idea in the history of the Universe and returning to camp on my own. The superficial reason for my tears is the dust, which has been engaged in an active takeover bid all week and that, by flinging this storm up in our face, appears to have finally won. Every surface inside the RV is dredged in it. *I* am dredged in it. I can feel it sandpapering my skin and lining my throat and lungs, a sensation that is beginning to feel like dry drowning.

So there are those tears, tears of discomfort and self-pity. But the longer they persist, the more they are feeling like tears of *frustration*. What I really want is to scream and rage and tear my hair out, stamp my feet and wail: *"It's not faaaaaair!"* I am less clear about what, exactly, isn't fair, but the overwhelming emotion in that RV is one of pent-up anger. I realize that I've been putting a brave (or rather *rave*) face on this feeling all week, drinking and drugging and pretending I've been loving every minute of my virgin Burn. When in fact, the experience has been equal parts uncomfortable and alienating.

Something I am ashamed to admit, even to myself. What does this say about my supposedly open-minded embrace of the Mystical World? For the seventy thousand freewheeling, peace-and-love denizens of Black Rock City, the temporary city that springs up to host the Burn each August, this week of "radical self-expression" represents the ultimate opportunity to experience life from a more numinous perspective. To get back to the wilderness of being human and to connect with Mother Earth, and with each other, mind, body, and spirit. Am I so unenlightened that I haven't been able to see beyond the lack of privacy and the stinking porta-potties? You're supposed to lose all attachment to luxuries like toilet paper at Burning Man, and in the process find yourself. To set your ego free, and in doing so gain an understanding of true community. How come it's been so hard to transcend my own selfish needs?

Outside, the storm has created a total whiteout, a bleak and eerie backdrop to my freak-out. Clashing repetitive beats from the two sound-stages neighboring our camp continue what has felt like an incessant, 24-7 assault on my nervous system. The dust is still swirling as dusk is beginning to fall, a few LEDs appearing like neon constellations in the otherwise forlorn landscape. My tears have subsided by now, leaving itchy streaks of kohl in the dust on my face, and I feel a pang of anxiety. How will my campmates have weathered the storm?

In my first magazine job, as style editor on a celebrity gossip magazine for teens, I was given the nickname Ruby Slippers—and, with twenty-four hours to go until The Man burns (the festival ends with the burning of a forty-foot wooden effigy), I wish I had a pair right now. Screw the rest of my crew, and screw my sorry unenlightened soul. I would like nothing better than to be able to click my heels together, chanting *There's no place like home,* and be transported back to Brooklyn, back to breathable air, and back to my own reality.

For the uninitiated, Burning Man is a weeklong arts festival that takes place annually in the middle of the Nevada desert. A sort of rave meets social experiment, the Burn is famous for its "gifting economy"—meaning nothing on-site is for sale (beside coffee and ice, it transpires—y'know, the basics). As such, attendees bring their own bars and music and art installations to be shared freely with fellow festivalgoers, while also agreeing to abide by the nine other "principles" of the Burner community, as defined by founder Larry Harvey in 2004.

---

## THE TEN PRINCIPLES OF THE BURNER COMMUNITY:

1. Radical Inclusion

2. Gifting

3. Decommodification

4. Radical Self-Reliance

5. Radical Self-Expression

6. Communal Effort

7. Civic Responsibility

8. Leaving No Trace

9. Participation

10. Immediacy

---

As a Brit who came of age in the 1990s rave heyday, I figured I knew festivals. After all, nobody has embraced the concept of getting spangled in a field in the name of communing with our higher selves through music as vigorously as the British—to the point there are now several opportunities to do so on any given weekend in the UK between the months of May and September (come rain or shine—usually rain). Perhaps it's because we're descended from a bunch of pagans.

And so the Burn had been on my radar for years. I was excited by the renegade vibe, but separated by an ocean, a whole continent, and requiring what sounded like an advanced degree in extreme camping, from London it had always seemed like the mother of all schleps. If getting to the middle of the Nevada desert was one thing, then getting yourself equipped to survive the week on-site was a whole other trip. It's recommended that you bring two gallons of water, per person, per day, for example. And that's before the conundrum of how, exactly, to create a week's worth of meals that "leave no trace" (let alone deal with food scraps going stinky in the desert sun) has even entered the equation.

Plus, the embarrassing truth is I only ever *really* enjoyed myself at a festival when I went to Glastonbury as the guest of a PR and got put up in a fancy B&B with a bunch of other journalists. We slept in proper beds and got to shower, and the couple who ran the hotel gave us a glass of chilled chablis before we got in our taxi to the festival site. Other times, I'd just about managed a night or two under canvas, so long as I'd had enough to drink—but by day three my skin was crawling with a full-body craving for clean bedsheets.

At what point I decided these experiences qualified me as Burner material will forever remain a mystery, but fast-forward to early summer 2014, and I am in the throes of organizing my very first visit to Black Rock City. For one thing, since moving to New York the distance to get there has shrunk by roughly half. But having recently launched The Numinous, my curiosity about the spiritual side of the event had also been piqued. Every which way I turned, I found myself in conversation with yet another yogi, techpreneur, or boho raver, waxing lyrical about the utopian founding principles of the event. In fact, something had become increasingly clear: among the Now Age set, the annual pilgrimage to Burning Man was a nonnegotiable. It had begun to feel like a case of be there, or be the ultimate spiritual square.

But that pre-Burn *prep*, though. By the time we set off on the mammoth forty-hour journey from NYC to Black Rock City (top tip: do *not* attempt to fly to Vegas and then drive to Reno in the same day, on a hangover, unless you wish to inflict a complete personality fail on anybody who has the misfortune to cross your path), I was also lugging a whopping eighty-pound case stuffed with the wigs, wearable LED lights, and industrial-strength wet wipes I'd spent the past two months feverishly ordering on Amazon.

I'd also got my numinous agenda set. I was going to kick off the week guiding my campmates in a meditation to meet our spirit animals, attend daily sunrise yoga sessions at a camp called the Mellow Mountain, and find myself engaged in constant deep and meaningful conversations about possible solutions to climate change with the leading thinkers in radical consciousness, having bumped into them on the dance floor at Robot Heart. I was also superexcited about getting really thin and tanned, from the biking everywhere and the forgetting to eat due to having my mind blown every five minutes.

But of course, Burning Man is also a celebration of pure, unadulterated hedonism—and a couple of days in, all my high-vibe intentions had been washed away by a pretty much steady stream of Coronas. We didn't even get to do the spirit animal meditation I'd so carefully prepared, as (a) it was impossible to get everybody sober in the same place at the same time, and (b) my campmates seemed way more interested in munching the sustainable, vegan, ridiculously strong magic mushroom truffles somebody had brought along from Portland, and meeting creatures from the fifth dimension that way.

But this was cool, I told myself, since I had always been pretty good at the hedonistic part of festivals. And since when did hedonism get such a bad name anyway? In the dictionary, it's defined as "the belief that pleasure, or happiness, is the most important goal in life."

For me, this echoes the concept of "kama," something I learned about in my yogic studies. Speaking to the fact that desire for pleasure is actually *what drives all human behavior,* kama is identified in the Rig Veda, the most ancient and revered of Hindu scriptures, as one of the four *purusharthas,* or aims of life—along with dharma (duty, ethics), artha (material prosperity), and moksha (the pursuit of liberation). The theory is that working to balance these four pillars (using the practices described by the eight limbs of yoga) is the key to creating a deeply and holistically satisfying existence.

And on paper at least, Burning Man is a technicolor metaphor for this philosophy. There's the *dharma* of being an active participant in bringing the event to life; the *artha* of assembling the necessary supplies to partake; the *moksha* of escaping the rules of the "default" world (Burner speak for life outside the festival); and, of course, the sheer *kama* of the sensory pleasures on offer—from an abundance of free massages and hugs, to a spin in the Human Carwash. Or all-day Coronas.

And for the first couple of days, I was more than happy to go about busily addressing the kama imbalance that can result when you work for yourself (#nodaysoff). But as the week wore on, life got generally dustier, weirder, and more uncomfortable. Something was out of whack. I also, thanks to Black Rock City being a total Wi-Fi black spot, began to experience a sense of restless unease I can now identify as extreme iPhone withdrawal. By day four, even through the tequila haze, I was aware that I'd long given up on hedonism and had charged headlong into all-out self-medication mode.

Because there's a fine line, isn't there, between the pursuit of pleasure and the avoidance of pain. From hedonism to escapism. If the tenth and final guiding principle of Burning Man was immediacy, or living in the moment, then more often than not, another moment spent hungover with no access to clean toilets, a shower, or a blessed moment of peace and quiet was NOT where I wanted to be. Cut to me wailing in the back of the RV. With hindsight it's so obvious—I was experiencing the mother of all comedowns.

But it also felt like more than that. What had really gone so wrong? Part of it lay in the fact I kept comparing life in Black Rock City to my experiences a decade and a half ago in Ibiza. This is the thought that kept resurfacing like a sand dune at low tide in my mind—as I applied fresh makeup over yesterday's glitter, downed another shot at an all-day dance party called Distrikt, and (finally) felt my being merge with the cosmos out in the deep playa (the empty desert right out by the edge of the fence) on a mind-and-body-bending cocktail of mushrooms and Molly.

What I got from "the Ibiza years" was a sense of unbridled freedom (*moksha*) in the pursuit of the pleasure principle (*kama*). No judgment, no limits, no rules. Want to head to the club straight off the beach, still wearing your bikini? Just had some MDMA and feel like having sex in the sea? ENJOY. Being a small and relatively unspoiled island in the middle of the Mediterranean, I also think a lot of Ibiza's rep as a "spiritual" party place is because a lot of the partying, and therefore a lot of the drinking and drugging, happens in very close proximity to nature. And like any shaman worth her stick of palo santo will tell you: you should only ever peek around the doors of perception with Mother Nature as your guide. The static electricity in cities is the biggest buzzkill.

I recently read an article titled "The Birth of Rave," in which the four British DJs who "discovered" Ecstasy in Ibiza in 1987—credited with kicking off the 1990s rave phenomenon when they brought it back to the UK—discuss that fateful summer. "(We were) all chilled out and loved up, thinking it was going to change the world, thinking that if everyone did (ecstasy) there would be no more wars," says Nicky Holloway.

"I found everything I was looking for," remembers Danny Rampling, adding a mystical side note: "I felt there was something deeper, spiritually, running through the whole experience. And I discovered something recently, through my own research. In August 1987, there was an event called the Harmonic Convergence, a global shift in unity consciousness through dance rituals, which is part of the Mayan calendar teachings." (An event I've heard mention of in various spiritual circles. And, interestingly, after the first "official" Burning Man was held on a beach in San Francisco in 1986—the event doubled in size and became cemented as an annual happening the following year, also the summer of 1987.)

It's an incredibly romantic story, but with not such a happy-ever-after. The problem is that, YES, humans have access to all sorts of substances that offer a window seat over paradise, BUT that drink and drugs are hedonism for beginners. As Ram Dass concludes in his 1971 classic, *Be Here Now,* following years of spiritual adventures with LSD: "No matter how . . . high I got, I came down. And it was a terribly frustrating experience, as if you came into the kingdom of heaven and you saw how it all was and you felt these new states of awareness, and then you got cast out again."

Which speaks to another very important factor in my own disillusionment with the Burning Man experience—which I've actually come to view as a pivotal moment on my path from Material Girl into a deeper connection to our magnificently Mystical World. If, somewhere along the line, drink and drugs had become my "default" route to bliss, then numinous experiences connecting to my higher self (Source, the Universe, Goddess energy, etc.), where doing my *dharma* had also come into the equation, had shown me a glimpse of true nirvana.

The sense of "alienation" I'd been experiencing? I can see now it was twofold. As much as I was unsure how the new me *was even supposed to behave* at an event like Burning Man, I was feeling equally alienated from what was rapidly becoming an outdated version of myself.

It took roughly two weeks of blissful post-Burn recovery (mainly spent marveling at the miracles of modern plumbing) to begin to process what had really happened out there in the desert, and the full download continues even as I write this, eighteen months after the event. In the moment, the experience was such a full-on assault on all six senses (including my sense of *self,* that is), it had been impossible for me to see beyond what was occurring in real time.

But this is also exactly what the last—and perhaps most relevant to life in the Now Age—of Larry Harvey's Ten Principles is all about.

*Immediacy* is defined thus in the Burner handbook: "Immediate experience is, in many ways, the most important touchstone of value in our culture. We seek to overcome barriers that stand between us and a recognition of our inner selves, the reality of those around us, participation in society, and contact with a natural world exceeding human powers. No idea can substitute for this experience." Or *no words*—making this sound also like the very definition of *numinous.*

"Immediate experience is, in many ways, the most important touchstone of value in our culture. We seek to overcome barriers that stand between us and a recognition of our inner selves, the reality of those around us, participation in society, and contact with a natural world exceeding human powers. No idea can substitute for this experience."

—BURNER HANDBOOK

*We seek to overcome barriers that stand between us and a recognition of our inner selves.* And isn't this what my whole Material-Mystical journey into the Now Age has been about? A return to an authentic sense of self, beyond the glamorous and seductive trappings of the material world?

I've heard people talk about how life on the playa makes you really face yourself. Uh, tell me about it. In my case, it also brought me face-to-face with so many of the different barriers there are to experiencing immediacy—to being content in the moment, connected to my higher Self, to my community, and to the natural world. In relation to my Burning Man experience in particular, these included:

EXPECTATIONS. Even if you haven't been to Burning Man, you know what Burning Man looks like, right? I actually kind of hated myself for not being "in awe" of what I saw out on the playa my first day. Was I that jaded? But I basically saw exactly what I saw in the images and YouTube clips I'd GORGED on before the event. In fact, and this may be too late, if you haven't been to Burning Man and you think you might go at some point in the future, I would advise a total BM hashtag ban starting now. The joy of discovery is a beautiful thing—and key when it comes to experiencing immediacy.

STUFF. Witness hundreds of Burners buying up literally the entire contents of Walmart in Reno in preparation for a week of "radical self-reliance" in the desert. Not to mention the aforementioned daily Amazon orders I placed in the months running up to the event. My thinking was you can never have too many pairs of vintage ski goggles. Turns out you definitely can. Not only that, out in the desert, the metaphorical weight of all that "baggage" felt like a ball and chain, anchoring me firmly to my preconceived notions about what my Burning Man experience would, and should, look like (and you know how I feel about the word *should*)—versus being open to whatever magic each day might hold, *and allowing this to unfold moment by moment.* In the words of Yogi Bhajan: "Travel light, live light, spread the light, be the light."

SUBSTANCES. See above comments about the fine line between hedonism and escapism. And the problem with using substances, alcohol in particular, as a route to hedonism is that essentially all you're doing is shutting down the "bad" feelings for a while, in order to experience more of the "good" ones—thus creating a barrier to the full and *immediate* experience of your true (whole) Self. Plus, to quote Brené Brown on this one: "Numbing vulnerability [*for example, and, man, was I feeling vulnerable out there on the playa*] also dulls our experience of *love, joy, belonging, creativity,* and *empathy*. We can't selectively numb emotion. Numb the dark and you numb the light."

CONSUMPTION. Versus *participation,* that is. There's a huge difference between showing up and "taking" part (consumption) in Burning Man/ life, and contributing in a meaningful way (participation)—and only as an active participant is it possible to experience the festival/life as it is happening. Otherwise you're forever an observer, on the outside looking in (an easy role, as a journalist, for me to slip into). I love the description of participation (Principle #9) in the Burner handbook: "We believe that transformative change, whether in the individual or in society, can occur only through the medium of deeply personal participation. We achieve *being* through doing. . . . We make the world *real* through actions that open the heart" (my italics). What had I participated in? Not even my spirit animal meditation. And what did I consume? Too many expectations, way too much stuff, and a shitload of substances.

SOCIAL MEDIA. Or rather, lack of it. Without the rabbit hole of Instagram to scuttle down as soon as, say, boredom, discomfort, frustration, [insert "negative" emotion here] set in, I became acutely aware of what an effective and all-pervasive tool this has also become for removing ourselves from the present moment—or "numbing," as Brené Brown would put it. Also, for enforcing yet more expectations about the way life "should" look and feel. My iPhone withdrawal? Being forced to confront all the things that *didn't* look and feel so great in that moment.

FEAR. A big one, THE big one, and hugely important since I ultimately think it was fear that blindsided my whole BM experience. Fear of life in the desert itself, fear of not fitting in, fear of falling off my bike, fear of dust storms, fear of weirdos, fear of my drink being spiked . . . you name it, I was afraid of it! Enter . . . overconsumption of expectations, stuff, and substances, to keep a lid on the fear.

If anything, these realizations make Burning Man one of my most numinous experiences to date—since cultivating awareness around the myriad ways I (*we*) have designed to numb out from the immediate experience of simply being with our true (sometimes ugly, uncomfortable, angry) selves is one of the cornerstones of thriving as a fully actualized human in the Now Age.

## EMBRACE THE BURNING MAN PRINCIPLES IN YOUR LIFE

RADICAL INCLUSION. Drop the Mean Girls act. This means accepting any and everybody as your brother or sister, since we all share a box marked HUMAN. (Yes . . . even the Mean Girls.)

GIFTING. Give freely of yourself and your stuff. And give because it feels good, NOT because you're expecting something in return.

DECOMMODIFICATION. Seek out experiences that are free, turn your back on brands, and embrace the idea of the "exchange economy." Need some new clothes? Arrange a swap party with friends.

RADICAL SELF-RELIANCE. Develop your inner resources. Strengthen your sense of self with yoga, meditation, and healing practices, as well as activities that expand your comfort zone.

RADICAL SELF-EXPRESSION. Celebrate your unique gifts, and not in a way that's designed to impress others. Try journaling, chanting, and karaoke (really!) to free your inner Voice.

## A RETURN TO THE DEFAULT WORLD

In the beginning of this chapter, I described how a lot of Now Agers view the annual trip to Burning Man as a *pilgrimage,* which is defined in the dictionary thus: "any long journey, especially one undertaken as a quest or for a votive purpose, as to pay homage." So what, exactly, are the denizens of Black Rock City paying homage to?

I think that ultimately BM is a celebration of freedom—or *moksha:* freedom to do our *dharma,* by contributing something meaningful to society; freedom in the pursuit of *kama;* and freedom to redefine what *artha* looks like on our own terms (our actual material needs, versus all the bells and whistles, the trinkets and baubles we've been sold on). Also, the freedom to make choices outside the "default" settings of

COMMUNAL EFFORT. Lean in to your community, meaning your family, your friendship group, your colleagues, the people who live on your street. What do they need? How can they help you? Reach out.

CIVIC RESPONSIBILITY. Clean up your side of the street, metaphorically and literally! Consider: How do my actions affect others? How can I make this a better experience for us all?

LEAVING NO TRACE. Recycle, recycle, recycle. Just say NO to the Whole Foods "double bagging" policy.

PARTICIPATION. Say YES to life. And ask not what the party can do for you, but what you can bring to the party.

IMMEDIACY. Put. Your. iPhone. Down. Through the window of e-mail and social media, it is possible to be all places at once. But only the present moment—present to the air that you are breathing, the food that you are eating, the words that you are speaking, and the person you are kissing RIGHT NOW—is real. Meaning only in this moment are you free to create the life you want, and to revel in the authentic, mystical, *numinous* human experience that is your birthright.

everyday life—choices about how to think, look, and behave, which it can often feel have already been made for us.

And we all want freedom of choice, right? Thing is, the more choices that are made for us, the easier it is to exist on autopilot. Meaning the less effort we have to make to tune in, and to connect to what our higher Self *truly* needs in any given moment. To practice *self-love*. An attractive proposition, since getting present with our deeper desires may often involve confronting what's *not* working for us (mind-numbing job, abusive relationship), or making "unreasonable" demands of others (higher salary, more fulfilling sex). Yikes!

Sure, despite my inability to engage fully with the immediacy of the event, for a little while at least my Burning Man experience actually made my "default world" a little less default. I was able to see things I had taken for granted (an RV park with a LAUDROMAT! Menus!) with fresh, appreciative eyes. As such, it's as if the experience restored a sense of "immediacy" to my daily life (until I became fully entrenched in my social media feeds again, at least).

But the biggest takeaway for me? Another definition of a pilgrimage is "a metaphorical journey into someone's own beliefs." And it might have taken a minute to unravel it all, but life on the playa was a unique opportunity to experience my personal transformation, from Material Girl to Mystical World, in real time. Next time—yes, I hope there will be a next time—I'll be leaving the expectations, the stuff, and the need to numb out behind.

# CONCLUSION

*Brooklyn, NY. September 4, 2016.*

"What's the book that changed your life?" It's a question that comes up a lot among people who identify as being "on the path" (or OTP, as my friend Elyssa puts it). Who has been the teacher, they want to know, and what have been the words of wisdom that have most inspired you to keep seeking?

Well, I can never just name one. When I first met the Pisces he was reading *The Alchemist* by Paulo Coelho, the story of a young shepherd boy who learns to follow his intuition and read the Universal omens in his quest for worldly treasure. Which, obviously, *I* took as a sign that here was a pile of man-shaped treasure right in front of me (especially since my family name was even Shepheard back then!).

*Eat, Pray, Love,* which I read as I was first starting my job at *Style* magazine, was another inspiration to march to the beat of my own drum, and I've quoted from Elizabeth Gilbert's *Big Magic* and Brené Brown's *Daring Greatly,* among other texts that have had a lasting impact on my worldview, in these pages. But honestly? The real answer to that question for me now is that *this book changed my life*.

Not that I'm, like, so in love with my own pearls of wisdom. Although there IS everything I've been saying—which I hope you've got loud and clear by now—about our own inner Voice *always* being our best teacher. Rather, it's been doing my research, actively walking my own talk, and living in real-life-human time the experiences I've shared with you here, that's caused the shift. It's one thing to read a book that moves you to tears (while nabbing a few killer quotes to post on Instagram), but physically living the lessons is what brings it all to life. And during the eighteen months it's taken to produce this book, this has led me to forge such a deep and unshakable connection to my truth, to *my path,* that life has become unrecognizable. In a good way!

At the age of forty, I feel physically healthier than ever. I have (mainly) regular periods, and I have been known to declare that my digestion is, for the most part, "flawless." The daily anxiety I used to feel about meeting deadlines, let alone A-list celebrities, is a thing of the past. When I splurge on designer clothes these days, they're usually secondhand (sustainable fashion at its finest!). And the thought of getting "out of it" with drugs or alcohol feels like a sad substitute for tuning *in* to my own carefully curated and lovingly tended reality. I know, I know, #smug. But also #sorrynotsorry.

And anyway, that's just the fluff.

In the intro I might have said some stuff about, I don't know, world peace. And I kind of embarrassed myself by including such a beauty queen cliché. But what I really meant was that, already, I could see how following my path into the numinous was making me kinder, more compassionate, more giving, and less self-absorbed. How seeking to truly know, accept, and forgive myself (how to unconditionally *love* myself), was making me *waaaay* less obsessed with accumulating stuff to make me feel good—and *waaaay* more connected to the fact that what feels really GREAT is helping others, creating really cool shit, and in some way contributing to the greater good.

Since then (yes, in the past eighteen months), I've gone from thinking of The Numinous as a cool girls' astrology site to seeing it as a platform for spreading this message as far and wide as I can (as well as a cool girls' astrology site). Based on my own journey with alcohol, I've started an event series for the "sober curious" called Club SÖDA NYC, which is designed to remove some of the stigma around choosing a more sober life, and to remind people just how high we can get on our own supply. I've launched Moon Club, a monthly mentoring program to inspire a new generation of seekers to become "spiritual activists" in their communities. And at the time of writing this, I'm organizing an initiative for World Peace Day titled #TuneInPeaceOut—based on the idea that the first step toward creating more peace in our communities (our world, why not!) is to seek peace within ourselves.

So this is the direction my life is going as a result of writing (and reading, many times over) this book. What has revealed itself as my wider path. Which is not, by any means, to suggest that you put it down and immediately start preaching peace, altruism, and sobriety (but also do, since that would serve my mission nicely, thank you!).

But what I hope you will feel inspired to do is begin, in earnest, a thorough investigation into *your* truth, and *your* path. The path of your ultimate health, happiness, fulfillment, and empowerment. And as a result, the path of your *dharma*. Not to mention have a bunch of fun, make some heartfelt new friendships, and enjoy endless adventures while you're at it.

How? Begin by getting to know your birth chart, with the help of any of the brilliant astrologers whose work is featured on The Numinous. Book a session with an intuitive or tarot reader who resonates with you (again, my recommendations are on the site, and everybody does Skype readings these days if you're not in the U.S.). Of course, do the yoga, the meditation, and the green juice (yada yada), but THEN pay attention to the wider changes you will very likely find yourself feeling called to implement as a result.

I often describe the practices and healing modalities I cover on The Numinous as "the missing piece in the wellness puzzle"—because, guess what? In my experience, when you clean up your diet and begin to take better care of the physical, you will automatically be asked (by the Universe, Source, your higher Self, etc.) to pay more attention to your mental, emotional, and spiritual well-being. And to make any necessary adjustments to your priorities accordingly.

Eddie Stern, my philosopher friend whom you met in the chapter on yoga, recently wrote a piece for The Numinous about the Hindu concepts of *sakala,* the reality we experience "with form," and *nishkala,* the reality that is "without form." In other words, our outer, quantifiable, world (body, possessions, money, social media, even the Universe) and our inner, unquantifiable, realms (knowledge, love, compassion, dreams, hopes, and potential). The Material and the Mystical. The here and now and . . . the numinous.

"In yoga," he wrote, "*knowing who we are* is the solution to all misery. For when we *don't* know who we are, we are limited by the external things we measure ourselves against (*sakala*). We measure, we compare, and we are miserable in doing so, because we always come up short. Yoga teaches that when we truly know who we are, we are immeasurable, pure consciousness (*nishkala*)."

In other words, it is in seeking to know the unknowable, to connect to the truth of our numinous nature, where our unlimited potential, and our true freedom, lies. And if I could wish anything for you, me, and (why not?) for all humanity, it's for us to be free.

# ACKNOWLEDGMENTS

Thank you firstly to my parents, for saying yes when my soul came knocking. To my mother, Nancy, my "other" Pisces and, in the words of Nayyirah Waheed, "The first place I ever lived." I am grateful and proud to be your citizen, and words cannot describe all you have taught me about what it means to feel and to be real. Thank you for reading my story with an open mind and an open heart.

To my father, Paul, for teaching me to think for myself (to create my own reality) and to always, always, always ask another question. Your Sagittarian skepticism lives in me. Except when it comes to astrology. Thank you for passing down your way with words, and for always being my friend.

Thank you to my brother John, for inspiring me with your scientific mind and your bohemian spirit. You have always been the coolest person I know, and your music feels like what my soul wants to say to the world. And thank you, Marysia, for your contribution to the spectacular cosmic cocktail that is John Henry Shepheard. The next-generation Pisces!

Rounding out the family shout-out, thank you, Bridget, for the horses, the heroism, and the Harrods Christmas sale, and to Felix for teaching us empathy for everything it means to be human.

Now then, Libby Edelson. Where to begin! This book began with you, and I will forever be in your debt for escorting me, with infinite loving care, fully onto the path of my dharma. You are charming, kind, and courageous, and your editing skills are second to none. Thank you for fighting my corner, for reining me in in the right places, for making me look clever, and for being an excellent therapist to boot.

Thank you to Carolyn Thorne at HarperCollins UK for your sparkling enthusiasm from the get-go, and thank you, Claudia Boutote, for including my Mystical World in your radical vision for HarperElixir. I can't think of a constellation of authors I would rather be a part of. Thank you to Alice Russell and Francesca Zampi at Found for helping get the rocket off the ground, and to Meg Thompson for becoming this project's adoptive parent.

To the Numinati! My soul family! This book could not exist without the wisdom each and every one of you has acquired on your journey, and has been generous enough to pass on to me in interviews for this book. Ophira and Tali Edut, Louise Androlia, Lindsay Mack, Betsy LeFae, Guru Jagat, Eddie Stern, Ellie Burrows, Bob Roth, Marika Messager, Wolf Sister, Chloe Kerman, Jennifer Kass, Elyssa Jakim, Alexandra Derby, Lisa Lister, Taryn Longo, Lisa Levine, Cindy DiPrima, Kerrilynn Pamer, Victoria Keen, Jill Urwin, Luke Simon, Erin Telford, Deborah Hanekamp: you are an endless inspiration to me.

Alexandra Roxo, sister. You came along too late for this one, but if I get to write another book you will no doubt play a starring role. Same goes for you, Biet Simkin. To ALL my Numinous contributors, and to the mystics and healers I have encountered on my path, oceans of gratitude for your words, your pictures, your energy, and your enthusiasm for being part of the tribe. A special thank-you to Gabriela Herstik, you funny, cute, clever little witch; and to the readers far and wide who are the reason we do what we do.

Thank you to Shelley Von Strunkel, the original purveyor of Mystical Glamour. To Kelly Cutrone, for giving The Numinous your blessing and welcoming us to NYC. To Aurora Tower and Laren Stover, for that one time in Café Gitane. To Arianna Huffington, for always replying to my e-mails. To Tiffanie Darke, for helping me to believe in me. To Alicia Keys, for showing us all how to be a woman in her full POWER. And to Martin Raymond, for being a mentor and a friend, and for inadvertently introducing me to the Pisces.

Simon Warrington. I knew from the moment I saw you that you would be my very favorite human, and you have yet to prove me wrong. This lifetime will not be enough to show you how much your love and companionship mean to me. Can we please do it again the next time around?

# GLOSSARY
# OF NOW AGE
# TERMINOLOGY

ABUNDANCE: Now Age speak for wealth, money, and material success. To be substituted in any situation where it might appear low vibe to openly discuss the former, in particular with regard to manifesting a six-figure salary, a new pair of Isabel Marant boots, or a fuck-off house in the country.

AGE OF AQUARIUS: Current astrological era, into which we began transitioning from the Piscean Age in the 1960s. Characterized by the toppling of hierarchical structures (a.k.a. power to the people), the rise of humanitarian values, the emergence of the global village, and a proliferation of new technologies.

ASCENDED MASTERS: Regular ol' human beings who have gone through a series of spiritual initiations and now reside as pure light energy in the sixth dimension (according to superstring theory, a hypothetical place from which whole universes can be perceived). To be called upon, along with our angels and spirit guides, in times of need, for assistance on job interviews, and to rescue us from disastrous first dates.

AURA: Biomagnetic field (also "biofield") of energy surrounding the body, via which we are connected to Source. Grows in size and brightness as you transition from low- to high-vibe life, along with the ability to attract more abundance and like-minded high-vibe individuals.

AWAKE: Adjective; energized and/or agitated state of being following an awakening.

AWAKENING: The realization, overnight or over time, that there is more to happiness and fulfillment than Isabel Marant boots, that we are all connected by a divine Source energy, and that it is our mission in our current earthling incarnation to free our soul, and the souls of our soul sisters and brothers, from suffering.

BLOOD MYSTERIES: Lost *her*story of how men's fear of periods led to the rise of the dominant patriarchy.

BURNER: Burning Man regular. Likely freethinker, spiritual seeker, party animal, and sexual libertine.

CHAKRAS: Seven centers of the energetic body. Keep the woo-woo flowing. Can become blocked due to negative emotional buildup, stored emotional baggage, or sudden emotional trauma.

DARSHAN: The act of catching with one's own eyes a glimpse of one's chosen guru or spiritual leader. Also, an experience of grace and connection (see "Numinosity") arising from the sight of either said holy being or an awe-inspiring natural spectacle—a sudden ray of light striking a mountain peak; Ryan Gosling in the shirtless flesh. Related to "puja"—a personal ritual for worshipping said idol from afar.

DIVINE FEMININE: The concept of "God" in female form, a.k.a. the Goddess. The awakening of which, within ourselves as well as society at large, is considered by many what will save humanity from spiritual and environmental Armageddon.

ENERGETIC BODY: Complex web of interactions of energy centers in the physical body, corresponding to the chakras. Also where feelings are felt, hunches are had, and all the woo-woo happens.

GONG BATH: Sound-healing experience in which the vibrations of the energetic body are "raised" as the participant is engulfed by waves of sound emanating from lengthy manipulation of a large brass gong. Related to "sound bath," in which the gong may be substituted for crystal singing bowls, wind chimes, didgeridoo, or a SoundCloud file of Tibetan monks chanting.

GRATITUDE: To be expressed daily, both as a practice for inviting more of all the good stuff into your life, and at risk of appearing unappreciative for the abundance bestowed upon you in this lifetime.

HERSTORY: The history of human civilization as seen through the eyes of women.

HIGHER SELF: Your soul, inner Voice, psychic voice, intuition, imagination, creativity, sexuality, spirit. A.k.a. the Universe expressing itself through you in human form.

HIGH-VIBE: (Antonym: "Low-Vibe") Adjective used to describe any experience, conversation, object, or foodstuff deemed to raise the energetic vibration of the participant(s); e.g., "This raw vegan cacao truffle cake is so high vibe I think it's actually *burning* calories."

ILLUMINATI: Evil cabal of celebrities, politicians, and rich people on a mission to manipulate the population and in doing so retain positions of power and influence. Possibly descended from aliens.

JOURNEY: One's life path.

LACK MENTALITY: The belief, propagated by modern consumer culture, that we can never have, or be, "enough." Also, that there is not "enough" (abundance, love, natural resources, Instagram followers) to go around. Can result in greed, hoarding, competition, and, in worst-case scenarios, global poverty and all-out war. A.k.a. root chakra problems.

MERCURY RETROGRADE: Thrice-annual astrological shit-show, during which the Internet will go wild with suggestions for how to "survive" it.

MOON CUP: The only acceptable form of sanitary protection for your Moon time. To be used with Thinx panties as backup.

NUMINATI: Benevolent and spiritually progressive answer to the Illuminati, on a mission to enlighten the population and in doing so alleviate the suffering of the world. Contributors to The-numinous.com.

NUMINOSITY: The occurrence and development of events displaying characteristics of a numinous nature.

NUMINOUS: That which is unknown or unknowable. Adjective used to describe any human experience that exists beyond articulation with language and therefore cannot be synthesized by man's technological advances.

OM: Primordial sound of the Universe. Syllable much used for punning within the yoga community.

OM (ORGASMIC MEDITATION): Acronym to describe the practice of orgasmic meditation, in which a designated "stroker" (usually male) stimulates the clitoris of the designated "strokee" (always female) for precisely fifteen minutes. Orgasm may, but generally does not, occur for either party.

PARADIGM SHIFT: Complete 360 of experiencer's worldview, relating to either one specific area of life or the whole dang caboodle, often as the result of an Awakening. For example, "Ever since I started OMing I've had a paradigm shift about how to communicate my needs."

PLANT MEDICINE: Hallucinogenic drugs provided by Mother Nature in order to facilitate Awakenings, emotional healing, trippy visuals, and/or Paradigm Shifts. These include, in alphabetical order and among others: ayahuasca, cannabis, iboga, magic mushrooms, peyote, and San Pedro.

PRANAYAMA: Yogic breathing techniques for the removal of energetic and emotional blocks in the physical body, with a view to facilitating the uninterrupted flow of life force energy.

SAGE: Cleansing herb burned by shamans and seekers to smoke out any malignant energies before and after ceremony/a really bad day.

SAGE BATH: The act of cleansing one's energy of basic bitches by dousing oneself in smoke from a burning bunch of sage.

SATURN RETURN: Astrological aspect occurring at age twenty-eight or twenty-nine, when relationship, job status, and sense of self have a tendency to go tits up, often leading to Awakening, emotional healing, and/or Paradigm Shift.

SEEKER: Person in the grips of Awakening, emotional healing, and/or Paradigm Shift, on a mission to find a spiritual panacea to aid them on their journey and bring meaning and purpose to this life.

SHAMANIC TRANCE: State of altered consciousness facilitated by a shaman with the aim of accessing personal information stored in the energetic body and/or subconscious deemed necessary for the healing process. Can be accessed using, among other techniques: hypnosis, drumming, visualization, song, plant medicines.

SPACE: Area in which ceremony, yoga class, or emotional outburst is about to take place, requiring said space to be "held" by responsible (i.e., emotionally stable and spiritually enlightened) space holder.

SURRENDER: The act of remembering (especially in the grips of Mercury Retrograde) that the all-knowing Universe has always got our back, and that we should just butt out and let it do its thing. Along with gratitude, to be practiced daily.

SWEAT LODGE: Hut made of natural materials and heated to extreme temperatures to be used in Native American shamanic traditions for ceremonial cleansing and prayer. Highly likely to cause fainting and hallucinations, and to bring on a Shamanic Trance, a.k.a. WAY more intense than hot yoga.

THE UNIVERSE: God.